Rastafari

Utopianism and Communitarianism
Lyman Tower Sargent and Gregory Claeys
Series Editors

Barry Chevannes

Rastafari

Roots and Ideology

Syracuse University Press

Copyright © 1994 by Syracuse University Press, Syracuse, New York
13244–5160

All Rights Reserved
First Edition 1994
94 95 96 97 98 99   6 5 4 3 2 1

Drawings by Frederick A. Wellner

The paper used in this publication meets the minimum requirements of
American National Standard for Information Sciences—Permanence of
Paper for Printed Library Materials, ANSI Z39.48-1984. ∞™

Library of Congress Cataloging-in-Publication Data
Chevannes, Barry.
    Rastafari / Barry Chevannes.
      p.   cm.—(Utopianism and communitarianism)
    Includes bibliographical references (p.   ) and index.
    ISBN 0-8156-2638-X (cloth). —ISBN 0-8156-0296-0 (pbk.)
    1. Rastafari movement—Jamaica—Kingston—History.   2. Kingston
(Jamaica)—Religion.   3. Dreadlocks—History.   I. Series.
BL2532.R37C47   1994
299'.67—dc20   94-18608

Manufactured in the United States of America

To the memory of my mother

Barry Chevannes is a senior lecturer in the Department of Sociology and Social Work at the University of the West Indies, Jamaica. He was a senior visiting scholar at the Institute of Social Studies in The Hague and the recipient of a Rockefeller Fellowship. Professor Chevannes has published numerous articles on Rastafarianism and is the editor of *Rastafari and Other African-Caribbean World Views* (forthcoming).

Contents

Preface

This study first traces the cultural roots of the Rastafari movement in Jamaica where it originated and then provides an ethnographic description of the movement in the city of Kingston. It argues that the worldview of the Jamaican peasantry, the direct descendants of "those who came" *after* Columbus, the Africans forced into slavery, resonates in the Rastafari. I call this worldview *Revivalism* from the religion of the same name and argue that the driving force in its formation was their determination to make the best of this new situation *on their own terms*, which meant resistance to European slavery and colonialism, both physical and mental.

The data come from fieldwork carried out in 1974 and 1975 for a doctoral dissertation at Columbia University. As much of the research was in the form of life-history interviews taken from thirty male and female informants, twenty-eight of whom joined the Rastafari movement no later than 1938 and two in the early 1940s, it is useful to clarify how the information was collected. It first took several months before I was able to find an informant of the 1930s vintage, who then put me in touch with others who in turn put me in touch with their acquaintances, and so on. This method is a form of network approach or what North American scholars call the snowball technique. As those who rely on this method would appreciate, there were many dead ends.

There were hazards as well. The first was the bias of the networking itself, which in my case I call my "Barnes bias." Brother Barnes, short in stature, completely gray, over seventy years old but extraordinarily energetic, was the first informant I found who qualified as the kind of Rastafari I was looking for. He joined Robert Hinds's King of Kings Mission in 1938. Bobbing and weaving on his bicycle through the slums of Kingston, he was able to mobilize and extend his network of former King of Kings colleagues and so provide me with other informants. The problem is that they were *his* network, and had I had the time I am sure I would have been able to find others. Indeed, it gives me now a great sense of sadness to reflect on the fact that these rich sources of history are probably lost forever. The result of my Barnes bias may be seen in chapter 4. My reliance on his network does not invalidate the data, but makes it necessary to caution against overgeneralizing.

Such caution is important, for ultimately oral testimony is no more than "prisms on the past" (Henige 1982, 5) refracted by personality, human necessities, social background and position, ethnic identity, social affiliation, and a bundle of other sources that provide the light by which one sees and remembers. In no other area is the caution more warranted than in the matter of how and when dreadlocks first came about. The prevailing theory up to the time of my fieldwork was the one that held that the practice originated among the followers of Leonard Howell and was disseminated through the movement after their dispersal in 1954 (Smith et al. 1960). Pursuing the Howell angle, Mansingh and Mansingh (1985) speculate on the plausibility of an Indian sadhu source, but without any evidence, oral historiographical or otherwise. Both hypotheses my research proved to be mistaken.

Although a draft of my work in the form of a report was available at the Institute of Social and Economic Research from 1978, Campbell (1980, 1985), unaware of it, concluded that the style was adopted from pictures of Mau Mau, whom the Rastas admired for their fearless resistance to the British. But relying on the testimony of Brother Wato, a Dreadlocks, and cross-checking with a non-Dreadlocks source, I traced the origin of the dreadlocks hairstyle to an organization known as the Youth Black Faith. This is set forth in chapter 5. Lo and behold, Homiak (forthcoming) now comes forward with yet another source, the Higes Knots. The remarkable thing about all these three positions (Chevannes, Campbell, and Homiak) is that they are not mutually exclusive at all, and none has the definitive grasp on how it really happened. Maybe Vansina (1973, 76) is right after all, and oral testimony "is no more than a mirage of the reality it describes."

A third major problem is the validation of the testimony. This is usually done in one of two ways, or both if possible, namely, through the use of other oral or written sources. I have done this validation where possible, but one gets the feeling that where it is not possible to validate through the written word, oral testimony is somehow tentative and cannot stand on its own. I would like to think that there was such a person as the "Seven Keys man" (chapter 3), even though I have not yet found any written sources. The prejudice in favor of written sources fortunately is changing as historians better understand the oral foundations of certain kinds of documentary evidence (Henige 1982; Ong 1982) and develop the techniques with which to wade through the distortions (an unfortunate word) inherent in oral testimony. Valuable knowledge that would otherwise be lost is more and more becoming available. After all it is *his*tory and *her*story and *their* story (*pace* dub-poet Mutabaruka). An excellent example is the work of Monica Schuler (1980) on which I have drawn in chapter 1. Erna Brodber's (1986) reconstruction of gender relations at the turn of the twentieth century and Evans and Lee's (1990) reconstruction of the history of a Florida town of African-Americans in the early decades of the twentieth century are other examples.

In the end it is the reader who will have to judge whether my use of the oral life histories gives the book any quality of authority. But I must make one disclaimer: It is *not* an oral-based history of the Rastafari. It is rather an oral-based account of the social origins of the movement and an ethnographic account of the processes it is currently undergoing.

But the study is more. It is an argument that has theoretical implications for the study of millenarian movements, insofar as it emphasizes continuity rather than break, ideas rather than action, culture rather than politics. Chapter 1 outlines the historical background for approaching the subject matter in this way. The remaining chapters show how the argument may be sustained through an examination of the social and cultural processes that led people to the discovery of Rastafari, and made it into a religious movement, and of the links it has with the past that give it so much of its current vitality, far more than are acknowledged or appreciated.

Following standard tradition in ethnography I have used fictitious personal names for my informants in all but two cases: Brother Wato, because of his historical role in founding of the Youth Black Faith and dreadlocks tradition, which would be otherwise lost, and with his permission, and Brother Barnes because as a member of the Combsome tradition, he pleaded to be heard.

Acknowledgments

Many persons and institutions have contributed to this book, and to them I owe debts of deep gratitude, in particular to the scores of Rastafari brethren and sistren, many of whom have since passed away. The Research Institute for the Study of Man under the late Vera Rubin, and the Institute of Social and Economic Research under Sir Alister McIntyre and later Dr. Vaughan Lewis provided research fellowships that made the fieldwork possible. Colleagues at the University of the West Indies and Columbia University made inputs into various chapters of earlier drafts: Lambros Comitas, Barry Higman, Rupert Lewis, Don Robotham, Maureen Warner-Lewis, Swithin Wilmot, and the late Derek Gordon, who was especially encouraging. In the postdissertation redrafting of the manuscript J. Gordon Melton and series editors Lyman Tower Sargent and Michael Claeys made valuable suggestions. The staff of the University of the West Indies Library network, especially Patricia Dunn of the West Indies Collection and Audrey Chambers of the Documentation Centre at the Institute of Social and Economic Research, and the staff of the Library of Congress proved particularly helpful in accessing local and overseas materials. I am especially fortunate for the friendship of Jake Homiak, Robert Stewart, Carole Yawney, Randy Hepner, and Stefan Palmié, who either placed their archival collections at my disposal or pointed out to me archival material I had overlooked. Dennis Edwards, Shirley Romain, Susan McDougall, Janice Murray, and Zanya Asiedu provided research assistance. Tartu Heron assisted in proofing and Abena and Aruba Chevannes in preparing the index.

A number of relatives and friends provided me with food, shelter, and much encouragement at various stages of the research and writing: Alma and Henry Ford in Luton, Walter and Thelma Chevannes in New York, Jake and Dianne Homiak in Washington, D.C., and Ronnie and Marcia Thwaites in the Blue Mountains of Jamaica. Finally I acknowledge a great indebtedness to my wife, Paulette, who helped to transcribe many of the tapes and provided me with the moral support without which I could not have completed this book.

January 1994   BARRY CHEVANNES
Mona, Jamaica

Rastafari

1. The Spirit of Resistance

Jamaica is a islan',
but is not I lan'

In this beautiful play on words, Joe Ruglass, the poet, folk-song composer, and flutist who has for years played with the Mystic Revelation of Rastafari, begins his poem that expresses the Rastafari rejection of Jamaica as a homeland and their yearning for repatriation.

The Rastafari ever since the movement's rise in the early 1930s have held to the belief that they and all Africans in the diaspora are but exiles in "Babylon," destined to be delivered out of captivity by a return to "Zion," that is, Africa, the land of our ancestors, or Ethiopia, the seat of Jah, Ras Tafari himself, Emperor Haile Selassie's precoronation name. Repatriation is one of the cornerstones of Rastafari belief. The fact that the majority of Jamaicans, including most of those who migrate, regard Jamaica as their home might make the position of Joe Ruglass and the other tens of thousands of the Rastafari seem very sectarian. The truth is, however, that the doctrine of repatriation is kindred to a lineage of ideas and forms of action four hundred years old. They arose first in response to European slavery and then, following emancipation, in response to the system of social, cultural, and economic oppression on which modern Jamaica was built.

Slavery and the Colonial Order

Our story begins with European slavery and is quite well documented for those who wish to trace it in all its details. Here the reader will find it useful to retrace its general features.

Beginning in the sixteenth century and continuing through most of the nineteenth, over 10 million Africans were forced across the Atlantic to the Americas, where they were bought by European planters and put to work as slaves on the plantations of the Americas. Countless others never made it. This extraordinary traffic in Africans was to replace the diminishing numbers of enslaved Native Americans, a turn of history that was not lost on the Africans.[1] Initially, most of them were drawn from the kingdoms of West Africa—from Guinea to the so-called Gold Coast—but as time passed and the demand increased, the European traders began pushing further east into Yorubaland and Igboland, rounding the Bight of Benin and loading cargos as far south as Angola. The slave trade had a profound impact on the social structure and economies of the kingdoms affected, not least because of the loss of many if not most of their best craftsmen, in addition to the alteration in the demographic patterns at precisely the time when the rapidly expanding European population was providing the social base for economic growth (Rodney 1982).

Of those who were brought, one-third reached the Caribbean islands, with Jamaica receiving under 700,000 (Mintz 1990, 33–34). Under slavery, despite the fact that all but a handful of Africans held the ascribed status of slaves, there emerged among them a system of stratification based on occupation. House slaves—those who worked in the great houses attending to the personal needs of the planters and their families—had higher status than field slaves. And among the latter, headmen and drivers not only exercised a measure of authority and power but were allowed important concessions such as keeping several wives (Patterson 1967). In addition, occupations such as trading or being hired out were preferred because they entailed greater freedom to move about.

1. The Rastafari notion of repatriation includes the restoration of the entire Western Hemisphere to its native peoples.

Among whites, the big planters, legislators, and colonial administrators composed the elite. Below them were the smaller landowners, parsons, bookkeepers, merchants, and attorneys, and a tier below these the skilled hands, many of them former indentured servants themselves. But as whites they all formed a class above the blacks.

Most important of all, however, stratification was also based on color: whites over blacks, and in between them a range of subtle gradations of color and status. The people of color, being the offspring of white male planters and black or colored female slaves, made up a manumitted and free group in the society, or else worked as house slaves. That was how Jamaican society was formed, and that was how it functioned. Two exceptions to the rule of color added some complexity to the situation: Jews, though white, lived a precarious existence, and until the nineteenth century shared the same status as the colored group; free blacks enjoyed free status with the coloreds but suffered along with the slaves the contempt of the rest of society for being black.

Emancipation in 1834 set in train far-reaching social changes in Jamaica, while giving momentum to others such as the consolidation of the coloreds as a political force (Heuman 1981). But of all the patterns originating under slavery, the one that proved by far the most incorrigible was—and still is—color prejudice. Its forms have varied, and although there is ample evidence of its diminution in recent times, it has by no means withered away. As late as 1992 one of the most popular DJ songs was celebrating love for *mi brownin'*, a new street name for a girl of light complexion.

The Peasantry

One of the most important social changes resulting from emancipation was the transformation of blacks from slaves to free peasants. The better to appreciate the rise of the Rastafari, it is important to dwell at greater length on the differentiation in the fortunes of this class that began to take place immediately following emancipation.

Gisela Eisner (1961) estimates that in Jamaica in 1838 there were just over 2,000 landholdings under forty acres each, but that by 1930 there were over 180,000 under fifty. The former slaves and their direct descendants either took advantage of the crises that gripped the big landholding class throughout the nineteenth century by buying up estate lands or turned to the inner recesses and rugged terrain of the island to fashion an independent life.

The growth of the peasantry in the first thirty years after emancipation was due to the movement known as the Free Village System (Paget 1945) and to the general decline in the sugar industry. The Free Village System was a response by the nonconformist missionaries, first and foremost the Baptists, to the reprisals taken by the planters against the former slaves who were refusing to work for wages they considered too low. The planters began widespread evictions from the provision grounds and from lands the laborers had been living on since slavery, motivated by the thought that by thus intimidating their former bondsmen they might retain a virtually captive labor force. Theirs was a historic miscalculation. In stepped the missionaries to buy up lands being sold and resell them in small lots to the people. Sligoville, Sturge Town, Clarksonville, Stewart Town, and many other free settlements sprang up.

The aim of the missionaries at first was to strengthen the bargaining hand of the laboring class by making its members less dependent on the estate, but they also saw this land redistribution as a means to strengthen the position of the church. The end result was that as more and more people opted for independent development, the peasant communities throughout rural Jamaica became the focal point for the development of a counterculture to the plantation system (Besson, forthcoming).

The planters in response to the sudden shortage in the workforce turned to a variety of labor sources that added to the social complexity of the island: liberated Africans, Germans, Chinese, and Indians.

In the meantime, West Indian sugar plunged into further crisis when the British Parliament passed the Sugar Duties Act of 1846, removing the preferential treatment Jamaica had enjoyed over European beet sugar up to that time. Between 1836 and 1865 the number of sugar estates declined by more than half, from 670 to 300 (Eisner 1961, 203).

The economic crisis presented historic opportunities for the blacks. It made possible the purchase of estate land under the Free Village System and through other means. It also made squatting necessary, as the abandonment of estates forced hired laborers into peasant production. In fact, after 1845 squatting was the main indicator of the growth of the peasantry. By 1865, leaving aside the kind of tenure, the number of land holdings under fifty acres had grown thirty times since emancipation.

The crops the peasants produced were either consumed or sold in the markets, but in response to what Arthur Lewis called the new era in the expansion of world trade, they soon took to the export market. Within ten years of an experiment in 1869 to ship bananas from Jamaica to the United States, bananas rose to become a major export crop. The total value of Jamaica's export to the United States rose from 8.6 percent of total exports in 1870 to 53.1 percent in 1890 (Eisner 1961, 270), an increase due almost entirely to the expansion of the fruit trade. Credit for the expansion of not only banana but of coffee production as well may be claimed by the peasantry. The peasants' share in the total value of exports rose from 10.4 percent in 1850 to 39 percent by 1890.

The sharp increase in the demand for these export crops naturally led to an increase in the demand for land, particularly land suitable for banana cultivation. The total number of landholdings less than five acres grew from 37,000 to 96,000 between 1880 and 1890, while those landholdings of between five and forty-nine acres grew from 13,000 to 16,000 (Eisner 1961, 220).

The colonial government, forced to pay attention to this industrious class, particularly after the Morant Bay Rebellion in 1865, instituted a number of measures to encourage peasant production: banks for farmers, an extension service to improve agricultural techniques, and the formation of the Jamaica Agricultural Society. By 1930 there were over 180,000 holdings of less than fifty acres each, of which 85 percent were less than five acres.

After 1930 decline set in as the lowest stratum of the peasantry began to lose its foothold on the land. By 1961, the year before independence, holdings of five acres and less had declined by 26 percent. This marked deterioration was paralleled by a rise in the number of larger peasant holdings, thus accentuating the social differentiation that had always been a feature of the Jamaican peasantry.

Writing on the period immediately following emancipation, Hall (1978, 158) distinguishes three groups among the agricultural population: small farmers, peasants, and laborers. The small farmer gave no labor on estates—indeed he sometimes hired labor—whereas the peasant, although a freeholder, occasionally drew earnings from the estate. The laborer differed from the peasant, however, in that the laborer mainly provided labor on the estate but maintained a provision ground on the side. Although it could be argued that the "small farmer" was nothing other than a better-off peasant, the distinction is quite useful in drawing attention to the social differentiation that had begun to take place after slavery. For example, figures researched by Hall (1978, 162) show that between 1840 and 1845 freehold settlements of less than nine acres recorded an increase of more than 2,000 percent and those between ten and nineteen acres an increase of 200 percent. Settlements of between twenty and forty-nine acres grew more moderately with an increase of more than 40 percent. Hence the main growth was among the very poorest.

Thus differentiation took place in two directions. First, there were the fairly successful who owned their own cottages and riding horses and thus exhibited a higher standard of living. Their fortunes did not always remain stable and were subject to deterioration. Nevertheless, they became the backbone of the export production of bananas and coffee.

The second direction was toward greater and greater impoverishment. Already in those difficult years of the early 1860s, reports were being made of "a destitute laboring population" (Hall 1978, 194), of "the number of poor persons . . . becoming greater for the last few years" (194), "of people wandering from estate to estate looking for jobs, of malnutrition and nakedness" (Robotham 1981, 46, 66–68). In the years following the Morant Bay Rebellion, the evictions and repossessions of crown land dislocated large numbers of squatters. As many planters switched over to banana and other exports, they often contracted out large portions of the estates to poor peasants, who remained tenants at will, subject to eviction and transfer at few day's notice (Robotham 1981, 51).

Race and color

No matter how industrious and socially differentiated the slave descendants in Jamaica were, very few were able to move up the ranks of the social order to the top, for color provided the principal stumbling block.

Throughout the post-emancipation decades of the nineteenth century, opportunities began to open up for peasants to join the lowest ranks of the middle class, as school teachers, ministers of religion, and clerks in the civil service. At first the impetus came from the nonconformist churches. Attached to every church was a school, where the brightest could be employed as teachers. Many churches also established seminaries for the native clergy; some of these seminaries grew to become high schools and colleges. As the Jamaican government increased its responsibility for elementary education and teacher training, limited opportunities for upward mobility increased apace. Education thus became the main vehicle for upward social mobility and achieved status either as clergymen, schoolteachers, sanitary inspectors, agricultural extension officers, or clerks in the civil service. Few blacks had the opportunity to advance to a higher status; among the outstanding individuals who did achieve greater disinction were Robert Love, a publisher and black nationalist, and J. A. G. Smith, the barrister. Others tried the technique of *marrying up*, marrying light-skinned spouses in order to "improve the color" of their children. The Anglicans did not elect their first black bishop until the 1950s, and as late as the 1960s an eminent judge was bypassed as chief justice because of his color. The story is also told of a black Jamaican who rose to become the head of the Central Bank in Haiti, and on returning to Jamaica in the 1950s applied for a position in one of the banks. He was curtly told that the only position available was that of janitor, which he could have if he so desired.

The late Derek Gordon (1988) in a study of upward social mobility in Jamaica between 1943 and 1984, adduced evidence to show that blacks advanced at a slower rate than did people of lighter skin color and ethnic minorities. He concluded that "the black majority is being held back by racial forces which operate directly in terms of economic power, as well as more indirectly through the medium of culture and ideology" (Gordon 1988, 278). One hundred and fifty years after slavery and thirty years after colonialism, black Jamaicans are still last in social rank, although they compose 85 percent of the population. Indians, Chinese, Lebanese, and other groups who became Jamaicans in the nineteenth century have moved up more quickly. Little wonder that there was a big outcry from the black intelligentsia when the member of one of the country's leading industrialist families, a white, was appointed special advisor to the prime minister after the 1989 general elections. Many voiced the opinion that there were others more eminently qualified but who were being ignored because they were black. Whether this argument was true or not, the debate that followed in the pages of *The Jamaica Record* between March and May 1989 confirmed, if confirmation was ever needed, that color based on racial origin still permeated the social fabric of the country.

The long and short of these developments is that Jamaica's social structure is not simply a matter of class, but rather of both class and color.

The complexity of this arrangement has led to a heated and sometimes bitter debate among Caribbean social scientists attempting to understand the social structure. On the one hand is a group of scholars led by M. G. Smith (1965) who, adapting the model of economic pluralism propounded by J. S. Furnivall (1948), developed the thesis that Jamaican and anglophone Caribbean societies in general are plural societies. Under the Furnivall model, ethnic groups brought together by the economic needs of the British colonies of the Far East mingle without really mixing; that is, they remain distinct ethnic groups, held together only by colonial power. M. G. Smith argued that the three-tiered system of class and color in the Caribbean comprised three separate racial groups, each with its own distinctive social, cultural, and economic institutions but all held together by the state.

Arrayed against the pluralism school is a long list of Caribbean scholars, beginning with Lloyd Braithwaite (1953, 1960) and R. T. Smith (1967) and including young scholars such as Don

Robotham and Charles Mills. From varying standpoints as widely different as functionalism and Marxism, they dismiss pluralism because it misses a fundamental aspect of Caribbean social structure, namely, the striving by those at the bottom to move up. In effect, while conceding the important cultural differences described by Smith, they argue that pluralism is more a defense of the already privileged than an adequate explanation of reality (Robotham 1985). Mills (1987), in particular, basing his argument on Gramsci attempts a rather successful reconciliation of the race and color versus class controversy: he characterizes the relationship not as either-or but as both-and, if we understand that color provided the ideological cover for class.

Indeed, slavery, in all its forms and manifestations throughout history was maintained by two methods, and European slavery was no exception. First, there was naked, physical force—the bottom line, without which it was impossible to maintain the enslavement of peoples. Each system, by its laws and social organization, ensured that arms were kept out of the reach of slaves.

But at the same time, all slave systems attempted to buttress slavery by the force of ideology. William McKee Evans (1980) has traced one of the most enduring forms this ideology has taken, namely, the myth of the "Sons of Ham," applied first by the Jews to the Canaanites, by the Arabs to the Europeans, by the Europeans to the Slavs, and seemingly by everybody else to the Africans. Europeans in Jamaica and elsewhere in the New World, however, went further. Some tried arguing that Africans were a species closer to the orangutan than to whites, an argument that convinced no one, to judge by the interracial mating and profligacy of the whites themselves. Instead, as I have already pointed out, the Europeans evolved a sophisticated and carefully calibrated hierarchy of skin tones, beginning with themselves at the very top and descending to pure African at the very base. To this pure African was affixed the aponym *Quashee*, the English corruption of the Akan and Ewe day-name *Kwesi*, "male born on Sunday." Quashee was depicted as not only black and ugly. He was, besides, morally debased, lazy, lascivious, and a liar.

Developed during slavery, these stereotypes produced effects that were still felt throughout the twentieth century. Physical characteristics were the target of abuse: coarse, tightly curled hair, broad nose, thick lips, and black color—all were rated negatively. The attack focused especially on facial features, the main source of establishing personal identity, rather than on the finer details of difference such as foot shape or arm length, and gave rise among the people to such practices as pinching children's noses to make them straighter.

A second line of attack was against the culture of the Africans. Strenuous efforts were made, if not to cause the people to forget Africa, at least to make them think of it as an uncivilized, primitive place. Day-names such as *Kwesi* and *Kofi* became synonymous with "stupid," and tribal names like *Bongo* synonymous with "uncivilized." The Creole language that developed from contact with English was considered the language of the illiterate and uneducated; to use it was to "talk bad," a practice forbidden in many households. As for the use of the drum and the dancing stimulated by it, these were regarded as too primitive for any self-respecting person.

In short, the subjugation of Africans by force was accompanied by the attempt to instill in them, both physically and culturally a sense of their own inherent inferiority, offset by a sense of the inherent superiority of the master race. That slavery lasted as long as it did and was followed by another 130 years of colonial rule attest to the strength of that force. And that the ideas and prejudices buttressing it still echo as the twentieth century closes attests to the strength of the ideology. But to draw the conclusion that therefore the subjugators have succeeded is to mistake the battle for the war, to mistake the retreat of Fabius Cunctator for defeat. Africans have resisted both slavery and colonialism; indeed even before they left the continent itself (Rathbone 1986; Clarence-Smith 1986). And they resisted in the same mode, meeting force with counterforce, ideas with ideas. And insofar as the Rastafari represent one of the most recent forms of resistance, it is all the more important that we examine the movement's pedigree. Horace Campbell (1985) has already linked the Rastafari firmly to that tradition beginning with the maroons, through the slave revolts of the eighteenth and nineteenth centuries, the peasant revolts of the nineteenth century, and the inspired work of Marcus Garvey in the twentieth. Whereas

Campbell's emphasis is on the political history, I will also include social, economic, and cultural currents.[2]

The Resistance

Marronage and Rebellion

Running away was perhaps one of the earliest and easier forms of resistance to slavery. But this action stood little chance of success unless unoccupied or untamed land could be found where slaves could establish communities and evolve their own social organization, patterns of kinship, culture, and defense. Thus viable maroon communities sprang up in all the mainland territories—Brazil, Colombia, Guyana, Suriname, the United States; and in all the larger islands—Cuba, Hispaniola, Jamaica.

Jamaica boasted four maroon colonies: Moore Town in the east, Scots Hall on the north, Accompong in the middle, and Maroon Town in the west. As running away was a crime, maroons had to defend their freedom. This they were able to accomplish successfully in a protracted series of struggles described as the First Maroon War.[3] The treaty of 1739 won the maroons their freedom and security but exacted from them the obligation to return all runaway slaves and to provide military assistance when called upon, and it denied them the right to enforce capital punishment.

True to the treaty, the maroons played decisive roles in the suppression of the Taki and Sam Sharpe rebellions, not to mention in the delivery of subsequent runaways, and, following emancipation, in the suppression of the Morant Bay Rebellion.

The Taki and Sam Sharpe rebellions were the only two that seriously threatened to bring the system of slavery crashing down, but every few years there was either some conspiracy or premature outbreak (Patterson 1970). The Taki rebellion of 1760 originated in

2. I make no claim to treat the issue of resistance exhaustively. For example, there were many slave plots and conspiracies that were nipped in the bud, not to mention other forms of resistance such as murder, attempted murder, work slowdowns, and economic sabotage.

3. The Second Maroon War of 1795 to 1796 arose from an incident perceived by the Trelawny maroons as a violation of the 1739 treaty and resulted in their defeat and transportation to Newfoundland and eventually to Sierra Leone.

the northern parish of St. Mary, where Taki lived, but was not confined there. The rebellion seemed to have inspired simultaneous uprisings and conspiracies all over the island (Hart 1985).

The Sam Sharpe Rebellion is generally regarded as the greatest, though it affected only the western half of the island. It proved to be the last rebellion under slavery and most certainly was the most organized. A Baptist deacon, Sam Sharpe led the revolt, the planning for which was effected through the network provided by the Native Baptist movement. Beginning first with a general strike at Christmas time, 1831, the rebels took to arms under a black regiment led by Thomas Dove but were defeated after a campaign lasting two weeks. The revolt hastened the official end of slavery two and one-half years later, in 1834.

The Morant Bay Rebellion of 1865 arose directly from the economic position into which the majority of the former slaves had been pushed by the plantocracy, but was compounded by race and color.

On Saturday, October 7, 1865, the case of a peasant accused of squatting was being heard at the petty sessions court at Morant Bay, the capital of St. Thomas-in-the-East. As the outcome of the case would have had direct bearing on their own fate, a large number of residents from Stony Gut, led by one Paul Bogle, turned up in court. Before the case was called up, one Geoghegan was tried, found guilty of assault, and ordered by the court to pay a fine and costs. Whereupon, the Stony Gut crowd countermanded him to pay the fine but not the costs, and a riot broke out. The following Tuesday, eight constables sent to serve a warrant for the arrest of Bogle were ambushed, beaten, and sent back to Morant Bay with the message that there would be a march on the following day to the town where the vestry would be meeting in session.

By this, it was clear that the rioters of the previous Saturday had become the insurrectionists and the rebels of Tuesday, for later evidence revealed that Bogle had sought the alliance of the maroons. And on that Wednesday he marched on Morant Bay at the head of one detachment while his brother, Moses, marched at the head of another, following an entirely different route. Indeed, the latter group arrived at the vestry meeting first. By the time Paul arrived, the courthouse was already on fire and the Custos, Baron Von

Ketelhodt, along with several vestrymen, lay dead as Moses' detachment dashed out from the flames.

But the uprising failed. The maroons hesitated before taking the side of the government, and the rebels failed to create a viable army, with the result that within two weeks the fires of rebellion were put out and Bogle captured and hanged. Eleven whites were killed by the rebels, whereas 439 peasants were slain in reprisals and more than 1,000 peasant cottages and huts burned. The governor, Eyre, called the retribution "so prompt and so terrible that it is never likely to be forgotten" (Hall 1978, 248).

To Curtin (1955), the Morant Bay Rebellion was a sign of a more general political failure by the ruling class to effect an assimilation "of the ex-slaves within the framework of European Jamaica" (162). As a result, the question of race lurked "beneath the surface of every Jamaican problem, intermingling with other issues and making all solutions more difficult." Hall, on the other hand, sees the rebellion as a localized riot, part of a pattern of other similar events caused by the general economic and social conditions. It was the handling of the rebellion that inflated it into a historical disaster in which the ruling class in panic surrendered its own political independence.

Robotham (1981), however, sees the Morant Bay Rebellion in terms of deeper underlying causes, namely, the general oppression of a class. The root of the crisis, he argues, lay in the precapitalist forms of relations that the plantocracy sought desperately to maintain, so that the "working people, the entire post emancipation economy, the social and political system remained bound to slavery, even in freedom" (Robotham 1981, 92).

Morant Bay indeed was the expression of a more generalized clash between the white oligarchy, on the one hand, bent on retaining its privileges and positions, and a newly emerged social force, the peasantry, on the other. First, the issue that ignited the passions of the peasants was a dispute over land between themselves and a planter. Second, the records show that the system of justice was corrupt, with many planters hearing cases in which they themselves were plaintiffs. The Commission of Enquiry that was set up to examine the causes of the rebellion received evidence that the rebels had their own alternative system of justice. Third, the raising of the slogans "Color for Color" and "Black cleave to Black" by the rebels could only have resulted from what they perceived to be generalized subjugation, so that the slaying of C. A. Price, a black vestryman, could be justified only on grounds that he had a "black skin but a white heart." Morant Bay signaled the arrival of the Jamaican peasantry and its claim, as an independent force, to a niche in the social structure of the country.

The next major rebellion was the 1938 Uprising, so called because a spontaneous general strike by the workers in all industries and services, who were at the time largely nonunionized, not only resulted in the total collapse of the Jamaican economy but triggered unlawful acts by the peasantry as well. The entire black population was, so to speak, up in arms.

Starting among the waterfront workers in the first weeks of May, the strike spread very quickly, engulfing workers on all the sugar estates. Even workers without grievances were forced into striking, and this included those in electricity, water, and transport. Factories, stores, and other trading establishments were forced to close their doors. In the countryside, bakeries were looted, telephone wires cut, roadblocks set up and manned, and, most significant of all, large tracts of estate lands were seized. The entire country was brought to a standstill. As I shall show later, the Rastafari were themselves caught up in this momentous event.

The army and police, assisted by reservists, were called up to quell the disturbance. They were unable, though, to prevent the birth of a new social order, for out of the uprising the independence and trade union movements were born. The immediate cause of the uprising arose out of general hardship. In the years preceding the events, the effects of the Great Depression of 1929 came down heavily on the poor. Unemployment, already severe, became most acute, as external migration to Cuba and the United States ceased. Bands of unemployed roamed the streets of Kingston looking, pleading for work. Alexander Bustamante gained considerable reputation for his letters to the press on behalf of the poor. It was only "natural" that the workers would have singled him out as a spokesman once they took to the streets. For Bustamante was a brown man, one who they thought would be better able to represent their interests to the whites. Bustamante set about organizing the workers in the Bustamante Industrial Trades Union (BITU).

At a deeper level, the cause of the outbreak may be found in the crisis of colonial rule: the brown middle class wanted its independence. Even before the events, groups like the National Club, building on Marcus Garvey's own work, were agitating for political reform. Thus out of 1938 came the People's National Party, led by an eminent barrister with an international reputation, Norman Manley, another brown man.

Together, Bustamante and Manley became the architects of Jamaica's modern political system, the former founding the Jamaica Labour Party (JLP) on his BITU base, the latter the People's National Party (PNP). These two political parties have been governing Jamaica since adult suffrage in 1944.

Migration

The people also resisted with their feet. With the opening up of the first opportunities in the last part of the nineteenth century, the impoverished section of the Jamaican peasantry took to migration. According to George Roberts (1957), in the 1880s migration to Central America at one point reached one thousand a month. From 1883 to 1884 an estimated twenty-four thousand persons migrated to Panama alone. There is little doubt that the rural poor, laborer and peasant, were the main force behind this movement. Roberts records the attempt by the governor in 1904 to allow the appeal by the United States for ten thousand workers only if a five-pound deposit was paid for every laborer "'to meet the burden which his leaving the island would probably throw on his parish under the poor law of the island for the support of these dependent on him.'" This condition was not met, but it clearly implied that the potential migrants came from the impoverished.

External migration continued for nearly a decade after the outbreak of war in 1914, mainly to the United States and Cuba. Most of those Jamaicans who left never returned, but settled in the host countries. Communities of Jamaicans may still be found in parts of Cuba, Nicaragua, and Panama.

The attempt to escape rural impoverishment led to internal migration as well. Here it is clear that from early after emancipation the internal movement of a section of the population posed a problem for the oligarchy, insofar as the vagrancy acts of 1834 and 1838 were aimed at suppression of the peasant. The movement of the rural population within Jamaica seems to have been a regular feature.

Without conclusive data to go on, Professor Roberts (1957, 152) nevertheless assesses that prior to 1921 the internal population movement tended toward Kingston not directly but in stages, "the migrants moving generally from one parish to another but always getting nearer to their goal." At any rate, this pattern was to accelerate in the years between the 1921 and 1943 censuses, then abetted by the cutting off of emigration outlets. Broom (1953) made the important observation that whereas the growth of cities in Europe was in response to the rise of industrialization, in the Caribbean it was the urbanization of the agricultural population that now offered an incentive to industrialization.

Kingston, established in 1692, became the capital of the island in 1872, the only parish that was then and is now totally urban. As it grew, it absorbed those sections of St. Andrew arched around it, and so in 1923 both parishes were incorporated as the Kingston and St. Andrew Corporation. According to figures provided by Colin Clarke (1975), the City of Kingston more than doubled between 1921 and 1943, and grew by 86 percent between 1943 and 1960 to nearly one-half million.

These figures do not reveal that this population increase was absorbed in the western area of Kingston and that area of St. Andrew immediately to the west of it. Thus in Western Kingston itself where the main markets were and still are situated, the Dungle, Back-o-Wall, and Ackee Walk became the most well-known settlements of squatters. People also squatted on all available lands west of these settlements, in the Jones Town, Trench Town, Rose Town, and Greenwich Town sections of adjacent St. Andrew.

Nor do the figures alone tell of the overcrowding, the disease, the parasitism, stealing, "scuffling," and other forms of social decay embodied by them. It is under such conditions that Rastafari became a hospice for the uprooted and derelict masses cast off by society and left to the mercy of the elements.

Cultural Reconstruction

Jean Comaroff (1985, xi–xiii) paid tribute to Monica Wilson for teaching Comaroff "that the anthropology of southern Africa was about the 'Reaction to Conquest.'" A similar claim could be made for Caribbean anthropology, as there is now widespread recognition that the culture of the peoples of the region has been influenced by resistance to slavery and plantation society.[4] This recognition marks an important departure from the acculturation approach by shifting emphasis from the dominance of colonial power and control to the resilience of the character of the subject peoples, in this case the African. It has shifted the discourse into an entirely new key (Langer 1951), raising again such knotty issues as the nature and quality of the linkages between continental and diaspora Africa (Chevannes forthcoming). It is interesting that Comaroff herself in a book about a South African people should be noting similarities between the Jamaican Revival and Rastafari religions, demonstrated in their resistance to the dominant opressive symbols and in the substitution of their own symbols. Borrowing a phrase from Vilakazi,[5] she says that like the Rastafari, "black religious innovation in southern Africa has likewise sought to wrest the Christian 'message from the messenger.'" And to Rastafari she might have added Myal and Revival.

The Myal religion first came to the attention of the Europeans in the Taki Rebellion of 1760, which means that it must have been in gestation for a while before that. At any rate, the political and cultural significance of the Myal religion is that it enabled a rebellion to be organized on pan-African instead of strictly ethnic lines for the first time in the history of the Africans in Jamaica (Schuler 1979). It was only natural that in conspiring to revolt, the rebels would have relied on the loyalty of those who claimed the same

4. The recent conference cosponsored by the Society for Caribbean Research, Berlin, and the Department of Anthropology at the University of Utrecht, was entitled "Born out of Resistance." It took place in Soesterberg, the Netherlands, in March 1992. (See Agorsah 1992).

5. A Vilakazi, 1962. *Zulu Transformations*. Pietermaritzburg: Univ. of Natal Press.

ancestors, spoke the same language, and worshipped the same gods. Myal changed all of that. Although Taki himself was Akan, through the power of Myal other ethnic groups were drawn into the revolt.

Little is known about the sructure of Myal beliefs and ritual in these early years, but it was noticeably different in the conception of "sin and sorcery, an offense not against God but against society" (Schuler 1979, 69). Speculating on the religion's origin, Schuler notes its strong similarity in characteristics to central African religious movements, one of which is a capacity to absorb external ideas. Shortly after the Taki Rebellion, Myal was absorbing and transforming Christian ideas.

Following the outbreak of the American War of Independence in 1776, a number of American planters loyal to the British crown fled to Jamaica, taking with them their slaves, among whom were a Baptist preacher named George Lisle (or Liele), Moses Baker, and George Lewis. Under abolitionist influence some planters allowed these men to proselytize the slaves. Lisle focused his work in Kingston, where he soon established the first Baptist church in Jamaica, using the class-leader system. Under this system the most talented converts were appointed leaders over classes of incoming converts, who as soon as they were baptized passed on the gospel to others. Thus the Baptist church grew.

In reality, however, it was Myal that was growing. For the class-leader system provided greater autonomy and freedom for Myal to refashion the symbols and teachings of Christianity into its own image, to snatch the "Christian message from the messenger." Only with this new development was it possible to pinpoint some of the teachings and practices of Myal using Christianity as a basis for comparison. In Christian teaching, the central relationship is between Jesus Christ, the mediator with God the Father, and mankind. Jesus brings mankind to his Father, and he does so through his Spirit. This complex theological doctrine was transformed by Myal: man's primary relationship with God was sought not with the Father or with Jesus the Son but with the Holy Spirit. Myal at first placed even John the Baptist above Jesus because it was he who transformed Jesus through the power of Baptism, and not the other way around. Where Christianity is transfixed on Jesus as mediator,

Myal was transfixed on the Spirit as possessor and sought him in dreams and secluded retreat. Whereas Christianity placed its emphasis on transmitted *knowledge* (doctrine, Bible, catechism) for conversion, Myal placed its emphasis on the *experience* of the Spirit. When followers found him it was to be filled by him, to be possessed. Possession by the Spirit thus became the quintessential experience of the myalized Christianity, replacing prayer and hymn singing. And this experience Myal ritualized in circular gatherings away from the plantations, where the worshippers danced and groaned until struck to the ground by the Spirit. In this state they remained until he released them, ready to be cleansed by the waters of baptism. The historian Edward Long, who did not disguise his contempt for the blacks, thought that this state, which he referred to as ritual death and rebirth, was induced by infusions of a drink made of calalu.

Meanwhile, George Lisle became so frustrated that he wrote to the Baptist Missionary Society in London, asking for help. When the Baptist missionaries arrived in the first decade of the nineteenth century, they could scarcely recognize a trace of Christian orthodoxy. Much to their embarrassment, the name "Native Baptist" was being widely used to refer to the more christianized forms of Myal.

In the periods leading up to and following emancipation, Myal took on the challenge of enforcing certain ethical values among the black population. Missionaries referred to the events in this phase as "myal outbreaks" because they were preceded by periods of relative quiescence. Myal was very anti-obeah. (obeah is sorcery performed by obeahmen who manipulate symbols in order to harm their victims). During this period, Myal's followers would mobilize from time to time to dig up and destroy fetishes planted by obeahmen, to imprison the evil spirits aroused by them or release those imprisoned by them, or to warn of impending disaster unless evil were subdued. Myal therefore was also known for its healing, a tradition that remained right up to the modern period.

Another important aspect of Myal was the charismatic leadership of the Myalmen, whom the missionaries considered autocratic and vain because of the total sway they had over their followers. Leadership under Myal was a function not of training but of gift, hence the obedience, deference, and respect leaders received. They were called "Daddy."

The missionaries, of course, could not but be biased, competing as they were for the allegiance of the same people. With characteristic logic, the way they saw it, one could not be a true Christian and at the same time worship Myal. But the people thought otherwise. They valued the antislavery and antiestablishment stance of the nonconformist missionaries, but they also valued their own approach to God. The solution they found was formal membership in the nonconformist denominations but informal participation in Myal. This was how it became possible for Sam Sharpe to be both a Native Baptist daddy and at the same time a deacon in the Baptist Church, and for tens of thousands of people to retain what subsequently became known as "dual membership." This was how it became possible that the Great Slave Rebellion of 1831–32, as it was called, organized by Sharpe under the very nose of William Knibb and the other missionaries, could have been blamed on the Baptists. The name given to it by the people at the time was the "Baptist War." And indeed it was. The Baptists rightly could not claim direct credit for it, but their class-leader system was critical in facilitating its organization.

Myal underwent yet another important development in the 1860s. This time a great religious revival begun in Ireland was sweeping through the anglophone world. When it arrived in Jamaica, it received overwhelming support from all the clergy, including the Anglican bishop who saw in the swollen congregations, the many confessions, and tears of joy the outpouring of the Holy Spirit. But when people began to *experience* the Spirit in their own way, dancing in the ritual circles, convulsing and groaning in possession, it became, in the bishop's eyes, the work of Satan.

Ironically—and this shows how far removed the world of the clergy and the world of the worshippers were from each other— "Satan" was being worshipped. In 1860 Myal as a religion was transformed by the intensity of the Great Revival into two variants, Zion and Pukumina, both under the general name of Revival. Zion, the first to become public, retained a closer semblance to Christianity, in the way the Native Baptists did. It made greater use of the Bible and other Christian symbols, but above all refused to show any respect for the belligerent and dangerous spirits that it acknowledged to exist but kept under control through the power of ritual symbolisms. Pukumina, on the other hand, emerged only after Zion did, in the early months of 1861, and for this reason throughout Revival it is referred to as "Sixty-one"; Zion is referred to as "Sixty." All spirits are powerful in Pukumina, which is closer to traditional African religions in which there is no equivalent of the evil spirit Christians call Satan; all spirits can possess and therefore deserve respect, an attitude also found in Vodun and Orisa (Shango).

To a far greater extent than most people realize, Myal and its later manifestation, Revival, have shaped the worldview of the Jamaican people, helping them to forge an identity and a culture by subversive participation in the wider polity. In one of my earliest encounters with the Rastafari, in 1969, I was surprised to observe members of the Reverend Claudius Henry's group showing signs similar to that of spirit possession because I knew that spirit possession was strictly taboo among other cult members (Chevannes 1976). Henry was believed by his followers to be the Second Person of the Holy Trinity. During a sermon he quoted from the bible the words "he shall rule them with a rod of iron," raising as he did so a rod hidden behind the podium. The act was greeted by a burst of enthusiasm and shouting. One woman experienced a fit of convulsions, and, without any reproof, she was given assistance by two other women who succeeded in calming her. My assumption at the time was that this kind of behavior was atypical of the Rastafari, with whom Henry's group had had serious doctrinal and ritual differences. Henry's church looked more like one of the Pentecostal or Church of God sects. They worshipped on Saturdays and had forced all members to shave their dreadlocks.

But shortly after undertaking the fieldwork on which this book is based, I became convinced that Revivalism had remained alive in the Rastafari movement. It was in January 1974, when all Rastafari observe Ethiopian Christmas, or the symbolic birthday of the emperor, with several days of celebration. As is usual, the activities of each day culminated in a religious service. The one I attended took place in a Rastafari yard located in one of the villages surrounding the Frome sugar estate in Westmoreland. Assembled were Rastafari of every age, males, as expected, outnumbering females. Chillum pipes, Dreadlocks, an abundance of ganja, colorful red, gold, and green garments, the drum rhythm now associated with the Rastafari, all gave this gathering its unique flavor. But the most striking feature to me was the closeness of the service to Revivalism. In the middle of the proceedings stood a table covered with a white tablecloth. On it were open Bibles, a glass of water and a vase containing a single branch of the leaf of life. This plant, along with ganja, is believed by the Rastafari to be sacred because it was discovered on the grave of Solomon. A period of vigorous drumming, singing, and dancing prefaced the more solemn part, which began with an opening address by one of the senior elders and intoning of "sankeys," as the hymns published by Ira D. Sankey are popularly known throughout Jamaica. These latter ones were familiar to the Revival tradition, and the local people joined in. A series of prayers from other leading elders followed, accompanied by soft humming in the background. Indeed, so close to the surface was Revivalism that a young Dreadlocks cautioned one of the villagers against bringing "poco-ism here." It was not at all clear what aspect of Pukumina he was referring to, but I would hazard a guess that the woman in question was beginning to show signs of possession. At all celebrations of this sort the local people sometimes join in the dancing and singing.

The character of Rastafari has been shaped by Revivalism to a far greater degree than is thought, and therefore an examination of the belief system of the Jamaican peasant is in order.

I use the term *Revivalism* to describe not only the rituals generally associated with the Revival religion, but also the complex of beliefs and values that underlie it. This philosophical use of the term is unprecedented. No one, to my knowledge, has sought to take a comprehensive look at the belief structure of the Jamaican peasant. Use of the term is fully justified because, unlike other African-derived religions such as Kumina that are narrowly confined to regional enclaves, Revivalism is national in scope and character.

God, Spirits, and the Dead. At the apex of this belief system is God, the Creator, commonly referred to as "Big Maasa" or "Maasa

God," a designation derived from the system of slavery itself. Just as the "Maasa" (Master) of the estate resided in his great house, so Big Maasa was believed to reside in the sky. The activities of the elements such as lightning and thunder are thought of as expressions of Big Maasa. For example, peasants jokingly explain to children the rolling of thunder as Big Maasa rocking his chair. Lightning is regarded with dread, and men sometimes swear by it, as in the exclamation, "God strike me dead!" Naturally, death by lightning is regarded as a divine act.

Except for actions of the elements, such as these, Big Maasa does not play any other important role in the Revival complex. He is like *Soko* of the Nupe people—"God is far away" (Nadel 1954). In the Revival religion the spirits occupy the prominent place both in ritual and beliefs. The spirits are always near and can be summoned by ritual. There are good spirits as well as bad spirits. The Pukumina cultists worship both good and bad spirits, whereas the Revival Zionists worship only the good ones, nevertheless believing in the existence of the bad ones.

Of the good spirits, Jesus is the most frequently invoked. Whereas God is perceived as far away, Jesus is thought to be near to men, having died for men. His benevolence earns him the frequently heard appellations "Father Jesus," or "Pupa Jesus," and at times one is unsure whether he is thus being identified as the incarnation of Big Maasa. He is also the same spirit as the "Lamb." Next, there is the "spirit," or the "Dove," whose actions are similar to the actions of the "Holy Spirit" as described in the New Testament, namely possession and inspiration. Then come the angels, archangels, and prophets. Because Jamaica has not experienced much of a Roman Catholic tradition, Revivalism does not have the proliferation of saints observed among the African peoples of Haiti or Brazil.

Belief in the evil spirits also shows the influence of Christian mythology. Chief among these spirits is Satan. Others, although given individual names, are together referred to as the "fallen angels," those cast out of heaven by God. They are bound to the earth or live underneath the earth.

The principal activity of the spirits, good and bad, is their possessing of individuals. The ritual paraphernalia and practices of the peasants bring out this possession. Possession is induced only by vigorous dancing and singing. Among the Zionists, the use of a red flag, a pair of scissors, or a Bible is designed to "cut and clear" away the evil spirits that hover over the congregation, ready to pounce on any individual. Specially gifted leaders can recognize them. Whether the spirit be good or bad, the belief that these spirits can enter into man is a fact of Jamaican peasant life. Likewise, their proximity and ready availability to man are also societal beliefs.

Except among the locally confined cults, such as Kumina and Convince, and among practitioners of Pukumina, the spirits of dead ancestors play but a small role in the life of the Jamaican peasant. However, the dead are thought to be very much a part of the world of the spirits.

In general, the attitude toward death and therefore toward the dead is one of fear of contamination. The rituals associated with death bear out this fear. At the first sign of death, the community rallies around to express sympathy and to offer help. On the first night a "set up" or wake is held. Nowadays, the corpse is taken away to a funeral "home" where it remains until it is time for burial. Meanwhile, if burial takes place in the family plot, the grave diggers pour a libation of white rum and fortify themselves with some before getting on with the job. On the day of the funeral itself, there is a great show of sympathy. Not to attend the funeral even of an acquaintance is considered a breach of etiquette. Consequently funerals are generally well attended. The larger they are, the "nicer" they are judged to be, and comments are often made that the deceased will be pleased. When leaving any building, whether the house or church, the corpse is always carried feet-first. In all the countless funerals over the years, I have seen this rule violated only once, and I think it was a deliberate attempt on the part of the minister to undermine the belief that the *duppy* or ghost, if carried out feet first, never travels backward and therefore never returns to haunt the places it has left behind. In the past, when burial used to take place within two or three days, the *nainait* or *turnin' out* ceremony was held on the ninth night after death, at which time the deceased is "turned out" of the house. The ceremony consisted of singing and games, but at midnight the house was swept thoroughly, the belongings of the deceased removed, and the furniture rearranged, the rationale again being that the duppy, should it return, will not feel welcome. Needless to say, this ceremony has the powerful psychological effect of bringing the period of mourning to an end. Nowadays, because few funerals take place under ten days after death, in order to accommodate the arrival of overseas relatives and to make better plans the nine night is held on the night before the burial. One year after death, or soon thereafter, the grave should be tombed (tombstone added). Failure to do so may merit the displeasure of the ancestor, who will make this known through dreams. The *tombing* ritual is thought of as providing a final resting place for the deceased. Until the ritual is performed a widow will wear black underwear to deny her husband's duppy intimacy with her.

Duppies are regarded as the inverse of everything human. They rest during the day, roam abroad at night, and must find their tombs and graves before sunrise. They never walk with feet on the ground; they talk with a nasal accent, laugh in a shrill tone, and cannot count beyond three. Knowledge of the habits and traits of duppies makes it possible for the living to maintain their distance by means of ritual. One ritual takes advantage of the duppies' love of counting but inability to count past three. The practice is to strike two sticks of matches, throwing each away. Next, strike the third, but simulate throwing it away. Result: the duppy chasing you will spend the whole night looking for it to reach the count of three. Recitation of the Lord's Prayer, or symbolizing of the cross are similarly effective measures. If the duppy is recognized as having been a Christian, a string of indecent expressions will serve just as well. When throwing water outside at night, failure to warn the duppies could incur the wrath of a drenched duppy. In short, all the practices and beliefs of the Jamaican peasants are underscored by the view that death, and things associated with it, are harmful and contaminating. An exception to this is the practice of obeahmen who invoke duppies to "set upon" people to do them harm. Baby duppies, Indian duppies, and Chinese duppies, very interestingly, have the greatest reputation in this regard.

And yet, paradoxically, the dead ancestors are a part of everyday world. In most rural communities interment takes place on the family plot. Besson (forthcoming) links the family plot to the institution of family land. The transmission of family land by cognatic descent bestows usufruct rights to all one's descendants but not the right to alienate through sale. The institution, Besson argues, not only represents a countertradition to the plantation system, but provides the kinship group with a sense of identity. As a part of family land, the family plot spatially and symbolically links the ancestors with their living descendants. Family plots are usually laid out in close proximity to the house, where they may be tended and kept clean.

Although there are no explicit rituals for venerating one's ancestors in Revivalism, ancestors are thought to exercise watchful protection over the living kin and from time to time will "dream" them, that is, warn or advise them through dreams. Ancestors are thought to visit taking the form of "bats," those large moths that will remain settled on the dark walls of a house for long periods of time. To chase them away is to offend the dead.

Nature. The Jamaican view of nature is concrete rather than abstract, manifesting itself in important animistic beliefs about natural objects and products. There are, for instance, certain beliefs about the influence of the moon such as its rays can cause insanity to the sleeper. In the agricultural cycle the moon's phases are important signs for when and when not to plant or reap certain products. Cassava is planted before the full moon, but bamboo if cut during this phase is easy prey to termites. Pregnant women or menstruating women are also thought to have a malignant effect on young crops, in the same way that the moon does in some of its phases— "The moon is like a woman—it goes through periods"— though the presence of the dragon plant in the fields is believed to neutralize this ill effect. Livestock mated in the new moon will bear females, and if mated in the full moon, males.

The moon is a symbol of fertility. The late Kapo, the well known Revival Leader and artist, was only twelve years old when he had the following experience:

"At about ten o'clock in the day . . . a spirit came within me and said I was to walk down the grade and look at what I saw. I looked up at a chocolate tree and didn't see anything unusual. But as I was about to leave I noticed an opening between some leaves on the tree which I had not noticed before. Through that opening I saw the moon. It was huge . . . Then the moon began to fall and it fell right down, as if it were going into the river. So I ran down to the river and asked my mother if she saw the moon and she said I was talking foolishness and the other women who were there began to laugh and some said to my mother 'You son want to marry.'" (Willoughby 1977)

Woods and thickets are regarded as haunted by duppies. These areas are different from the "bush" of the peasant farmer, the latter being cultivated. Some rivers, at certain holes or pools, are thought to be the abodes of river mummas, female water spirits. Among trees and plants, the towering cottonwood tree is the sacred home of spirits. The pawpaw if it grows too close to the house will sap the fertility of the male occupants. The oil-nut tree is commonly believed to bleed red if its bark is bruised on Good Friday. The croton is used to mark graves and to keep down the duppies of the dead, as well as to mark property lines. The dry coconut is a ritual object in Revival Zion—smashing it on the ground is one way of preventing possession by an evil spirit. Among animals, the frog is regarded as evil. Warts, called *Kokobeh,* are believed to be the result of frogs spitting on an attacker. For this reason, boys stone the frogs to death. Frogs are also used as portents, brought along for appearances at court, more often than not with mouths firmly padlocked. The rat-bat, which makes its appearance at night, becomes the bloodsucking vampire common in a number of folk tales. The howling of dogs and hooting of the *patu* (owl) are omens of impending deaths.

Mankind. In Revivalism, mankind is created by Maasa God, and the Bible records the true story of that creation. As a creature man is subject to all the forces mentioned above: God, spirits, the dead, nature. Nevertheless, the Jamaican view is that human beings are also capable of manipulating those forces to the benefit of the living. The animism just described, far from resulting in the paralysis of man before nature, is used to secure ends. The dead are invoked to serve the living usually in the form of harm to others. Also, the good spirits are heavily relied upon to heal and the bad ones to bestow wealth.

The multiple soul concept noted among African societies is also part of the outlook of Revivalism. Man has a *soul,* as the Bible says, and this soul goes to heaven or hell on judgment day. But man also has a *spirit*. This spirit wanders off during sleep and its experiences appear as dreams. Its failure to return to the body is tantamount to death. Each person also has a *shadow*. This shadow is not the same as the spirit, but is rather like an extension or reflection of self that can be separated from the self by being captured through obeah. The self can be harmed by imitative magic performed on the shadow. Separation from the self does not result in death, but in madness. A mad or "foolish" person is one who has "lost his shadow."

Mankind, in the worldview of Revivalism, is sinful, tending more toward evil than toward good, capable of generosity, friendship, love, and so forth, but only by struggling against the bad tendencies. Black color, according to this worldview, is one of the signs of this debased nature. Personal and social conflicts are the bases for philosophical comments on the nature of black people, their lack of solidarity when compared to other ethnic groups in the country. Sayings such as "That's why black people will never come to any good" or "Black people is him worst enemy!" or "You see fi wi black people! Dem is the worst set of people!" are common and reflect attitudes that Peter Wilson (1973) has called "crab antics." They are the result of repeated failure to carry through to success a struggle against economic and social oppression. Many, for example, are quick to point out that Garvey was "carried down" by his own black people. Alexander Bedward told Martha Beckwith that in heaven his skin will be transformed to white like hers (Beckwith 1929, 69-70). In these negative sentiments and comments we have evidence of accommodation to the status quo.

The position of women in the peasant worldview is an ambivalent one. On the one hand, women are respected, perhaps even feared, for their powers of fertility and command greater allegiance and love from males and females alike than do their male counterparts. The honorific title *Mada* (Mother) is bestowed on any woman who by her counsel, advice, and caring earns the affection and respect of the community. Hence, all female Revival leaders are called Mada. Because motherhood is considered the highest fulfillment of womanhood, the greatest evil that may befall a woman is sterility. And because the symbols associated with healing are mothering symbols, most Revival healers not surprisingly are women (Wedenoja 1989).

On the other hand, the control of women by men is reinforced through myth and symbols. The Adam and Eve myth justifies women's generally unequal place in the family and in society. This and other myths from the Bible reinforce the peasant worldview that women are treacherous by nature. The three outstanding Old Testament types are Eve, Jezebel, and Delilah. Myths like those of Ruth and Anna, taken from the same sources, but which emphasize positive qualities, are not generally known. Thus we find proverbs such as "Woman deceitful like star-apple leaf" (the upper face green and the lower brownish), or "Beautiful woman, beautiful trouble." Another saying makes the point that the perfect woman is as scarce, or nonexistent as a *white* jangkro.[6] In the market a woman may never step over merchandise displayed on the ground (Warner-Lewis 1990). The effect on male toddlers walking under the legs of a woman is believed to be stunted growth.

But man is, after all, man; and he must have relations with woman. As long as he keeps her happy, all is well. Two related preoccupations are money and sex. The folk song "Ooman a 'ebi load" tells of the man's problem on payday, "when di money no nuff," and Cundall and Anderson (1927, 118) cite the proverb "Ooman an' wood neber quarrel". They interpret wood to be firewood, but this does not make sense. "Wood" pronounced with an *h* substituting for the *w* (as in "hood") is a common but vulgar reference to the penis. The meaning is therefore clear: sex keeps a woman happy.

Male ambivalence toward women is handsomely captured in the following sketch from the late nineteenth century. The setting is Port Antonio, the central figure is Zacche, a tailor whose shop is the scene of his misogynist ideas:

This creature, Zacche proceeded, is like a lucky bag whichen children buy for a quattie because it has a pretty face upon it, and because it is supposed to contain first class sugar plum and maybe, such a thing as a diamond

6. Scavenging vultures in Jamaica are called *Jangkro*, also spelled "John Crow." A great banyan tree in the central park of downtown Kingston used to be one of their nesting places. The name *jangkro* is a curse word and insult, as in "Dutty [dirty] jangkro!."

ring. But what do the children find? . . . De sugar plum all make out a Plaster of Paris, and de ring . . . well sutt'nly, that is a kind of loop for the finger, having de likeness of a ring and made out of cheap brass wire. Gentlemen, it is no diamond ring at all (Cries of "For true, for true, 'pon my word").

Sutt'nly . . . woman is useful, but so is dildo, whichen as you know makes a real first class fence, but has more prickle and "macca" and is more ruinous to the flesh of a human person than plenty people can have a conception of. Woman, I say, is useful, but so is dildo; woman is amusing, but so is monkey, which is more deceitful than any other animal in this world; woman walk softly, but so do snake and scorpion; woman mean well but so do black spiders; woman is attentive, but so is sandfly and mosquito; woman is bewitching but so by all account is the very devil himself. (De Montagnac 1899, 110–111.)

There was however another side to Zacche.

Irene was caught mixing lime juice and sugar and water for the man to drink who declared that woman were worse then poison . . . The truth is, Irene was of use to him, and, what would not then have been believed, he was a great admirer of "de soft sex them!"

"What did you say?" she asked "Indeed you don't know what you said. I suppose you will tell me you sleep well at night now?"

"Well sutt'nly, I do not" he answered with a mischievous twinkle, "whichen *you* should know." (De Montagnac 1899, 131–32)

In Revivalism the supernatural world communicates with the living through dreams and visions. The folk tradition has worked out norms for deciphering them, many of which find their way into secular life. For example, in dreams or visions handling feces means a promise of money, blood means death, death means marriage, and so forth. Gamblers purchase their lottery numbers according to the objects or events dreamt about. The principle behind the attention given to dreams is that every dream has some meaning, even if not yet known. Therefore dreams are sometimes recalled and deciphered only in the light of subsequent experiences. This is one of the ways conversion takes place. Such dreams are called visions.

Healing and Divination. In manipulating nature and the supernatural, Revivalism is heir to an elaborate tradition of healing. Healing is an art. Its sphere of relevance applies not only to physical and mental illnesses but also to what one may call social "ills" as well, such as unsuccessful love affairs, litigation in courts of law, revenge, and so forth, which have their roots in social conditions. We may distinguish two levels, the physical and the spiritual. The physical level spans both folk practices and modern medicine, whereas the spiritual level comprises balm and obeah.

No special training is required to practice folk medicine. By growing up in the culture, one becomes familiar with various herbs and plants and their uses; one learns to identify those natural remedies used for bellyache, constipation, colds, fevers, ulcers, "bad blood," and so on, or those used as prophylactics. Ganja is considered a panacea. A brew made by steeping the green matter in white rum and leaving the mixture buried in the earth for nine days, is thought to make an excellent tonic. Similar techniques are used with other herbs, barks, and roots. The "wood-root" culture among young Rastafarians is well known.

Modern medicine is also given its place in healing, probably, as vom Eigen (1987, 7) believes, because it is more effective in treating diseases, whereas "Jamaican folk healers are more effective at treating 'illness problems', the functional, social and psychological concomitants of disease."

Folk healing, or balm, which has been receiving some attention recently (Wedenoja 1989; vom Eigen 1987), rests on three fundamental assumptions about the nature of mankind. The first assumption views the human person holistically. Not only may physical illnesses have spiritual causes but mankind is such an integral part of the cosmos that it is impossible for there to be disease without God providing a cure, whether through nature or the spirit or both.[7] The second assumption is the power of the spiritual over the material. Illness requiring the healing powers of a Revival, or folk, healer may range from physical symptoms, such as pains and ulcers, to the purely spiritual, such as a streak of bad luck or being pestered by an unknown spirit.

Folk healing is a charismatic gift. The healers of highest repute diagnose by divining rather than by inquiry as a physician would do. Hence cures invariably involve ritual, whether ritual bath, psalmody, or amulets and charms.

---

7. Many Jamaicans express the conviction that there is a cure for AIDS, only that nobody has found it yet.

Finally, there is obeah proper. Here animate and inanimate objects take on sacred characters. For example, exudia such as hair or nail clippings can be used to hurt the owner and therefore are disposed of specially. Through obeah, spirits and duppies are invoked or exorcised, witnesses in litigation silenced, predial thieves intimidated or hurt, employers forced to re-employ, or business ventures ensured success.

The difference between the two levels of healing is one of degree, though the degrees may be so great as to constitute differences of kind. For example, there is nothing magical about the use of the fever grass bush for fevers, but the folk healer must perforce be an expert in herbal remedies, since in most cases supernatural causation is attributed only after first working on the assumption of natural causation but getting nowhere. The Jamaican peasant when sick does not first consult the healer or the obeahman, unless the etiology of the illness is self-diagnosed as being spiritual. Folk healing is usually the last resort. Generally speaking, the sequence is first bush remedy, perhaps on the advice of neighbors or friends, then medical practitioners. Only when these fail is there a search for a spiritual cause. Natural effects have natural as well as supernatural causes.

Hence divination occupies an important place in Revivalism. A good obeahman or Revival leader is a "four eye man," two eyes in front, like everyone else, and two in back with which to see back into the past and into the future. Nothing is hidden from him. Good healers are also consulted for "readings," that is, to foretell one's fate. Resorting to the obeahman or healers is not always necessary in order to determine the future or to probe the unseen. The Bible and key or the ring and glass of water technique used. Chapter 9 contains a good example of the use of the Bible to uncover guilt. But to deal with matters that involve divine supernatural causation, only the healer or the obeahman can be consulted. Although they are necessarily versed in other levels of knowledge, divination is their specialty.

To summarize, mankind is viewed in a dialectical way. On the one hand, he or she is subject to supernatural forces, to sin and fate. One's place in the world and in society is predetermined by and from the creation of Adam and Eve. "What is for you," a proverb says, "can't be un-for you." In this he or she is the passive object of other forces. On the other hand, mankind is capable of mastery over the supernatural, the natural and the human world. through dreams, bush medicine, magic, and divination. The "secrets of knowledge" can be his; armed with them one is capable of great feats. In this sense man is man the actor, the initiator, and manipulator. Great store is placed on the acquisition of "knowledge." The obeahman is frequently referred to as a "science man."

The Idealization of Africa

The emergence of Myal, its development into Revival, and the reconstruction of a worldview in response to European subjugation and dominance provided solid foundations for the later achievements realized by the Rastafari. But there are certain other aspects I have so far neglected to mention, that deserve singular treatment.

As is well known, the Rastafari view Ethiopia as Zion, and therefore the movement has been regarded as an extant example of Ethiopianism. As used by Sundkler (1961), Ethiopianism described the secessionist church movement in southern Africa, both those seceding from white control, beginning with the Wesleyan minister Reverend Mangena Mokone in 1893, and those seceding from the secessionists. That Mokone called his breakaway faction the Ethiopian Church was owing to the identification of the name *Ethiopia* up to that time not so much with present-day Ethiopia, then more commonly referred to as Abyssinia, but with Africa. It would seem that at first Ethiopianism in southern Africa was directed mainly against white nonconformist churches, for immediately on breaking away, Mokone affiliated with the African Methodist Episcopal Church (AME) in the United States and invited its leader, Bishop Henry Turner, an ardent repatriation advocate, to visit South Africa. Turner's visit, says Chirenje (1987, 66) "gave an impetus to Ethiopian activities in South Africa as well as in neighboring territories." When the Ethiopians later seceded from the AME, it became clear that the main driving force of the movement was independence. In this respect the term also came to include independent churches of an apocalyptic kind known as Zionists (Shepperson 1953, 10).

Ethiopianism in North America and the Caribbean owes its origins to the "Ethiopian references in the Bible which had a liberatory promise and which, when contrasted with the indignities of plantation bondage, showed the black man in a dignified and humane light" (Shepperson 1968, 249). This influence was especially true of Psalm 68, verse 31: "Ethiopia shall soon stretch out her hands unto God." Strictly speaking then, Ethiopianism in Jamaica can be said to have begun only with the introduction of the Bible toward the end of the eighteenth century, not before. But were we to confine our approach only to that period, significant aspects of the tradition of resistance would be missed. Moreover, in the context of the forced removal of Africans from their continental home, even the cherished memory of Africa becomes an important piece of the ideological mosaic. Therefore, for the purposes of this discussion I prefer to speak of the *Idealization of Africa,* a broader concept in which Africa or Ethiopia becomes a symbolic point of reference, whether as ideal home—hence denoting repatriation—or as source of identity—hence identification.

Four periods in the Idealization of Africa in Jamaican history are discernible: (a) the pre-Christian period, up to 1784 with the arrival of the Baptist preacher George Lisle; (b) the period of Christian evangelization from 1784 to 1900; (c) the Pan-African years, from the launching of Robert Love's Pan-African Association in 1901 and Marcus Garvey's Universal Negro Improvement Association (UNIA) in 1914, to 1930; (d) the Rastafari years, from the coronation of Emperor Haile Selassie in 1930.

The pre-Christian period. Monica Schuler (1980), combining oral and written sources in her social history of indentured BaKongo who came to Jamaica after emancipation, found among them a tradition that held that the ingestion of salt prevented them from flying back to Africa. Many of their ancestors had dreamed of return but could not because they had found it impractical if not impossible not to consume the traditional salted fish and pork imported as food for the slaves and now for the working class. Exploring the significance of these ideas, Schuler explains that according to BaKongo cosmology a barrier of water called *kalunga* separates the living from the dead, and the BaKongo identified kalunga with the Atlantic ocean after their contact with the European slave traders. America, therefore, was to them the land of the dead. Once taken there, there was no way that any but the exceptional could return except through a salt-free diet. "So in Jamaica to resist eating salt may have been a metaphor for resistance to foreign ways. . . . Thus, only those who were faithful to African ways were worthy to return to Africa" (Schuler 1980, 96).

Similar beliefs, she claims, could be found in nineteenth- and twentieth-century Cuba. It is therefore quite possible that this tradition existed much earlier, because slaves were being shipped from central Africa early in the eighteenth century. But the linking of salt with exile and the avoidance of salt with repatriation may have been much more widely African. Warner-Lewis (1990, 15) speaks of a belief from the slave period "that slaves who had not eaten salt were able to fly back to Guinea" and notes that the yearning to return there "is one of the most pervasive themes in slave song discourse and recurs in many accounts of slave burials." The dead were thought to return to Africa, a belief that was also common in Vodun (Breiner 1985–86, 34). In Revivalism, salt is taboo to the spirits. At the set up ritual a saucer of salt rests on the table around which the mourners sing, and from it they occasionally take a pinch. If, then, salt intake excludes the spirit, total salt avoidance would have the opposite effect, namely, the intake of the spirit and possession of higher spiritual force, of such magnitude as to enable one to fly back to Africa. A common Jamaican expression, *yu salt* or *'im salt*, preserves the tradition linking salt with the loss of spiritual force. It is used to refer to a streak of bad luck or misfortune.

Thus Rastafari salt avoidance, under the Ital rubric, is probably linked to ideas of spiritual force and repatriation prevailing from the time the earliest Africans were forced across the middle passage into bondage, though, as Littlewood (1993, 272) points out, the association of salt with the spirit world is also common in Europe. The extent, therefore, to which most Jamaicans have become reconciled to adopting the island as their land may be measured in the adoption of "salt fish," a slave food imported from Newfoundland, in combination with the slave dish of ackee, a west African fruit, now the national dish.

If the examples given so far represent the idealization of Africa based on African ideas, then the following represents an example based on the European idea that Africans were the Sons of Ham. In 1748 the Jamaica House of Assembly received a petition from a slave by the name of "Cadjoe" asking that a proposed bill before the House be amended so that slaves be given the same rights as mulattoes and Jews as far as sworn testimony is concerned, and be tried not only by jury but by their peers.[8] The petition began:

To the Honorable Edward Manning Esq. and his Associates Representatives of the Town of Kingston & P.

The humble petition of the Innocent Distressed *Sons of Chus* Commonly called the Negroe Slaves, of the said Town and Precinct in behalf of themselves, and one hundred and six Thousand of their Brethren, unjustly and inhumanly detained in Thraldom and bondage in the Island of Jamaica.[9]

"Cadjoe," the writer's way of spelling Kojo, or Cudjoe, later in the petition made one reference to "us the *Ancient Desendants [sic] of the Grandson of the Patriarch Noah*" and another reference to the fact that the bill if passed would "prevent us getting possession of the *Promised Land*."[10] His petition was read into the minutes of the sitting from the sworn original dictated and signed with his mark. The assembly did in fact pass an act in 1748 granting "manumitted blacks and browns the same rights in court as those who had been born free" (Heuman 1981, 5). Quite likely then, this was the main concern of Kojo. The details of the petition, the social and political circumstances around which it was drafted, the personalities involved are all important questions to be resolved. What group of persons passed the myth on to them, from about what time, and how we do not yet know. We do know that slaves had already adopted the Hamitic myth from the middle of the eighteenth century and identified with the ancient Kingdom of Kus. The reference to the "Promised Land" is more problematic. Because there was nothing in the text to suggest that Africa was meant, I am inclined to conclude that it was being used metaphorically. That in itself is quite significant, for it indicates some familiarity with Zionist ideas, no doubt through the Bible.

8. *Journal of the House of Assembly* 18 May 1748, Archives of Jamaica 1B/5/1/13. See Appendix for the full text. I am indeed grateful to Dr. Robert Stewart for leading me to the existence of this petition.

9. The emphasis is mine.

10. Also my emphases.

The period of Christian evangelization. With the introduction of Christianity from the 1780s on, the name *Ethiopia* began to be used. Lisle called his church Ethiopian. Later, in the early nineteenth century, the passage from Psalm 68 was used quite liberally by the Baptist minister William Knibb in his sermons and prayers, making clear his identification of the slaves with Ethiopia, and in the publication of his weekly paper, *The Baptist Herald and Friend of Africa* making clear his own position as well.

Robert Stewart (1983, 275–76) has shown that the missionaries throughout the nineteenth century kept alive the idea of returning to Africa, not however as repatriated exiles but as missionaries to Christianize the natives of Africa. Some Jamaicans did go, as teachers and missionaries, but there was, he says, "little positive regard for African culture in itself." Nevertheless, there existed individuals such as the anonymous writer whose call posted on the Lucea wharf gate was couched in phrases calculated to stir sympathy and support:

I heard a Voice speaking to me in the year 1864, saying, "Tell the *Sons and Daughters of Africa* that a great deliverance will take place for them from the hand of Opposition. . . . The calamity which I see coming upon the Land will be so grievous, and so distressing, that many will desire to die! But great will be the deliverance of the *Sons and Daughters of Africa*, if they humble themselves in sackcloth and ashes like the children of Nineveh before the Lord our God. A Son of Africa." (Quoted in Stewart 1983, 294–95; emphasis added)

Or those like one Reverend Gordon whose words might have been taken from a speech of Marcus Garvey, except that they were delivered in 1875, fourteen years before Garvey was born: "Some people . . . are ashamed to own their connection with Africa, but this should not be, since it must be admitted, that she once held the most prominent and influential position in the world, and that from her, thro' Greece and Rome, the British Nation received the first elements of civilization." (Quoted in Stewart 1983, 280) This was to become a favorite theme of Marcus Garvey.

The Pan-African period. Marcus Garvey owed much of his formation to the influence of Dr. Robert Love, whose journal the *Jamaica Advocate* became the main vehicles for Pan-African and anticolonial ideas and race consciousness from 1894 to 1905. In 1901

Love launched the Pan-African Association in association with H. Sylvester-Williams, another Pan-Africanist, from Trinidad,

1. To secure the Africans and their descendents throughout the world their civil and political rights;
2. To ameliorate the condition of our oppressed brethren in the continent of Africa, America, and others parts of the world. (Quoted in Lewis 1987, 30)

Love's cry was "Africa for the Africans."

The way for Garvey was paved also by the activities of a number of religious street preachers, at least two of whom, Isaac Uriah Brown and Prince Shrevington, laid claim to Royal African lineage (Elkins 1977). It is possible that the defeat of the Italians at the hands of the Abyssinians in 1896 stimulated such claims to royalty. Brown, who tried to pass himself off as "Royal Prince Thomas Isaac Makarooroo of Ceylon," was arrested for sedition in 1905 after advocating a strike for higher wages and nonpayment of taxes. He told his audiences that after emancipation each slave was to have received sixteen acres of land in compensation but that the whites took it, and he was going to land his own troops to get it back. After serving his one-month sentence, Brown sailed for England, where he tried passing as "Prince Thomas Makarooroo," nephew and heir apparent of Menelik of Abyssinia. "Prince Shrevington Mitcheline" also tried passing in Britain as the crown prince and grandson of Menelik II, but Elkins mentions nothing of his activities in Jamaica. A common motif running through the background of Brown and Shrevington is their travels abroad, a necessary annex to their royal credentials. A third preacher, Higgins, popularly called "Warrior Higgins," quite possibly because of his scuffles with the police and his fiery preaching, was active in Jamaica from 1897 until he died in 1902. He founded a Revival group, the Royal Millennium Baptist Missionary Society, commonly known as the "Millennium Band," and aroused black consciousness with his frequent condemnation of the whites. Another preacher, identified only as "the Seven Keys man," is mentioned later in chapter 3. These preachers kept alive consciousness about Africa among the urban and rural poor, paving the way for Garvey.

Undoubtedly the most successful preacher was Alexander Bedward, the leader not merely of a Revival band but of a movement, with affiliated groups all over Jamaica and in Colon, or Panama. He too had traveled, but as a migrant worker to Panama. Bedward first came to public attention a few years before the end of the nineteenth century, when he headed a mass following, whom he fired with hatred for their own oppressed condition, calling them the "black wall" that needed to rise up and throw down the "white wall" that had surrounded it. He even stirred memories of the "Morant War," which had taken place thirty years before. Bedward was arrested for sedition but sent to the mental asylum. On release, he continued his activities as a great Revival healer and preacher in August Town near Kingston, until 1921 when on a march to the city "to do battle with his enemies," he and eight hundred of his followers were arrested and put away. He led his followers directly into Garveyism by finding the appropriate charismatic metaphor: Bedward and Garvey were as Aaron and Moses, one the high priest, the other prophet, both leading the children of Israel out of exile.

Marcus Garvey's middle name was "Mosiah," a fact to which the people would have attached great significance given the strong tradition of wordplay in Jamaican culture,[11] Mosiah being suggestive of a cross between Moses and Messiah. Too much is already known and written about the life, work, and impact of Garvey throughout the African world, continent and diaspora, for me to trace these subjects.[12] I wish, however, to single out two recurrent themes in his idealization of Africa: Africa as symbol of identity, and Africa as home.

Like the many preachers before him, Garvey tirelessly used the biblical references to the name Ethiopia, the mere mention of which "excited powerful emotions in the hearts of Christian Blacks" (Lewis 1987, 168). When therefore six years after founding the UNIA and building a powerful international mass movement, Garvey summoned the First Convention in New York in 1920, the name *Ethiopia* was adopted as the focal point of identity for blacks the world over. The fortieth demand in the *Declaration of Rights of*

11. See Abrahams (1983) and Brathwaite (1986).

12. Among titles appearing in the last fifteen years are Martin (1976, 1983), Hill (1983–85), Stein (1986), Lewis (1987), and Lewis and Bryan (1988).

the Negro Peoples of the World read: "Resolved, that the anthem 'Ethiopia, Thou Land of Our Fathers,' etc., shall be the anthem of the Negro race."

The Universal Ethiopian Anthem
(Poem by Burrell and Ford)

I

Ethiopia, thou land of our fathers,
Thou land where the gods loved to be,
As storm cloud at night suddenly gathers
Our armies come rushing to thee.
We must in the fight be victorious
When swords are thrust outward to gleam:
For us will the vict'ry be glorious
When led by the red, black and green.

CHORUS

Advance, advance to victory,
Let Africa be free;
Advance to meet the foe
With the might
Of the red, the black and the Green.

II

Ethiopia, the tyrant's falling,
Who smote thee upon thy knees,
And thy children are lustily calling
From over the distant seas.
Jehovah, the Great One has heard us,
Has noted our sighs and our tears,
With His spirit of Love he has stirred us
To be One through the coming years.
CHORUS—Advance, advance, etc.

III

O Jehovah, thou God of the ages
Grant unto our sons that lead
The wisdom Thou gave to Thy sages
When Israel was sore in need.
Thy voice thro' the dim past has spoken,
Ethiopia shall stretch forth her hand,
By Thee shall all fetters be broken,
And Heav'n bless our dear fatherland.
CHORUS—Advance, advance, etc.

No one who has stood to the singing of one's national anthem on some important or historic occasion, or the anthem of a group or a movement, can fail to imagine the emotional power transmitted by hundreds and thousands of people of African descent singing this song. Hearing old Garveyites sing it even today or the Rastafari sing their own adaptation of it is enough to convince one that the anthem has lost none of its power even if the Garveyite movement has. It undoubtedly stirred the same passion then as the "Nkosi sikele i Africa," the national anthem of the African National Congress of South Africa, does today.[13]

The other aspect of Garveyism, the one that was to have a well-recognized influence on Rastafari teachings, was his Back to Africa ideas. But somewhere lost in the many glosses on this by scholars writing about the Rastafari is Garvey's thinking behind his Back to Africa programs and schemes. A return to Africa was not in Garvey's mind a sort of mass exodus to right past wrongs. "We do not want all the Negroes in Africa," he said. "Some are no good here, and naturally will be no good there" (Garvey 1986, 122). What he dreamed of was the creation of a nation spearheaded by the UNIA with the help of those willing to work and sacrifice for it, strong enough to defend the interest of black people and force the respect of the rest of the world. In this he was influenced by the attention the League of Nations had been giving to the restoration of Palestine to the Jews and by the recognition being given to the nationalist aspirations of Ireland, Egypt, and India. "Africa is the legitimate, moral and righteous home of all Negroes, and now, that the time is coming for all to assemble under their own vine and fig tree, we feel it our duty to arouse every Negro to a consciousness of himself" (Garvey 1986, 122). Race consciousness in this sense meant falling in line behind the UNIA to realize for the African race what was clearly being realized for others. "As far as Garvey was concerned . . . the African, wherever he lived, had

13. At the singing of "Nkosi sikele i Africa" in the assembly hall of the University of the West Indies, Mona, on the historic visit of Nelson and Winnie Mandela to Jamaica in 1991, many academics, white and black, not to mention other staff and students of the university and other visitors, their fists clenched above their heads, sang this anthem as a sign of their identification with the struggles of the people whose hopes it represented.

no government to speak to his interests" (Martin 1976, 46). The creation of such a government was the principal aim behind the back to Africa movement.

The Rastafari period. As I hope the preceding discussion has shown, the idea of repatriation to Africa was not suddenly sown in the head of the Rastafari by Marcus Garvey. Garvey's ideas crowned the long history of similar ideas and feelings by virtue of the international mass character they embodied. But they also came at such an opportune time that in light of events that followed they clearly marked a turning point in the history of the idealization of Africa.

Those events were the ascent of Ras Tafari to the throne of the Ethiopian empire as Emperor Haile Selassie I in November 1930, and the interpretation that was given it by several persons. Selassie's titles were "King of Kings, Lord of Lords, Conquering Lion of the Tribe of Judah, Elect of God and Light of the World," titles some of which the Bible also gave to the Messiah. Among those individuals who made this link was Leonard Howell, the person generally credited as the first to preach the divinity of Haile Selassie. Howell claimed to have been a Garveyite, but as Hill (1981) shows Howell was influenced also by Reverend Fitz Balintine Pettersburgh. "Ballantine's supreme Book of Royal Rules for the Ethiopian Western Repository" (34), published in Jamaica in 1926 under the title *Royal Parchment Scroll of Black Supremacy*, Howell plagiarized in *The Promised Key*, which he published in 1935. Others preaching the new doctrine included Joseph Hibbert, Archibald Dunkley, Robert Hinds a former associate of Howell, and Altamont Reid. Among other influences cited by Hill in the growth of Ethiopianism were *The Holy Piby*, written by Robert Athlyi Rogers in 1924, and the outbreak of the Italo-Ethiopian war in 1935.

The invasion of Italy by the fascists aroused a wave of anger throughout the hemisphere and in Africa. In the anglophone Caribbean, including Jamaica, people sought to enlist as volunteers (Weisbord 1970). The event stimulated the formation of groups such as the Ethiopian Alliance of the World by the Garveyite St. William Grant (Hill 1981) and the flow of ideas through the pages of the Garveyite paper *Plain Talk*. Through a series of articles in *Plain Talk* L. F. C. Mantle was "instrumental in crystallizing the ideology of Ethiopianism" (Post 1970, 196), by identifying all blacks as Ethiopians and as Jews, placing Ethiopia at the head of Egyptian civilization, and connecting modern Italy with Ancient Rome. These ideas are now common throughout the Rastafari.

Of greater far-reaching if unintended effect was an article published in *The Jamaica Times* by Philos in 1935. Philos alleged that blacks all over Africa were flocking to an organization known as *Nya-Binghi* or "Death to the Whites," which was founded in the 1920s by a Congolese King. Now the head of it was none other than Haile Selassie, whom its members revered as God and on whose behalf death was sure admission to heaven. Intended to scare the whites into preemptive action, it had the effect, says Post (1970, 204), of the Ethiopian movement "accept[ing] the Philos article as a perfectly natural white reaction to something which was in fact true—a league of black people against the whites, headed by Haile Selassie." The Garveyites, he says, cited it as proof that the League of Nations had never intended to help Ethiopia against the Italians, whereas the Rastafari members appropriated the name.[14]

In this chapter, I have presented the forms of social and ideological oppression undergone by Africans and their descendants in Jamaica, on the one hand, and on the other, the social and ideological forms of resistance to this oppression leading up to the rise of the Rastafari in the 1930s. To see one side without the other is to see but a partial picture. The history of the country is like that of two wrestlers, locked in a combat of cosmic proportions like Jacob and the Angel, tumbling through four hundred years of different shapes and forms, expending different levels of energy but still fighting. In a way it is a spiritual battle for control of the central prize, the *I*, the self. The shape and the form that it took in the 1930s brought the combat to a new level, it is true. But we miss the full picture if we fail to see its historic cultural and social connections.

14. Post's general argument is that Ethiopianism in the 1930s fits Engels's definition of ideology as false consciousness, a construct in which ideas derived from past epochs are able to digest new facts by fitting them into their own structure.

2. The Uprooting

When asked what Jamaica looked like, Columbus is said to have crumpled a piece of paper in his hand to dramatize the fact that deep valleys and gorges, steep hills, and mountains account for over 70 percent of the land surface. On these lands today, the very worst for any sort of agriculture, lives the peasant population.

The majority of the early Rastafarians came from the landless and small cultivator class of peasants. Not all of my informants could give a precise idea of the amount of land their parents owned or rented, but of those who could, eleven fell into the 0 to 4 acres category, three into the 5 to 9, and three into the 10 and greater.

The categories are somewhat arbitrary and do not themselves state the real condition of the people who possessed them. For example, the mother of one of my informants inherited eighteen acres in St. Mary from her own mother, on which she planted coconuts and other food provisions that she herself then sold at the markets in Kingston. By 1929 she had to move to a nearby district in order to give her twelve children a chance to attend school. Marketing provisions were, however, not enough to provide a cash income so she gave it up to work as a domestic for the manager of the Beverley property, while the children continued gathering food from the family land.

In a second case involving thirteen acres, capital was clearly a problem. The thirteen acres were held in three different places, making it three times as difficult to produce the sugarcane this peasant planted and to manufacture the wet sugar his wife and daughter sold at the Savanna-la-Mar market in Westmoreland. The family had two mills to crush the cane.

Some of the time, there is no animal to look after the bulding of the cane. At the yard where the three and a half acres is, he sell a half acre, and he go and get some money from the Building Society and put with that money and buy a mule to help crush the cane. Well, it never stay no time the mule die. One morning I just wake up and see the mule lie down under a chocolate tree. Well, the cane stay there and rotten. Persons come and make a mess of it, and all things like that.

In addition to this loss, his wife took sick and was confined to bed for a very long time. We have then a peasant who, to advance as a farmer, had to sell a part of his land, and in addition borrow money that must be repaid at interest. Then he lost the investment altogether.

The one other person whose father owned more than nine acres of land, ten to be exact, came from upper Clarendon. The land is now family land. Back then, in the 1920s, it still did not afford the family much of a prospect in life; therefore, his father had to seek employment as a drayman for a Chinese man "and a next gentleman by the name of Mr. Miller."

Thus, the differentiation among peasants, which we discussed in the preceding chapter, gave only a global picture of the situation and should not be taken to mean that those owning any but the smallest tracts of land were guaranteed even a measure of prosperity. The main reasons for this difficulty were the poor quality relative to the size of the land and the inavailability of capital. Peasant agriculture in Jamaica takes place on lands that are the least fertile and that are subject to erosion. Ten acres of rugged terrain may not be as profitably exploited as two or three acres of flat, fertile, and well-watered land. This point had been made repeatedly by the late George Beckford and by others calling for land reform that would give the peasants who need no further proof of their industry some of the land now consumed by the large plantations of a senile sugar industry.

Having suitable land solved only part of the problem. The peasants still faced problems of capital. The Peoples Cooperative Loan Banks were set up precisely to solve this. But apart from the fact that their capitalization was low—£40,000 available among forty branches in 1928 (Eisner 1961)—access depended on legal tenure and therefore was denied a large section having the customary tenure through the institution of family land. One alternative was to join a building society. In 1874 the Westmoreland Building Society, the second of several building societies, was established. The building societies accumulated capital by selling shares either at lump sum or by monthly subscription. Whatever method was followed, to be a member of a building society implied having either some form of cash savings or a steady cash income. The drive for cash has been an important feature of the Jamaican peasantry, even in its proto-peasant phase under slavery (Mintz 1974) and later in its development of the internal marketing system. It was responsible for the energetic role played by the small and medium peasants in the production of export crops such as coffee and, later in the nineteenth-century, bananas.

Not all peasants produced for export. Indeed, mainly the medium and larger proprietors did, those owning between ten and fifty acres. The small peasants relied mainly on the internal marketing system, for which they engaged in diversified production. Even sugarcane was grown for domestic consumption and the local market.

My parents were very poor. My stepfather was a cultivator, but the land that he lived on was very small, so he have to constantly work on the small land, acre and a half. The land was his own. He raise one cow and two pigs and all those things. Meanwhile he is in the field working, my mother had a donkey and she used to go to the market. She carry water coconut and boil a little peas and other little food. It was short distance from the home but she had to sell a little to help us live, to buy our clothes and so. After that now, she thought it was too hard for her and she started to practice to take the bough of the coconut and plait them to make hat, and sew it with her hand to assist us a little better, because people always buy the hat, people in the district and people in Mandeville. When the sun hot upon people head they wanted a broad hat. So she got along a little better. Until doing that now, she bought a machine and start to practice to make our clothes. So she go in Mandeville and buy some cloth and make pants and little girl suits so that she could sell. At that time now I was a girl and a boy in one. I had to wash them clothes, clean floor, cook the food and all those things. For that reason my education I could never get.

In this case, there were ten children to support. The reader can note the transition from merely marketing what was produced on the one and one-half acres of land to engaging in crafts. According to the informant, plaiting straw hats was more rewarding than marketing coconuts, and dressmaking more rewarding than the latter. While these activities brought in cash, the labor of the children helped to preserve the family's standard of living, but, as this informant tells us, at the expense of an education.

Wage labor also went hand in hand with land cultivation. To most whose means of living off the land was meager, wage labor was a necessity. As was true of the first free settlers after emancipation, a large number of the rural population was made up of only "part time peasant." One mother "just have a piece of land. And it just have a few fruit trees on it and being a woman she want a little money. Sometimes you have drought, so till the earth open up and nothing can't plant." So she took to walking four miles to the large Clarendon Park estate where she found work "weeding grass." I already cited the case of an informant's mother who took to domestic labor in spite of owning eighteen acres, and the owner of ten acres who hired out his services as the driver of a cart. Even children helped the inflow of cash. One of my informants told of how he used to "weed grass" or reap pimento berries for sixpence a day in St. Elizabeth, in order to buy his school clothes, and another of how as a child he performed task work on a nearby estate in St. Ann.

Wherever possible, poorer peasants rented land from richer farmers or from the big landlords. These they planted out in subsistence and cash crops.

Mi father was a cultivator in a place name Seville estate, just a little ways out of St. Ann's Bay. In those days, when you got two acres, you got plenty. So him plant it out in banana and sell it to di wharf.

Mi father was a carpenter, but at the same time he works a large field, around five acres. He was paying rent to a gentleman on the Stettin property. I would say is over 800 banks of yam he plant. He has a large banana plantation dat sometimes one cutting he can cut twenty stem of bananas.

The tenant, it is obvious from these two examples, could do well provided he had access to more suitable and fertile land such as was available from the large estates. But renting land carried the risk that one could be thrown off at short notice. The new owner of Seville estate in St. Ann decided to eject all the tenants on his land to turn the place over to cattle grazing. "An' after six months him take 'way di whole to raise cow, and mi mother don't have no supportance for us. An' him tek it 'way, leggo cow in deh and di property turn down entirely, dat nobody couldn't understand how it so hard."

Precapitalist Relations

Labor relations in the rural Jamaica of my informants were in many cases based not on a wage contract but on forms of relationship generally called precapitalist. In St. Elizabeth, for example, the owner of a large property would lease his land to the small cultivators, but require that they hand it over after one and one-half years in exchange for a fresh piece. The purpose of this arrangement was that the landowner would get his estate bushed and cared for without paying for it. Some enterprising peasants also cashed in on the practice, by leasing large tracts of a property and then subrenting each acre to three or four tenants at a time. "But after the time up, suppose they lease it for a year or two years, after the two years up you have to give him back because you cultivate it off already. You turn it back and then you go and get a different piece. Sometimes Browney lease the land to a certain amount of people, and then we rent from these tenants and cultivate." Thus the upkeep of properties that were rented out portions at a time on a short-term basis was maintained not by wage labor but by moving the tenants around from developed to less-developed or ruinate pieces. This was one form of precapitalist relations. Other forms existed also.

The father of one informant died and left his children a piece of the rockiest land in St. Mary, so stony, he said, that all they could grow on it was sugarcane and this they would squeeze for breakfast during the 1914 war years. To support the family, the oldest sibling used to husk coconuts on the Industry property. According to the informant, when Jones owned the Industry property, it was a "blessing."

It had coconut, banana, breadfruit, orange, pear, everything, you know. But not one day a man ever hold you and say you steal his things. You pick coconut, you pick pear, you pick orange, you look wood—everything that was on the property; and the man never one day ever complain yet. Those people were blessed people, the Jones' them. And they had a barbecue where people use to get job picking pimento. And them give out land to cultivate, to plant coconut. And you work the land until the coconut come to a state now, and them give you another piece. Otherwise when you cultivate grass to feed the cows, you don't plant the grass until the last crop. Suppose you going to plant three crops of food, you don't plant the grass in the first or second crop, because you would have to reap it too early. But these people were blessed people, man.

What advantage did the property get from giving peasants the land to use free? To the peasant the landowner was just kind. But the picture is clear enough. Jones had two main interests, having enough coconuts to maintain copra production, and having enough grass to feed his herds of cattle. Instead of hiring a permanent team of workers, he would parcel out the land to poor peasants, whose interest was in using the land to feed their families, but in a way that had to coincide with Jones's interest. If, within the three years that he had use of the land, a peasant were to plant the grass first, then he would have to wait a whole year to plant food for himself. Therefore, he planted Jones's coconuts and his own food for the first two years, and by weeding his own food prevented the coconuts from being stifled before they reached a certain height. In the third year he planted the grass, and moved on to another patch. Thus, he paid for the use of the land not with money but with labor.

Such forms of exchange included the church also. Although peasants generally do not regard the church in this light, some of my Rastafari informants did because, as Rastafari put it, the oppression of black people is effected through church and state. Thus, whereas most would see the traditional "harvest" as a necessary act of thanksgiving to God "from whom all things flow," the Rastafari sees it as naked exploitation:

My father-in-law and my mother join the church. They paid dues like, yearly. When all this time my father-in-law and my mother did have a nice cock-chicken in the home and a nice bunch of banana or a nice bunch of plantain that could be sold for money or we could enjoy, they cut it down and give it to Parson. Parson take from some people and him sell it back to the same people.

The proceeds from the harvest went to the upkeep of the church and to the clergyman's family.

In the Moravian Church each parson had total jurisdiction over the church lands, and from this he was expected to live. The land was called a glebe, and was equivalent to the benefice of the feudal church. On his glebe in Manchester, Parson Jenkins required his members to plant corn.

And we plant the parson corn. In planting these corn the members chop the bush and the land where the corn was to be planted. The parson and his son and daughter and wife stand by and looking. Them get two kerosene pan of sugar and water and a lot of crackers and rum to give these people. They chop a big lot of land and when the bush dry, those same members come back and they burn it and plant the corn. All the parson do is continue mixing sugar and water and rum.

One thing strike me most of all is when the crop come in: parson take the same corn and boil porridge and give the people to shell the corn. They call this shelling patch. Two and three nights of shelling pure corn. Well, when the corn measure and ready to be sold, none of the members don't know about that. They know how much corn Parson make; they know how much bushel, but how much money him get them don't know. It work up to a time that I see Parson buy all car. The car that he bought new, my mother coming from Porus market, Parson pass my mother around two and a half miles. My mother see the car before him pass and call to him. She is a member of the church. Him and his wife and him son and him daughter in the car . . . the car don't full. When my mother call to him, him go on as if him never see her and him well see her! But she couldn't get a drive in the car. And him come home and my mother had to walk her foot come up.

The voluntary nature of this labor service to the church resembled the "digging," an old but popular form of collective labor, but only superficially, the important difference being that Parson had no obligation to reciprocate in kind, and it is clear that in this case Parson Jenkins did not. But what irritated Baia, my informant, is the class and status differences that the Parson maintained between himself and the very congregation whose voluntary labor he alleges allowed him to acquire the symbols of his position.[1]

One practice that might be considered another form of labor relationship was the rearing of poor peasants' children by the more well-to-do peasants and farmers. I hesitate, however, to classify this arrangement with the other forms discussed above, because the practice often involved reciprocal ties of real and putative kinship that extend beyond mere labor exchange. For example, one of my informants was given away to his godparents, owners of a large property and bakery in the parish of St. Mary. He was their general handyman, receiving no payment other than food and shelter, but was allowed to earn his own cash by planting four or five squares of banana. This is an example of the tradition of customary adoption still quite common throughout the country and which does not fit the definition of disguised labor exchange, as some of the cases I shall presently cite will bear out. For now, I only wish to point out that if children who are adopted prove lazy they are returned.

Social Pressures

I would like now to discuss some of the social pressures on the poor peasants, as they manifested themselves in the lives of my informants, and the way they set about coping with these pressures.

First, there were the often bitter disputes over family land, which Jean Besson (1987), following Peter Wilson (1973), describes as "crab antics." Because, as she argues, family land is not simply another form of tenure but a symbol of kinship identity as well, attempts at exploitation by individual members of the group whether through production or alienation are often opposed by other members. For this reason, family land tends to lie idle and underutilized.

Brother Williams reports that his father owned three and one-half acres of land, separate from the land that his mother herself inherited from her mother. Before Williams's father wandered off

1. As a boy I do remember the Anglican parson in our district who rarely gave anybody a lift in his car, but when he did placed the person on the rear seat. He wore, besides, the "bowler hat" white English colonials used to wear.

on his itinerant preaching, his father left an acre for him under the care of his aunt, but she sold the land. Similarly, Sister Portia's mother died leaving two and three-quarter acres for Portia and her sister. Cousin Franklin, with whom Portia went to live after being thrown out by her father, sold it. "I went over to a next cousin and tell that Brother Frank sell the place, for them did never know. And she say if me want it to go to court, she will take it up. I say, 'no, mam, mek it stay. Him know why him sell it, and im have im reason why im sell it so.'" Sister Portia refused to take the matter to court, but that did not mean that she approved of his action. Sister Lali also reported having received an acre from her father, which her bigger sister sold.

Brother Anton's grandfather cut up his family land, leaving his daughter, Anton's mother, an acre. Forced by poverty to move to Kingston, she left the land:

She did have a bad daughter, who leave her a Kingston and come country and sell out the place to mi cousin over there so. And when me hear and tell her 'bout it, she coming everyday about it till she dead. Since him, mi cousin, dead, fi him wife take it sell it to mi uncle wife. Den fi mi brodder come a fight them fi it, till it all go a court; and lawyer take it sell it to a next somebody.

Anton's example shows some of the complexity in family land. It was, he explains, sold by one of his sisters, "a bad daughter," meaning someone difficult to control, to one of their cousins. As Edith Clarke (1957) explains, family land could be passed on by mother or father. Although land bequeathal gave unlimited rights to all one's descendants, male and female, it excluded all those relatives not related to the original ancestor. Anton's cousin therefore was a relative on their father's side.

The motive behind the litigation was either to establish the correct ownership of the land, or to enforce the principle that family land should not be sold outside the kin group. Family land gave the right to use but not to dispose of land. Ownership rested with the sib group as a group. In passing on the land, a parent might specify which piece was to be used by which offspring. But the main principle distinguishing family land from other lands was its inalienability. Its sale was discouraged.

Even if Sister Portia had taken Cousin Franklin to court, there was no way the courts could have enforced restitution because family land was not a custom recognized by law. Justice was achieved, in her case, by retribution, and in Brother Anton's case by the machinations of an allegedly unscrupulous lawyer.

In considering the families in which the early Rastas were socialized, two things are immediately striking. First is the very large size of the families. I say families, meaning mother, father, and children, rather than households. Informants remembered how many offsprings their parents had, but often were unable to tell who also lived in the household. Nevertheless, we can get a rough idea of the number of mouths a mother had to feed. Two out of every three of my informants came from families of five or more children. Indeed, of the fifteen who were specific about the sizes of their sib groups, seven came from families of ten or more children.

A second feature was the high ratio of mothers to fathers. Of all my informants, only four reported having been supported by their fathers. Some said that their fathers died early, which fits in with the shorter life expectancy of males, whereas the rest reported simple neglect.

My father was a fisherman. He was a master painter and also a mason, and mi mother she sell around. They were living together but separation come in the midst of them, that the father say im don't concern with me, I am not his child. So im wouldn't support me. Well, the mother now, she can't throw it away. The father im can do it, but the mother have to keep it.

Here the father rationalized his negligence by denying paternity. And as this informant so well observed, men can quite easily deny paternity, but women cannot deny their maternity.

Other fathers simply wandered off, one as an itinerant preacher, another to seek fortune abroad or to set up a new household. It does not surprise us, therefore, to find tremendous bonds of love and loyalty between these Rastafari and their mothers who were alive at the time of research.

Faced with the pressure of raising children on the threshold of starvation, mothers resorted to one of several possibilities or a combination of them. Some of these activities have been already discussed, such as wage labor, and renting land. Many peasants were artisans; engaged in handicrafts; or peddled fruits, foods, and other wares. In a developed or rapidly developing modern country the growth of industry transforms peasants into urban workers. But as Broom (1953) argues, what took place in the Caribbean was first urbanization and then, in response to it, industrialization. In the meantime, people live as they can, giving rise to a very large informal sector. Witter and Kirton (1990) estimate that for the period of 1962 to 1985 the average size of the informal sector was between 14 percent and 34 percent of GDP. We can therefore assume that the trend observed in connection with the early Rastafari has not declined since the 1930s; if anything it has grown.

Another coping strategy was giving away the children to either near relatives or strangers. Brother Roy was first sent to a cousin in Ocho Rios, where he endured "bad treatment" for three weeks before his mother sent back for him. He was then sent to another cousin in Lime Hall, this one childless. This latter cousin failed to send him to school. Finally, he was sent to still another cousin, but this time outside the Parish of St. Ann. "Him was mi cousin, but not so near, but still family. Anyway, dem give me away a Clarendon and dat was in 1908. And from a go to dat place, dem never sen' me to school. I in the bush all day long, feed cow and pick grass."

The order of choice for giving children away seems to have been first to relatives, which would account for the willingness of Brother Roy's family to send him two parishes away. Other children, however, went to godparents and even strangers.

Parents were as anxious to be relieved of the extra mouth to feed as were strangers to receive additional domestic labor. Brother Duggie knew neither father nor mother.

Mi father must have emigrate to America, but mi mother I don't know her either. In those days, long time days you know, things were so hard when a person sometimes in the country they have their children, they can't make two ends meet, they give them away to who would like them. I was given to this female with her children. Them just like me. Two of us was twins. Mi sister died and them take me.

"Them just like me" sums up the effort often made to fit such children into the structure of warm and affectionate relations. Duggie fitted in well. He supervised the other children, even to the point of punishing them. Quite proud of his integration into this family, Duggie was also fortunate. A worker who carried coal and banana on the wharves, his foster mother sent him to school, where he struggled to the fourth standard before setting out to find a job. He remained faithful to her up to her death, for when he heard she was alone and sickly and that her own children had either died or migrated, he left his sisters and came to live with her.

Others were not so fortunate, and quite evidently met with severe hardship. At eight years old Sister Gladys was given away to a woman in Kingston, through a go-between who was asked if she knew of a little girl who could work. For many years Gladys cooked, washed, and cleaned. Then someone also told her about another woman near Port Maria in St. Mary. "And going in St. Mary now I believe I would get good. Instead of getting good I get bad." The new "mother" was a higgler who operated in Kingston. By the time Gladys returned to Kingston, she was old enough to seek employment.

Sister Dixon had a similar story. Her mother was mentally ill, and Dixon was passed to the care of an aunt. Then came a woman from Anotto Bay, "Mother Simmonds." "She say she like me and she want me for she have no girl child; she have one boy child and she would like to have a girl child where she are. Mi aunt now say to her: 'I gwine give you Coolie pickney, but you must care her.' And is dat she do." Mother Simmonds was, it seemed, some sort of Pukumina or Revival leader, and on discovering that the young girl could sing well, she took her with her on all religious sojourns. But the child did not approve of Mother Simmonds and regarded the "adoption" as "dem thief mi 'way."

These examples of customary adoption bring out important aspects of kinship rarely discussed in the literature. Under customary adoption, adopted children generally retain their surnames, as well as knowledge of and social relations with their blood relatives, but they are fully integrated into the extended family, up to and including inheritance. This often gives rise to bonding between members of the sending and host families and sometimes to exchange of gifts. Not only would it be unfair to classify such an arrangement as disguised exploitation of labor but it would also miss an important dimension that Caribbean ethnographers and others have noted, namely, the love for children. This affinity for children explains why in all the complexities of the family structure, children move around between relatives and, in customary adoption, strangers.[2] The practice of giving children away to relatives or strangers was not uncommon, and children were not afraid of the separation, it seemed. Their expectations were in many cases high— "Dat time there, pickney woulda did glad if anybody, you know!"—though a frequent complaint was "bad treatment."

Another form of coping was institutionalizing children at approved institutions. Here, the Alpha Approved School played an important role. Two informants reported having been sent there, both of them after having lived with relatives. Sister Hall passed through several hands after the death of her mother in Nicaragua before reaching Alpha. "Den now, mi faada say im would prefer bring me over to his mother. Den to take shame outa his eye, my auntie, his sister, take us and raise us. And den, when she couldn't manage now, she take us and put us into Alpha three years after." There is no suggestion here that only "bad" children went to Alpha, although it ought to be expected that the heavy pressures on parents and guardians would have reduced their ability to control the socialization of children.

Many mothers took to migration in order to cope. Portia's mother migrated from Manchester to Monymusk, where she found work with an engineer on the estate until her death. Sister Lali's mother also migrated. In her case, she was working with an engineer sent to build the railway line in upper Clarendon and followed him when he was transferred to St. Catherine. After his recall to Canada or the United States, she came to Kingston. Two other informants reported that their mothers left the countryside directly for Kingston. In cases like these, the children are left with grandmothers and other relatives.

2. Alice Walker, describing the Jamaica she saw in 1984 as "a ravaged land," overheard "a 13-year-old boy offer his 11-year-old sister . . . to a large hirsute American white man (who blushingly declined) along with some Jamaican pot" (*Mother Jones*, Dec. 1986, 45). The impression is that the boy is a pimp, hustling both sister and pot. On the north coast tourist strip anything is possible, but it is also possible that the boy was offering to give his sister away to a white family. Many poorer families will offer to give children to better-off people who show interest in them, confident not only that the children will retain their identity and kinship contacts, but also that if they do well they will in fact help their kinsfolk.

Migration

We come now to consider the migration of the informants themselves, the process by which those who became the first Rastafari ended up in Kingston, and the general problems they had coping with the inhuman conditions and social disorders that characterized the growth of that city. They did not always pass directly from country to town, but as Roberts (1957) shows of the general pattern, more often than not they stopped in other parishes to look for work. The sugar estates were one frequent source of employment, either seasonal or permanent, the opening up of Northern Clarendon by rail in the 1920s another. Once having left home, however, they seldom returned to resettle.

For most of my informants, migration began at an early age. Several informants, however, left the country as adults. Hall was a young man of twenty-two when he joined his mother in Kingston, and Roy was about the same age when he settled in Kingston after returning from Cuba, whereas Morris was close to thirty on his return from Panama. Barnes was thirty when he visited Kingston for the first time for seven months, and, therefore, several years older when he settled for good. Missis was twenty-eight when she left Westmoreland to work with the family of a lawyer, and Lali was old enough to have been a higgler.

All the rest began their sojourn as children or teenagers. Anton said he was ten when he left Manchester, and his wife was eight when she was given away. Biini was nine when he took things into his own hands and absconded. Others were of school-leaving age, that is, around fifteen or sixteen. Powell made it quite clear that he was still in school when he left Trelawny.

The youthfulness of these migrants is a further indication of the pressures felt by the Jamaican peasantry. They left to "look life" elsewhere rather than remain in the countryside cultivating dry patches, often without prospect of owning land or of genuine improvement in life.

Some informants spoke of being haunted by Kingston, of being haunted into leaving home, into traveling. Downer was one such person. A young man of twenty-three, he had learned two trades from his father, was already an experienced cultivator, had a girlfriend and a child, and seemed to be settling down to the kind of life already lived by his parents when he decided to leave. "My concept never design fi stay home. I don't know what it is, but I feel that I must go out, my whole aspirations and my conscience never settle that I must stay in Trelawny." That was his way of expressing his desire to go out and exchange the life of a cultivator for that of a worker. And so, the Friday night, after gambling the only half-penny he could spare and winning a shilling on top of it, he equipped himself with a flask of rum for ninepence, a pack of Needlepoint cigarettes for a threepence, and a box of matches for ha'penny, and set out accompanied by a younger brother and the brother's girlfriend. They walked the whole night from Stettin in Trelawny to Kendall in Manchester, a distance of thirty kilometers, where they awaited the train heading from Kingston. They alighted in Spanish Town, all three practically penniless, and rented a room for two shillings a week. The following Monday, the brothers found work on Caymanas estate, but the conditions of work being bad, Downer left it and proceeded into Kingston where he found lodging with an uncle on "Pound Road," as Maxfield Avenue was then called.

Sawyer, who as a child and adolescent experienced being given away twice by his mother, first to a relative, then to a well-to-do peasant godmother, looked on Kingston as a place to which he had to go.

Mi mind just haunt me fi leave. Say you go out and leave to go to town, I always say I want to go town. But somebody say to go into town and live, you has to go to a work, grab a work there fi keep you. So, through I know this Chinaman Lin See Young—Lin See Young him have a bakery in our district and him sell out business and come to town—through I know him and him know mi father, I come in town and ask him if him could give me a job. Him say he could, but I would have to live in town so that when him need somebody him just know right where in town mi live and send direct to me.

With all his savings, Sawyer came to Kingston, rented a room, and awaited the call from Lin See Young. His migration was planned. He first took the good advice of somebody with experience, then set himself up with a promising job prospect, before making that important step. An indication of the momentous nature of the move was his decision to take with him his savings of fifteen pounds, a considerable sum of money in those days.

Barnes also used a similar phrase to describe why he came to Kingston. His spirit, he said, was urging him to return to Kingston, where he had spent seven months with his sister. A trained tailor, he had been put to work by a cousin during that short visit, making cheap "reach-mi-down" pants for sale to some stores. He also learned to cut jackets according to the style in fashion, a skill he took back to the country very successfully. Yet back in St. Mary, he felt "mi spirit urgin' to Kingston." And among the many experiences he cherished about Kingston, there was the following:

Dream is something you have in you mind, and you go to sleep and you dream about it. But vision, now, is [about] the thing to come. Sometimes is years before it fulfill, but you remember it. It was what cause me to come to town to know what I know now.

The first one I got, I was living with my sister. One day I was passing and I saw a man making a splif. Dat time, Coronation market was at Burying Ground, and him sit by the market making a splif. Dat time, I never know them, but I hear about it, but I never smoke it before. And I went to him and asked him for a draw. One of the fellows say "Don't give him!" and I say "Give mi." They were strangers to me, eighteen, twenty years—young men. And them give it to me and I take about six inhale. And while I going on, I say, "How them say this thing so dangerous and I don't feel anyway?" I was going to look for a friend at Oxford Street. So when I turn up Oxford Street I feel like mi eye shutting down, like I want to sleep. and I went into the bed and lay down. As quick as I could lay down, I see a little woman about four foot. She tie her frock and throw it over—is a tall dress, and piece dat throw up go right over till it reach the tail. At dat time I did trust a sweepstake ticket fi six shillings. She say to me, "You buy a sweepstake ticket and you struck a good number." She tell me di number too. She read the number that was on the ticket, and I go on till I wake up from mi sleep. And when the time come to pay for the ticket, I never had the money. I had to turn it back. And the second time I gwine smoke again, she dream me again. And she tell me dem playing peaka-pow at Princess and Barry Street.[3] And she say, "Mark so: 8 at the bottom line." That time is only one bank, so vendor go round and pick up the post. Right in front of my cousin shop, him had to hide from a police raid. And im turn back the money to me. And I never dream her again.

3. Peaka-pow is a popular Chinese lottery.

And I went home but my spirit urgin' to Kingston. And when I came to Kingston, I hear this doctrine, Rastafarian doctrine, but I never accept it.

Barnes was trying to say that he would never have become a Rastafari had he remained in the country, for it was mainly in Kingston that the doctrine was being preached at the time. Therefore, that urging he had was the urging of his spirit guiding him into the movement, first by getting him to leave the country for good. He was haunted by the association of Kingston with his fortune, having twice been given instruction how to win and twice having to turn it down, the first because he lacked the money, the second because of a police raid. Ordinarily Barnes would have called his experience a dream, as most Jamaicans would if told in sleep to buy a certain sweepstakes number. But when two years later he made up his mind and came to Kingston and found a greater fortune than he could have imagined, the Rastafari, the dream of the "little woman about four foot" became a vision.

In the following two cases a conscious drive for upward mobility was the main factor pulling these informants from the country. Apologizing for his lack of education, Faulkner observed that if things were then what they are today, "peradventure you woulda know me, but I would perhaps be a doctor or so, because my brain is very good, and I have the ability and I have the intention to be uplifting in that way." But without education his chances of getting anywhere were bleak. So when a superintendent of Road Works who was cutting a road through the district asked Faulkner if he would like to come home with him to take care of his horses, Faulkner jumped at the opportunity. His father was very glad, "because they know I would be more elevated when I got with that man, more than where I was. Because in those days the country parts was very backward, and they see that I had something." First, he went to live in Stony Hill, at that time a part of rural St. Andrew, and only after several years of being required to perform work on Sundays, his day off, without pay, did he leave to work as a domestic servant for a prominent elite family in a lower St. Andrew suburb of Kingston. All through his early career as a worker, Faulkner retained attitudes of subservience and deference, which he thought were important if he were to get ahead.

For Brother Powell, opportunity knocked in similar fashion. In the early decades of this century, "two-tone" rubber sole patent shoes were in fashion among dandies. "All dem man wear a shoe like that, you come like a King." One afternoon the truck driver for a small businessman in Albert Town, Trelawny, called the young Powell and asked him to clean his shoes. That evening, Powell said, everybody had to ask who had cleaned them, so well polished were they. The following morning the driver sent for the youngster and started him on a new life, traveling to and from Balaclava.

Naturally he taught Powell how to drive. Powell followed him to live in Manchester, where he soon established his own independence living with an aunt in Christiana until he got a job driving a sports car. One day, while tightening some bolts underneath the car, fire from his cigarette ignited the car. For the next two weeks, he took to the "woods and canefields" in hiding before trying his fortunes once more in the larger town of Mandeville. There, he remained for a few years bouncing from job to job, first cleaning out the market, then as a general helper at the hotel, then packing bread in a bakery, then cleaning stables.

I was there a while until I leave him and go to a man named Henriques, who was a dentist, and I start to drive for him. I work for him about two years, but I was seeking a better job, and I want to come to Kingston. But he was a man that like me very much. His wife was so much of a nice woman. You know, since I was a little boy, I have always been loved by people because I have one tendency, I like to show you manners and respect. And I can tell any man, from the experience that I had in my own way—I am not trying to exhibit—but in my own way of living, I find that manners and respect and a good approach; these three things plus honesty of purpose, is the basic principles of man's life as I see it.

These basic principles are not far different from those that motivated Brother Faulkner, though Powell's are expressed in a more moralistic way. For all his claims, however, Powell was not above breaking these principles, as he did by lying to Henriques in order to get out of that job and head for Kingston. Unlike Sawyer, who first made sure he could obtain employment, but more probably like the thousands of others who trekked into the gaslit city, Powell took the next ride he could get, without being too sure what kind of employment he would find, without knowing, even, with whom he was going to live.

The lure of finding better jobs, of improving oneself, and of achieving something in life are sentiments that motivate people into pulling up their roots and changing their status. It is interesting to note that on the scale of jobs, domestic work ranked higher than higglering, the decisive factor being not the wages offered (for domestic wages were lower), but the social standing of the employers.

Others who found their way into Kingston did so with consciousness of the hardships that pushed them. For Brother Watson it was simply the fact that, "I never see it what manner me mother would able furnish a trade. We have to jump around to Mahoe Hill, a long journey, and sometimes we have heavy load to carry, for we have no beast fe carry load." Mahoe Hill was the place where his mother owned and cultivated several acres of land. With eleven other children to support, Watson's mother gave her consent for him to work with a family who operated a dairy farm in Stony Hill. The job paid four shillings a week for work that started at four in the morning and lasted until dusk. Part of his chores entailed shoving a cartload of bananas all the way up the steep hill from Constant Spring, at that time the outer limit of the city, a journey of three miles. One day in Constant Spring he met a cousin who reproached him for having left the country only to look after cows and who invited him to work digging marl alongside him.

Watson has never gone back home to St. Mary despite the fact that over there lie eighteen acres of family land, a portion of which he is entitled to, despite the proverbial Rastafari love of the land. He expresses his reason thus: "I have never been away so long, and to return now empty handed, it doesn't look so wonderful." Those who leave their homes, he seems to be saying, whether for foreign parts or for the city, leave for a better life; to return without achieving it is a sign of failure. In the words of others describing their own situation in the country, "things was rough; couldn't get on there," or "it was very slow and wages was very small." Brother Roy, however, was very specific as to what prevented him from returning to St. Ann following his brief spell as a sugar worker in Cuba: The price of bananas rose, and the wealthy landowners threw all tenants off the land. There was nowhere for him to cultivate.

Sister Portia's mother left Manchester to work in Monymusk, and there she died. Three years after learning this news, her father came out from Panama and took Portia to live with his wife and children in Kingston. She was already an adolescent when the family then moved to St. James, where her father took a job as headman for the Pringles. There Portia got pregnant. Her father, to protect his social standing, cast her out. Finding her way back to her mother's relatives in Manchester, she spent three weeks trying but unable to adjust, for, as mentioned earlier on she discovered that her cousin and head of the household had cheated her out of a piece of land left by her mother. She obviously could not go back to St. James, so she took her only sister and boarded the train to Kingston.

Portia's story is a good example of the power of ideology to destroy human relations and displace people. According to the ruling ideas prevailing in the 1930s, families achieved and maintained their respectability and status through marriage and legitimate birth (see Henriques 1953). Sister Portia was one of countless young girls who were forced out of their parental homes to protect their families' social standing. Her father climbed up from migrant origins to become headman of one of the banana barons of St. James, and he was a practicing Anglican and a man of standing in the local community. An extramarital pregnancy in this family threatened to undermine all he had achieved. Portia's first choice of refuge was not Kingston but her mother's relatives in Manchester. Kingston was decided upon only to avoid conflict over family land.

A few of the informants found their way to Kingston directly from their places of birth, without any prior movement. Some came under the protective custody of a parent of a near relative. Others had some prior knowledge of Kingston, which attracted them to make the break. The more prevailing pattern, however, consisted of a movement that brought them to other parishes closer and closer to the city. From the rough infertile hillsides, the sugar areas of Clarendon and St. Catherine often provided good stepping stones to Kingston. Even in the cases of Brothers Watson and Faulkner, who lived less than thirty miles from the city, the movement to Kingston was gradual, involving the two outlying towns of Stony Hill and Constant Spring.

Once they arrived in Kingston, migration did not cease. A good illustration is Portia. With great difficulty she managed to save enough money, as a higgler, to buy a piece of land and put up a shop in Trench Town. Her conjugal partner was a very poor man from Mocho in Clarendon. Together they eventually decided to sell out and go back to the country.

We go over there and one of his cousin sold me a little piece of land. Told me that is an acre, more or less. But di time was so hard, we couldn't manage was to pay him, until the time dat he wanted was to get pay for it. And he take something and measure off part of it and sold it to a next man. Well through we couldn't manage to pay him, we satisfy with the little part what did leave. After a time and I see how things hard over there, I say, "No!" I put up di little place for sale and I get it sell.

Then she joined her son in Kingston.

Brother Powell, too, did not rest in Kingston. After several months without luck, except for casual, day-to-day employment, he got on a truck heading back to Manchester. Failing to achieve his desire there, he returned to Kingston. Later he found work in St. Thomas, then in Manchester, and back in Kingston again.

The movements in and out of Kingston continue up to the present. When interviewed, Anton was back on his family land in Manchester. Inki spends part of his time farming a piece of land in St. Catherine. And for weeks at a time, Barnes, a tailor, leaves Kingston to tend a piece of citrus land in Clarendon. Indeed, my knowledge of other younger Rastafari and non-Rastafari indicates that this is not an uncommon practice. And there are others who report a similar practice of combining city life with country life. The differences between town and country in Jamaica, for at least some section of the urban population in at least one respect, is not very sharp: the passage from one area to the other and back again is accomplished with ease. Occupational multiplicity (Comitas 1973) thus has an urban-rural dimension.

Social Conditions in Kingston

Not all of those people who came to Kingston had relatives to receive them. But those who did were given only enough time to adjust to the change. The longer they took to find employment, the greater was the burden on relatives. In some instances, the relatives would help them in the search, but in the end the young migrants would be expected to leave. In Brother Dawkins's case this expectation took the form of withdrawal of hospitality. His uncle began to indicate displeasure by leaving his dinner in the kitchen instead of serving it on the table like that of the rest of the household. Dawkins's refusal to touch the food precipitated a conflict, during which the uncle demanded the room back.

There is no doubt that having a relative to stay with in Kingston made it easier for the migrant. Those who did not have relatives there stayed with friends or even strangers.

I come to town in 1938, the first of March, one Wednesday. I come 'pon the bus—Syrian man dem call Shadoub bus. "Highgate Special" it name. Come in town about nine to ten o'clock. I know a lady who have a place, name Miss Thompson. 'Im come from my district and 'im have place in town, and I know all her children dem. An I leave and go round there and ask them if them know where I could get a room. And dem say dem have a room dere. I buy a cot, till I coulda able fi buy bed.

Sister Portia came to Kingston already pregnant, accompanied by her younger sister. She went to Allman Town in search of a friend, only to find her no longer living there.

I go to di gate and ask dat I understand dat is there de person dat I was looking for live. And after when I went in di yard, when she say dat she, the person, not living there again and she don't know the direct place where she living. I stood up by di gate, you know, with that sort of consideration like "where I going to go?" Night was coming down then, for it was about five o'clock. She say I mus' come inside. You know how some people how dem stay? Well, I go inside and I put down the things that I bring, me and my sister. And she say, "Well, you can stop in this room until tomorrow you can go and look for her." Anyway, she give me some thin things to sleep, and a little cot; me and mi sister sleep in there. The next morning dem say dat dis woman was living at Robert Street, and I go to Robert Street and I didn't find her for dem didn't tell me the number. So I came back. She say is one and sixpence a week for the room, and if me want to stay there mi can stay. Well, I stay there, me and mi sister, and so it go.

Sister Portia's host was herself from the country but had been living in Kingston long enough to own a house. She interpreted sympathetically the lost look on Portia's face and offered help. The two of them became excellent friends: "She was a nice woman, I tell you. She act a mother part for me. For when I have the baby, she stand up to see that I will get through."

The hospitality extended by absolute strangers in an expanding city and the new bonds of friendships that were made were actions and responses that must have been repeated thousands of times. Even Sister Gladys, on leaving St. Mary to return to Kingston, lodged with the same person who had taken her from her mother to work at eight years old. This suggests that the "bad treatment" and less than satisfactory conditions were never so bad as to require severing the relationship completely.

For many like Powell, however, there was neither relative nor friend, therefore not even the luxury of a reference point from which to begin looking for someone.

Nobody at all man, mi a little stray boy. Mi a look living and me a hunt. Mi get drive 'pon truck and mi come here and me never go back. Just rest a town. Mi sleep under house, I kotch at a yard, find a little girl friend— you know, I run joke and you have to love me after I make the joke with you—if I had a two shilling, I'd say, "Sister beg you some cookies," and all that, you know. Therefore, is those kind of life makes me get along alright. I can even remember fairly well when I take a tree leaf for hammock, kotch up there and early morning I come down and stretch out the body. I don't have any family in town. I usually up and down the street.

Other migrants were reduced to experiences like that, including sleeping on sidewalks. Finding oneself alone in the city was common enough. It proved the need for the Salvation Army Hostel, where migrants and visitors to Kingston could spend the night for a penny.

Many worked out a "partner" system, by jointly renting and paying for a room. One informant subrented a portion of a room, which entitled her to move in only a bed for five shillings a month. Generally speaking, rent was payable not in advance but at the end of the first week of occupancy. It was referred to as "live to pay" rather than "pay to live." Ackee Walk on the western edge of Kingston soon became a large slum. In the 1930s it was owned by East Indians who, according to informants, used to mass produce shacks for rent, called *wapn bapn*. The rental rate varied from one shilling and sixpence to two shillings and sixpence a week.

But lodging was not the only nor perhaps the first necessity. There was the matter of sustenance. Although some people like Brother Watson (whose cousin told him, "You stay here! Anything mi eat, you eat too!") could be sure of something to eat regardless of whether they found employment, most rural migrants had to face what one informant called "hunting the shilling" every day.

The main activity on which the economy of the country rested at that time was the production and export of bananas. Consequently, there was a great deal of work around the port, loading fruit or refueling with coal. "Every bunch you carry you get a brass. But after you get a hundred brass you change it and get two and six [shillings]." Earnings for the day depended on how many bananas came in by the train and on how many bananas one could carry. Three hundred brasses were not an impossible target. As each worker passed with a bunch of bananas on his or her head on the way to the checker, there was a man who chopped off the stem and the shoot: "Him have a sharp cutlass and him a go bam! bam! Mark you, him keep hand steady. Him don't stretch over him hand, so him can't cut you." This process of chopping off the stem while the fruit is being carried on the head is described by Lord Olivier (1936, 441–42).

Work was hard, but workers found ways to beat the system. Sister Dixon used to load ships with coal at the rate of a penny per basket, and a large basket it was. "We can't carry di big basket, you know what we do? We bend di basket so, and put all a jacket in there, and put cardboard in there. And den it hold one shovel and it light that you can help yourself. You have fi know how to use you brain fi work, or else dem mash you up. Mi wouldn't living till now." She claimed to have run up as much as fourteen shillings in a day, which at a penny per trip per basket amounted to nearly 170 trips.

At rates like these, work on the waterfront was undoubtedly among the best Kingston had to offer at the time, and to hold a job there, when one was available, must have been a privilege. The work enabled Anton to help his mother and support himself, for he was living on his own in Ackee Walk.

The period of the twenties and the thirties was also a period of expansion of the baking industry, and it absorbed quite a few workers. The larger bakeries were owned by coloreds, the smaller ones by Chinese. In both large and small bakeries, conditions of work were extremely oppressive.

The Three Star Bakery, for example, employed at least thirty people in production, plus other workers on the streets who distributed the bread in pushcarts and vans. Top pay was eighteen shillings a week, and this went to the tableman or the ovener. At the bottom were those who received eight shillings for stamping the baked and packaged bread as it came out on a sort of assembly line. The working day began at 4 A.M. On Monday, Tuesday, and Wednesday it ended at 5 P.M. After returning to work at 4 A.M. on Thursday, the workers worked right through to 5 P.M. on Saturday. Then they received their wages. On Sunday they returned at 3 P.M. and worked until midnight, to begin at 4 A.M. the same morning. Thus the workweek for bakery workers totaled 109 hours. Wages amounted to two pence an hour for those at the top, and less than a penny an hour for those at the bottom. On the weekends the employees worked without sleeping and ate meals on the job.

At the famous Hannah Town Bakery, the hours were identical to those at Three Star. At Easter the workers were required to bake right through the week, nonstop from Sunday afternoon to Thursday night, producing the famous Easter bun. The lowest-paid workers received seven shillings. There was no lunch break. "If dem ketch you eat even a bulla [cake], you pay fi it." Yet it was not economic exploitation that forced Sawyer to quit.

Him take liberty with mi girlfriend. She come and call me to ask me something. I just say to the foreman say I beg him a little time to go talk to her. And im come at the gate and begin to curse her, call her dirty and stink. I tell him, "No!" I feel he is a Chinaman and he come and see me in dis country and me working. Him shouldn't take no liberty with me, cause I wouldn't take that liberty with his wife. Dat time him have de bakery at Franklin Town, now. Im cry bankrupt at Princess Street and him wife go to Franklin Town and open dat bakery, call it "Gold Medal Bakery," on Cumberland Avenue, and up there we was.

In the rebuke "I feel he is a Chinaman and he come and see me in dis country and me working," the "me" indicates "me, Sawyers," of course, but also "me, the black man."

The owner had declared Three Star bankrupt and reopened the bakery in his wife's name, no doubt to escape paying taxes and paying off creditors, a loophole this upwardly mobile entrepreneurial class must have stretched to the limit. His wife was not Chinese, but a "red nayga" from St. Elizabeth, and this, more than anything else tells us something about his social and economic origins: rural and probably of retail-trading background.

Working similar hours for a "fair complexion" man, Brother Dawkins reported collecting four shillings at the end of his first week. He was refused more work on the grounds that "you only can clean tin sheets and you are not a baker."

Domestic labor provided another source of employment. At the time, female domestic labor enjoyed no monopoly over male domestic labor. The yardboy was as prevalent as were the cook and the maid. Both performed menial tasks under conditions generously saturated with prejudice based on class, color, and race. In domestic labor, race and color were the more pronounced factors behind both abuse and patronizing behavior. At the same time, however, the antagonisms were often mitigated by the inevitable development of some good personal relations. The following cases bring out these points.

In 1928 at the age of fourteen, just in from the country, Baia began knocking on gates until he found a job as gardener for the Tracey family. He did not live in, but received lunch. Wages were nine shillings for a seven-day week. The Traceys had two small children, and in introducing Baia to the job, Mrs. Tracey demanded that her gardener refer to them as "Mister Roy" and "Miss Elizabeth." Baia resented this. "I have many brothers and two sisters. My mother never teach me to call them 'Mister' and they never call me 'Mister.' Why should I call a white man child 'Mister' smaller than myself?" Nonetheless, he complied—it was his first job. The job entailed running errands, gardening, and other chores, but most odious of all was cleaning his employer's boots every evening. The odor was repugnant enough to Baia without Mrs. Tracey's insisting that to clean them well he had to shove his hands inside. Day after day, Baia's resentment grew, and he took the first opportunity to leave.

Opportunity came about for Baia in the following manner. Nearby stood the famous South Camp Road Hotel. One day as he passed on the way to buy ice, the hotel manager, a white man, offered him twice the pay he was then getting. He agreed to start the following morning. If he walked off the gardening job, he could expect no pay from Mrs. Tracey, so on returning with the ice he feigned a serious stomach ache and got himself dismissed with pay. The missis was far from impressed. Clever as Baia thought he was being, they probably did not fall for his act, and once confronted with his ruse realized his intentions. At any rate, the relationship did not permit him to go to them with any story, true or false, and have them believe him, so he played on it, knowing they would see through his real intentions. Not a fool, his employer, without any ado, dismissed him. "When I come outside the gate I look 'pon him and say, 'Looks pon you! You want me to come say "Sar" to you little boy, and dem no good looking like me! You see, mi no fool! See mi money there. You want to put me in slavery. Go'way! Look how you red!'" The cussing off, which followed from the safe distance of the street, was for Baia the fitting and necessary punctuation to this introduction to class and color in Kingston, as well as reassertion of his own self-esteem. It is clear that the Traceys were colored, because Baia cursed them as "red" rather than as "white." On the Jamaican color scale a "red" skin person is of very light complexion and therefore a notch above "brown." These shades of difference may not be great, but Jamaicans tend to be preoccupied with them—they are an important part of good looks. Thus even as he hurled abuse at the Traceys for being red, Baia felt particularly sure that it was on account of his looks that the hotel manager chose to call him when he did. "I come out to buy the ice. That time, very young, shine, good looking and all that. Very nice at all times, comb properly. I have good clothes that I put on. When I done work I always bathe my skin and put on clean clothes. So I looking alright." But what did he mean by good looking? Baia's hair was curly, not woolly. The name *Baia* in fact is one of several Jamaican names for male Indian, though he was not Indian. "When I come to Kingston first, people thought I was a Indian, and the Indian also believe that I'm just an Indian like them, but you call it mix. My father was a true maroon. My father mouth black, just like a pot, and his eyes is like fire. My mother is also a maroon but the blood as rich as my father." So it was from the maroons, the "royal tribe" of black Jamaican peasants, that Baia believed he gained his good looks.

Descent from the maroons is still regarded among Jamaicans as positive mark of noble background. Many of those who claim maroon ancestry sometimes appeal to a curly or softer hair texture as proof. They maintain, therefore, a visible difference from common blacks. Although there could be a basis for this mythical claim by Maroons,[4] it is more than likely another example of racial ideology that grades physical traits using the European as the standard. The closer to the norm, the greater the value. Though black, and arriving less than three hundred years after blacks started coming here, Indians with their straight hair and narrow noses have found a niche above Africans; and the Chinese with their fairer complexion and straight hair but flatter noses, a niche above Indians. Proud, not ashamed, of his new nickname, and conscious of his "nobility," Baia probably smarted under the imperious demands of his employers. They, for their part, showed by their insistence on having domestic helpers address their children formally that they were conscious of maintaining the class/color distinctions of colonial Jamaica.

After three months in the hotel kitchen, Baia's pay rose from eighteen to twenty-two shillings a week. His task was to kill and clean the birds and to clean the fish. Parts, such as the head and liver, which did not find their way to the tables of guests found their way into Baia's soup pot. Jealous of such bold action on the part of a newcomer, his fellow workers secretly told the boss that Baia was filching some of the meat as a regular practice. One day, it happened that the boss came to confront him just as Baia's soup began to simmer. Surprised that use could be found for such parts of a fowl and liking the taste, he asked Baia to leave him some the next day. And so the two of them got on excellently.

4. Kofi Agorsah (1992) produces archeological evidence to suggest an Arawak (Amerindian) presence in the early Maroons settlements.

Him like me because I'm not chatty-chatty. In the evening time him carry mi in him car and go up to St. Andrew. Him take out all a man wife in the car. Sometime him take mumma and daughter and leave the daughter in the car with me. But mi no like them white people because them raw. Them have a high smell. Sometimes they definitely force themselves to rub up against me, but me can't show them definitely what it is I feel. You can't cope with them that way. Well, his wife now—say every night him come out, him say that I must tell di wife that where we go is places that we go drink and merry-make and play games and all dem tings. Well, when we come, she is always pumping me and I telling her what him tell me.

Baia has his own prejudices against whites, but to "cope with them" he was forced by circumstances to suppress his true feelings of repulsion. Thus, even though they got on well on the surface—indeed, according to Baia his boss defended him against his own white social circles as "my black son . . . you can't stop me from owning him"—there remained feelings of racial animosity not far from Baia's consciousness.

The management changed while he was recuperating from an attack of typhoid, and he lost his job. Nevertheless, his patron showered gifts and visits on him during his illness, eliciting the comment of his sister: "Boy, you come a town a lucky time! White man draw up a gate and say, 'Where is Richard?'—that's my real name."

Baia's patron was almost certainly not from the local white community, which, whatever it might have thought or done about adulterous relations, would not have tolerated the flaunting of social conventions such as he practiced. Jamaican whites had well worked out codes about treating their servants and as Brother Duggie experienced, some expatriates, unlike Baia's patron, did learn.

For a period of at least six years, beginning in 1930, Duggie worked as a gardener and a waiter for the officers of the British army sent to serve in Jamaica. Each of his four employers paid the same twelve shillings a week. The last had a wife "that walk about Jamaican people and find out how dem handle dem servant, and she want to bring rule on me." At each of her frequent dinner parties the servants were required to stay and clean up after the guests had departed and to return promptly at six o'clock the next morning. The attitude of local whites and coloreds, it would appear, was that even reasonable concessions to servants would "spoil" them.

Brother Faulkner worked for a wealthy pen-keeping family, Jamaican whites. At twelve shillings a week, his job was to polish the car and look after the garden. "They treat me so nice. And if I look about anything and it look very good, them give me a extra money away from my pay." He also got lunch every Sunday. All the servants were provided with unfurnished accommodation. A wage of twelve shillings was not much, and Faulkner found a way of increasing it.

I go to market on Friday. The lady I used to work with dem call her "Big Missis." And she gi me a list and she tell me "Go to Cross Roads market and buy these things." and how I get the money: through she is white people, when she go to the market dem charge her more than I because dem is white people. Me will go now and say, "Lady, I want some yam to buy. I want about ten pound but I can't pay the price you want, you know." Big Missis may go a market last week and she may see yam at say 20 cents a pound. When I go this week, the price may drop to 10 cents. And she estimate the amount of money I get and check it to see how much it can buy. Now when I go I say "I want some but I cants afford to buy them for 20 cents. Sell me for 15 cents." But true she a white people dem charge her a higher price. And when mi done now me find meself a rich man, for the little 12 shillings per week can't pay me; I have fi feed meself the whole week.

Here we see Faulkner manipulating the racial class structure in order to compensate for what he felt was a low wage. He could not demand more, not only because he could not if he wished to retain his job, but also because of the element of patronage inherent in domestic service.

But the lady did love me very much, because she find out that something is in me. If she is in a room, she has a washer, a cook and a butler, and I am working outside in the garden. And if she want a drink of water—now, dem have a bell and dem tell me say two call belong to me. And when I got inside she say. "David, please bring me a drink of water." She says, "You know the reason why I want you to give me this water? When you give me this water I drink it more digested. I feel more satisfied than when the other servants give me the water." Dem careless. But me now, when she send me for the water, I wash the glass and saucer and a waiter. And when I done wash the glass I get some hot water from the stove and throw on the glass, so no rawness whatsoever is there. And when I go and she drink it, it nice.

The glass of water ritual helped to reinforce Faulkner's illusion that he was getting ahead, by maximizing his opportunities relative to other servants. In the end however, he was dismissed as servants can be dismissed—ignominiously, for borrowing some money Big Missis gave him to pay her milk supplier. He quickly found employment, using the same subservient attitudes. "I know plenty gentlemen in authority to give work. And once you go to them in a decent way you can obtain work. But if you go in a rash and feisty manner they don't care much about you." He was far from wrong.

As bad as the condition of male servants was, that of females was much worse. Sister Missis worked for a member of the intelligentsia, a lawyer. "They took me as a slave maid." For seven shillings a week she cleaned and tidied the rooms of the four-bedroom house, did the laundry, and cooked. In the evening, dressed in the cap and uniform of a nursemaid, she walked the twins whom she had to care for in addition to all the other tasks she performed. Seven shillings in 1929 was more than what others like Gladys or Portia got, but it was 70 percent less than what Faulkner got, and Portia worked more hours.

It must not be forgotten that the lower social strata also employed domestic help. After the birth of her son, Portia found a job paying two shillings a week at Kingston Gardens, then a middle-class suburb. Forced to take the child to work, she had to tie him to a tree, "as if you tying out a dog or a horse."

For, through di people dem is mulatto and I working wid dem, dem wouldn't allow the child to go up and down into dem place. One day, when she used to send me to Camp—for her husband was on the contingent gone to war; she used to send me to Camp every other day for her supply. I remember one day when I came back and see mi baby, I cry. Him dirty from him head to him foot, plastered with the mess. And I cry and I say "Lord, if you father didn't dead, I wouldn't have to be working and you stay like dis." I tek him and I wash him and tie him back again.

Domestic help was not always a mark of social status or color. Better-paid workers and small entrepreneurs also employed domestic labor. For example, during the First World War, Portia worked as a domestic for a soldier at one shilling and sixpence a week. In the late 1920s, Sister Gladys took on a job cleaning a man's house for one shilling a week, "and when dem see it look too bad the lady put on sixpence." She even worked for a shilling a week cleaning a man's two-room apartment and carrying his lunch. She carried his lunch every weekday and cleaned on Saturdays. She did not have to cook—his sister-in-law did that. She bounced from job to job carrying lunches. When she reached two shillings and sixpence a week, she was employed by a caterer to carry thirteen lunches a day plus twenty-five pounds of ice for workers at the railway station. Work began at 6 A.M., at which time she bought food in the market. She then helped with the cooking and left at 11:30 A.M. Her chores for the day were fulfilled when she returned after lunch and washed the dishes.

Discussion

The paths leading to Kingston as a final home were direct for some of the founding members of the Rastafari, but for most, they involved detours. With or without detours, however, the city of Kingston marked the end of the journey, with a population that expanded from 89,400 in 1921 to 379,600 in 1943. There people found menial and low-paying jobs with harsh working conditions that reminded some of them of slavery. But there were alternatives to wage labor, such as higglering, an occupation that bridged the distance between town and country. For some, higglering had begun in the rural towns, with Kingston offering an enlarged opportunity, but for others, the art was first learned as a means of surviving in the city. The market area of Kingston, even before the building of Coronation Market in 1937, was fairly concentrated. Redemption Ground and Chigga Foot Markets were situated within two blocks of each other, and not far away was the Railway Station where citrus and bananas were brought in for shipment. In this area of the city there sprang up a lively bustle of pretty trades and crafts. One informant found work on the waterfront for a while, then following a layoff turned to higglering, then to the life of a small shopkeeper, then became a cultivating peasant, then returned to higglering. Brother Faulkner, after his dismissal from domestic labor, found work in the Public Works Department of government. He then took to operating a lunch cart in one of the markets so successfully that he was able to employ wage labor. Later he met with financial ruin and returned to wage labor. Brother Sawyer knocked about between sporadic employment in baking and peddling oranges. Brother Powell tried a hand at peddling trinkets before being employed as a driver. The list could go on and on. Some, like Barnes, learned to peddle ganja or to live off gambling. Other showed a capacity for innovation: Brother Inki said he was the first to develop a handcart with four wheels and a steering rod; Baia claimed to be the first to convert discarded rubber tires into famous sandals he called "power."

Every personal history of striving to make a living in the city was punctuated with wage labor and the entrepreneurial activities of the "self-employed." Indeed, there is a strong sentiment among the Rastafari, even today, that they would rather work for themselves than for others, and the basis for this sentiment lies in the existence of such alternatives to wage labor.

Nevertheless, such sentiments are not expressed by the Rastafari in any but ideological terms, and the experience of racism and color prejudice in the social structure by people fresh from peasant life must have acted as an important stimulus for them to leave the labor market world of "Babylon."

Racism and color prejudice were integral parts of the colonial world, the necessary outgrowth of exploitation on a world scale of non-European peoples. In the British Caribbean, the racial superstructure was crowned by white colonial expatriates (like Duggie's masters), beneath them local creole whites (Faulkner's masters) and, further down, the colored (Baia's and Portia's first employers).

Judging from a remark made by Duggie that one of his employers went to some trouble to learn from the local whites the racial codes of conduct with respect to servants, and judging also from the flaunting of those codes by Baia's second employer, it would appear that local whites were far more assiduous in keeping blacks in their place than were the expatriate whites. This practice, in turn, reinforces my point that the colored middle class reproduced ideas about race to consolidate their own power. The inhuman treatment of Portia's child was accurately explained by her as due to color rather than to class—"through dem is mulatto." Another Rastafari informant also remembered being fired from his job for "thinking you are a white man," when all he did was wear an expensive sports shirt to work.

The reactions of the most racially and socially oppressed were not devoid of their own contradictions. For example, almost at the same time that he nurtured deep resentment at being treated as an oppressed black, Baia nurtured within himself feelings of ethnic superiority because of his softer curls and maroon ancestry. Later his coming under the patronage of a white expatriate pleased not only himself but also his relatives as an event of good fortune, despite the division it created among other workers (some of whom were also trying to ingratiate themselves) and despite Baia's own racial prejudices. In a similar vein, Faulkner was proud of having most-favored status as a servant, a response that comes through clearly in the previous excerpts, notwithstanding his low pay.

Given the rural origin and character of the early Rastafari, it is not surprising that they brought with them into the city elements of the outlook of the peasantry. Explaining some of the forces driving her off the land, Sister Portia recalled the injustice meted out to her by her own cousin in selling the only piece of land left by her mother. Rather than trying to take him to court, she resigned herself to fate. "Justice" was done several years later. "Three months after him go to Cuba him was a dead man. Three months after him dead in Cuba the biggest son dead. The other one turn idiot." Belief in retribution is not confined to any one class; it plays a great role in explaining personal misfortune and catastrophes. "Leave him to God!" is the expression of the Jamaican peasants' undying faith that injustice cannot prevail against the hidden hand of fate. Other elements in that outlook can be cited. For example, from the very start of the trek toward Kingston, visions and dreams served as guides along the path.

3. The Enlightenment

I now seek to examine two of the principal factors that led founding Rastafari members to the enlightenment in the Rastafari message, and then to discuss some examples of the cognitive framework within which their very personal decisions were made. In Chapter 1, I traced the long history of political, social, and cultural resistance by blacks in Jamaica to oppression during and after slavery. Particular attention was given to the different forms of cultural reconstruction and, within that focus, to the belief system and ethics of Revivalism. That chapter ended with a brief evaluation of the sense in which Garveyism could be considered a turning point in the history of the idealization of Africa. I now proceed, through the life stories of the founding members, to examine these two factors: Revivalism in order to begin to trace its continuity with Rastafari, and Garveyism in order to show certain breaks in that continuity. The discussion centers on (a) the Revivalist outlook; (b) the idealization of Africa; and (c) the processes of conversion.

Revivalism

In order to describe the religious outlook of the people earlier in the pre-Rastafari period, I shall draw on Sister Dixon, the only informant who was attached to the Bedwardite Movement. The picture she paints is in two parts. The first describes Bedwardism in general terms, the second in the context of the 1907 earthquake. Bedward's headquarters were in August Town, now a part of Greater Kingston but at that time a settlement adjacent to the Mona Estate on which sugar cane was grown.

Bands from all bout come. When I go up there I was a little child. I can remember when my parents carry me up there. I have an aunt named Mother Burke. She is Bedwardite woman, a Baptist. Captain Goldson was the Captain for Bedward, Minister Dawson, Minister Steel, Minister Edward, nuff of dem. Twenty-four Angel and seventy-four Elders. And when him baptize the people down to the river him march them to parade at the big church. I was a small child but I remember that him baptize nuff people.

And 'im was carrying on with the work. People from foreign, people from all about come there and baptize. Pure God water. Go dere now and go by the riverside where the medicine come from, a little hole; the water spring up from the hole near the river but 'pon the land. And im consecrate it and is dat water heal the people. And the stone is right there now.

Is there Minister Dawson stand up and preach till the sun rise. Manley and Busta went up there to try the medicine. And the doctors could not get the people, for him mostly attract the people there. For some Catholic people did went there and them acolyte did get better by the water. It was a Father go there which the wife of a friend, and dat friend tell another friend working at the white people that him have a boy who was a acolyte in the Catholic path, and this boy get cripple, sick, and Father was tending to him but him can't get better. And this woman now tell him about this man in August Town. And the white woman bring him son up there.

And dem keep this June meeting, this three day fasting. Some of the people tek up the fasting 12 in the day to 6 in the evening and some tek it 6 in the morning to 12, and break it. And some tek it 2 day and break it 6 in the evening. Is so the band of people dem march and go up dere and baptize. And who want to keep it up three days them go under a tree by themselves. And they have a nurse to get their mouth wash, bring basin and wash their mouth. You have to have your mouth cleansed, for dem don't eat nothing, no drink, nothing. And dem break it in three days; in the evening dem go pon de parade and break it 6 o'clock. The three day people call it June meeting. And the people dem that break the fast baptize. All baby and all baptize in the river.

Sister Dixon's account is hampered by the fact that she passes from one point to the next as memories flash into her mind. Thus, remembering that a "June meeting" was held for the son of the white woman, she goes on to describe it without finishing all that she probably wanted to say.

The Bedward movement comprised a network of loosely attached Revival groups, besides having a church organized around Bedward himself. Mother Burke, Dixon's aunt and foster parent, was herself the leader of one of those groups. The groups functioned autonomously of their center of gravity but paid recognition and allegiance by visits to August Town for baptism and other rituals. That was why, no doubt, Minister Dawson was among those deputized by the prophet Bedward to baptize.

Within Bedward's own church, as it existed in August Town, there was clearly a structure of offices comprising ministers, angels, and elders (Simpson 1956). Later Rastafari mention seventy-two elders as comprising their own "house," or group, but here, according to Dixon, the number is seventy-four, probably an error because the number seventy-two has biblical reference.

There were three main features which had strong roots among the people. The first was baptism as the main form of salvation. Children as well as adults were baptized. Their belief in the spiritually cleansing power of water by virtue of their African and Christian background (Herskovits 1958, 232–35) was all the stronger. Baptism took place in the early morning exactly at sunrise. The bands journeyed through the night in order to greet the rising sun, the symbol of strength and fertility, as I shall presently illustrate in more detail. Second was the belief in the efficacy of fasting in order to prepare oneself for spiritual battle. The prototype of this was obviously Jesus' fasting for forty days. When Bedwardites fasted, and contemporary Rastafari fast as well, they let nothing pass their lips, not even water. Consequently, before breaking fast their mouths had to be rid of its dryness to get the saliva flowing again. Third is the main feature of Bedward's fame, healing. For this he was famous in and out of Jamaica. He used to consecrate, bottle, and dispense water that even now still flows out from underneath a large rock and into the Hope River. We are told that foreigners used to come to August Town to see the prophet. Bedward himself, as mentioned in chapter 1, had been a migrant worker to Central America before getting called to serve God, and so was probably known back there. The "foreigners" were likely also migrant Jamaican workers. However, Bedward was sufficiently famous to have attracted not only the poor, but people from the other social strata as well. Dixon does not mean to be taken literally when she says that Manley and Busta visited August Town. Even the way she uses the names of the two political figures is an indication that she means "people" of that sort, namely, "politicians and dignitaries." At any rate she does mention a white woman and her son.

Sister Dixon was a little girl when the earthquake struck Jamaica in 1907. She remembers the day of the catastrophe quite well. It had begun, she said, with the death of a little boy killed by a streetcar. Her aunt, Mother Burke, was holding a morning service.

Is the morning the boy dead. And after the crowd gone and dem carry the body to dead house, me stand up at the gate and me see this man come, the man have hair 'pon him ears ya so, two side, and im black and im lip red. Big man and im stout. And I remember him put im hand on mi head and say, "Little one." Meanwhile the people dem still in the church. Him have on a white gown and a basket in im han'. And im say, "Can I go in?" and I say, "Yes, you can go in."

And I 'member I see the man go in and im stan' at the doorway while everyone inside. And Captain blow the whistle and tell the members dem to stan' up. And when the man go in the hymn was dis:

> Before Jehovah's awful throne
> Ye Nations bow with simple joy
> Know that the Lord is God alone
> He can create, He can destroy.

All the members them sing it and when dem finish him turn to them and say, "Everybody is in peace?" And the people dem say, "Yes."

And him put him hand on the Cup and him do so, rattle the cup like, and him say, "I don't come to preach. My master send me to King Street to say that by 3 o'clock he is going to speak." And him bid goodbye.

And when him come out now him go out North Street and him stand at North Street and Regent Street corner, over pon this hand—I remember it, and him put on a blue gown and when him put on the blue gown now him was looking at the sun like this—eyes straight in the sun. And that time the sun hot you know! And pure pickney! For me run follow him, through me see him with this blue gown. And when him gwine move off, him tek off the blue gown, put it in the basket and put on the full red gown.

And the people dem say "Where dis obeahman come from?" Me tek mi ears hear dis. And children anxious fi follow him. And him tek a step go towards King Street. Hear what him going sing now—him have two shake what you shake into him hand, and im say:

Aaron and Moses, mi Lord
Aaron and Moses
Aaron and Moses, mi Lord
Aaron and Moses
Fire da bun generation
De fire da bun
De fire da bun generation
De fire da bun.

The narrative follows this prophet all the way to downtown Kingston where he enjoined the retail merchants to close their stores. One of the merchants sent for the police who, with a sub-servient clicking of heels and salute to the white manager, sent the "warner" pitching headlong to the ground and arrested him for lunacy. That afternoon came the deadliest of a series of earth tremors that lasted a few seconds but which seemed to many the end of the world.

J. J. Williams who was in Jamaica at the time of the earthquake described his own experience of a young woman who tried to warn her father of the catastrophe. He went on to say that when finally he reached Kingston the following morning: "I repeatedly heard stories of a weird prophet who, it was said, had passed along the city's streets some hours before the disaster, sounding a cry of warning." (1934, 2).

The event was most significant for Sister Dixon because it had been foretold by a Warner. This figure has not entirely disappeared from the religious life of the people. Occasionally in Kingston one may still see the warner, usually female, enrobed, head wrapped in a turban, armed with a Bible and a palm frond, going out among the "highways and byways" and warning the people to avert immi-nent danger by turning from evil. In respect to this warning against evil the tradition shows affinity to Myal. The role of warner there-fore had two aspects to it: that of prophesying the future and that of calling society to account for its corrupt violation of God's moral laws. Both aspects were integrated, in that the failure of men to lead upright lives merited the retributive justice of God, administered in catastrophes such as natural disasters. For example, the destruction of the pirate city of Port Royal in 1692 was commonly regarded as an act of God against the most sinful city on earth (Parry and Sherlock 1957, 89). Such beliefs find their substantiation in that most popular source of oracles, the Bible, where God is conceived of as working through nature, earthquake, lightning, fire, and so forth, to restore or to establish a moral order.

The 1907 warner took his message not only to the poor but to the rich, whose privilege at the expense of the exploitation of the poor was precisely the kind of order Revivalism sought to change. Up until the 1930s, according to informants, stevedores and casual laborers were subject to harassment for walking home via King Street, then the center of expensive shopping in Kingston. The reason was thought to be their unsightly appearance to tourists. The act therefore of a black constable clicking heels and saluting a white store manager was symbolic of servant-master relations between black and white. Racism, in its many forms, was one of the main targets for attack by Revival leader Bedward himself.

With the decline of Revivalism as an organized religion, the warner role passed to the Rastafarians. One of our informants was herself a warner before becoming a Rasta and continued warning long after her conversion. Dunkley, one of the founders of the doctrine, used to warn. He is said to have gone about the city prophesying the destruction by fire of the Roman Catholic convent. I am told that the same was also true of Robert Hinds.

The warner in the episode was said to have stood up for some time gazing "straight in the sun." Far from being the isolated idiosyncrasy of a madman, sungazing had roots in the wider context of Revival ideology. The sun is regarded as the giver and generator of life, a symbol of male strength and sexuality, just as the moon, receiver of the light of the sun, is the symbol of female fertility. The point is worth dwelling on for some moments, and I shall draw upon other Rastafari who also express the same ideas.

Baia was by Princess Street one day, in the early forties, preaching the doctrine to those who came around the market. A policeman interrupted him.

"Move off from here, dirty, nasty Rasta!" Mi look at him. Mi say "You dirty more than I, you know, for blood is on your side, and blood around your waist. You don't see that? You are sinking in blood! See, it reach your waist!"

Him lift his staff, lick after me and mi escape from it. Mi feel mi hand go down so—that is a next one hold me. When him hold me, now I used to practice looking in the sun when I'm alone, drawing up communication. So I pulled them to the corner and look in the sun and when I come back and look in them eyes I see them squint. So when them squint, I draw them back and I look back again. And I look back in them eyes and I see them drop them head.

Baia's reference to blood is to the red seams on the outside of the trousers and to the red band around the waist of uniformed constables. According to Baia, the effect of his looking in the sun was to force the policemen not to be able to look him in the eye, hence the detail that they dropped their heads. The sun thus assisted him spiritually. There is, according to Baia, some sort of magnetism in the sun.

The sun is attached to a human being, for a man to have some connection with a spiritual being. Because the sun—no one could stop it from rise, no one could stop it from set. It's attached to a man and the moon also is attached to a woman. One light is greater than the other and the magnet from the sun should be able to assist while you thinking alright and moving correctly towards that. It can assist you in working spiritually. You arise in the morning early, you take a bath, a few psalms when the sun is rising and you can feel a different current.

Taking a bath first thing in the morning is an act of purification, after sexual intercourse, in preparation for the replenishing power of the sun. In sexual intercourse a man is thought to lose his seed to the woman (MacCormack and Draper 1987) and thereby become as weak as she is, if not weaker, a position or order that needs to be rectified, for it is she who draws her power from him and not vice versa. Folk brews such as Irish moss (a kind of seaweed) are credited with transmitting sexual power, a belief capitalized on by the producers of certain stouts that have the power to "put it back" and to allow one to acquire greater potency.

Sister Dixon gives the symbols of sun and moon practically the same interpretations, and goes even further than Baia. In a vision she saw a brown man dressed as a doctor and carrying a leather bag, and a big black woman. The man invited himself into her house and asked to sit on the bed. Out of the bag the woman took a red flower and placed it in a glass of water. The man drew his spectacles from out the bag and inserted a thermometer in her mouth. Then he withdrew it. That done, he took out a key and opened his chest, both sides opening like a book, "like a Bible leaf." Inside she saw another man with his arms outstretched. "Look as far as you can see," she was instructed and saw blood gushing from his chest and being sucked in by the man inside. Who was the doctor? she asked rhetorically. None other than God, the Father.

The Father! The Father is in you!, mother and son. How you deliver yourself? You come from your mother's womb. Here is yu mother, down here [*pointing to her genitals*], and here is the son, [*pointing to the heart*] and here is the head of Christ [*pointing to her head*]. The son of God is in man. The Father dwell in man. You don't hear people say you can't see God the Father? You see God the Father everyday. Three spirit in one. Don't this [*pointing to her genitals*] receive the baby and this deliver?

She then connected this vision with another in which the Father commanded her to go out and testify, not about Jesus, as she used to do, but about Selassie. In this second vision she saw "the Emperor and his six brothers with him."

And me see the moon a come down and me see the sun a go up. Man a go dat way and woman come this way. And seven of us stand before the Almighty, Jah, amen. And stand up and see him. Him work, you know, him have on him blue pants like you. Him a worker, black man, him have beard. The moon was coming down and the moon rest over my head. And a woman coming away from over the ocean. And when she come she stand up side of me and she make seven. I was make six. I and she go and stand up at the throne room crying. And you hear them speaking about throne room? Is a rock he sit on! But them wattle the place, in the sea. And when I stand up before him, I look into the sea and I see a man. You see like snow?—Is the holiness of him. Him sit over a four cornered table, and see him ya: him a peep out 'pon me. And him draw in, the magnet of him. I determine I want to see him. It's the sun what you see. A big pool was before him and him fasten down there and the hole have No. 1, No. 2, No. 3, go right up, take him time going up. The moon coming down, the moon coming down, the sun going take him time coming up. A man come so, the woman go so. And when I look, I see the sun coming out of the sea. Puppa! It terrible and dreadful to see the sun coming out of the water. Is a man, you know! I don't see nothing but firelight. And the moon coming down, and the moon come right down and the water cool it. And im look 'pon me and hear what him going say to me: "Go and tell them that I will send a little rain and a little breeze!"

Sister Dixon then gave a single interpretation to both visions. To her, they were a part of her conversion process, whereby she came to the full understanding that God is flesh and blood, not a dead soul in the air.

For, up in the air, if somebody did live there, with a heap of—beg yu pardon—shit would come down on us! Him is right here with us. The moon stand to represent woman and the sun represent man. Christ love man, for man is the foundation of the earth. Man is God and God is man and he is living—translate himself in spirit inna all of unu [you], never die. For if him tek away his breath from we, we never live, we die. That's what the vision mean, for him show me the three spirit in one. How come you go to a woman and have children with her? You is a power. You is a high man. You is a ruler. I am only a helpmate unto you, but you must treat your wife good. Don't care how you see the man old and bend, him is a ruler. Every woman represent Jesus Christ mother standing before you.

What Sister Dixon did was to link the religious belief in the love of God to man's practical experience of sexual love. The head sees and loves; this is expressed by the heart, through the organs of the sexes. It is the Son therefore who expresses sexual love. Dixon speaks of the Son delivering and the female genitals receiving the baby, thereby suggesting that love of the Father is expressed through the Son's delivering the baby to the woman who receives it in her womb. Thus, man and woman are not equal; one delivers, the other receives. She cannot receive unless or until he delivers. She waits upon him, even as the moon waits upon the sun. Both do not rule the sky at the same time; his coming up is her going down. The man completely dominates. Although a man should treat his wife well, there is no doubt who is the ruler: "How come you go to a woman and have children with her? You is a power." Life, human life, comes from the man. It is the man who originates it. The woman only nurtures life for him; she is only a "helpmate." She therefore is not God, though she may be God's mother.

If we keep these ideas in mind when we come to discuss the sexual taboos of the Rastafarians, in chapter 6, we shall better understand how it is ideologically possible to justify the subservience of women. For if man, not woman, is God, then the role of the woman in the household and in the religious movement as a whole must of necessity be lower.

Idealization of Africa

All those founding members of the Rastafari whom I interviewed who were fortunate to have heard Garvey either in Kingston or in country before he departed Jamaica in 1934 considered thsmselves Garveyites, not because they were members of Garvey's UNIA—they were not—but because they agreed with and defended the principles for which he stood and the policies he pursued. Garvey's movement was a mass movement, staunchly defending the black man against racial oppression and upholding the principle of a free Africa. In Garveyism, therefore, we have one of the ideological foundations of the Rastafari religion.

Attitudes toward Africa

As I have demonstrated in chapter 1, Africa was far from unknown to the people before Marcus Garvey. As Africa became a symbol of the primitive and uncivilized in the mind of the European, so also was it upheld by the slaves and their descendants as home or as a place to be proud of. In the clash between these two sets of values many conflicts were waged.

As a child "going to school I read about Africa—that it was a dark continent," remarked one informant. "Dark" meant unenlightened—by the standards of Christian civilization—pagan, heathen. "Is only parson used to preach against Africa. Him say the people over there are monkeys. Yes, parson call me monkey. That's why I don't like parson, for them preach against Africa from I was a youth." This informant was born before 1900. The position of the church, as mentioned before, was to paint a picture of backwardness that would stimulate missionary activity among blacks, who it was felt would be better able to transmit the gospel there than would whites.

Consciousness of Africa came not only from institutions like the church. Africa was alive in the family traditions.

From I was born coming up, I like to hear a black man talk. And I always stay among older men to hear them talk, especially about Africa. Mi mother talk about Africa all the time. She said the time will come when all black man must return to their homeland. And she talk about how dem ketch us in Africa and take us as slave. She always counsel us and tell us how the white man ketch the black people and bring us here. She talk a lot about Africa.

For this informant it was not unusual to catch bits and pieces of a conversation of older men on the topic of Africa. And it was in the family itself that some children came to understand about slavery, about Africa. Said Missis, "Mi mother always tell me that things that I am going to see she not going to live to see it, and we foreparents come from Africa. I always ask her what we going to see, and she say when we come up we will see it. Well, 1929 I saw Mr. Garvey." With Sister Missis, however, maternal teaching went beyond mere suggestion and placed the experience of slavery and oppression in the framework of religious belief.

Mi mother said those Africans that are in Africa, they don't come out in no slavery. They remain saints. They don't know what we know in the outer world. We are a sort of disobedient people, that's why we are cast out into the hands of the enemies; because we were disobedient to God. We would not hear what he say. And he said he don't want to discard the whole land of Israel, so he would just cast us into the hands of our enemies and let we feel their hand. He will stretch his hand the second time to take us back to his land. And that's what she told me.

Missis's mother, in the image of the Israelites suffering in exile, used a common theme, centuries old: disobedience earned us our exile, and gained us suffering unknown to the Africans who remained saints.

Other informants were able to trace their family traditions about Africa many generations back. One claimed her family had received its surname from one of the ships that brought the last batches of slaves to Jamaica, and another could cite example after example of how his family cherished the memory of Africa, enjoined to do so by a great-great-grandmother.

If the subjects of forced migration from Africa and subsequent enslavement were alive in the traditions of many peasant households, there is no reason why these themes should not also have been the object of religious or other preaching. Several informants, when asked what they knew about Africa, kept referring, in passing, to "the Seven Keys." I took little notice of this reference until Dixon described the "tall, strapping man, him mout' red, big hand, big lip, big nose." He was "from foreign." According to Dixon, the man came one day to Oxford Street, stood beneath the piazza of a Chinese shop, and shouted out, "Take seven key to breathe God's word, Deuteronomy to seal!" A large crowd gathered, including children, and with readings from the Bible and hymn singing he began to teach the people about Africa, "where the living God is." Soon he formed a religious sect known as the Seven Keys and included children in it. "Him start to teach the children to wear full white, black shoes and white thing 'pon you head." He encouraged adults to read, using the literate to teach the illiterate. He was finally arrested and, Dixon believes, deported.

Dixon is firm that the Seven Keys man was not a Jamaican but a foreigner sent to do God's work. But as we know from Elkins (1977) street preachers like him were common, and as I noted they all presented themselves as having gone to or come from "foreign." Foreign credentials enhanced their credibility among the people. Elkins, whose account is based on newspaper accounts and colonial records, describes how "Prince Makarooroo" was embarrassed into silence when recognized by someone from his home parish. Most certainly, the Seven Keys man was not a foreigner; he was a Revival leader whose followers wore white turbans. He therefore was not deported but quite possibly left the island after his release from prison.

The significant thing for us is that, appearing on the scene some time before the Garvey movement, he added another brick to the citadel of ideas that served as a defense against racist ideas. Nothing in Sister Dixon's testimony allows us to conclude that his message was subversive. We can only judge that it was considered subversive from the fact of his arrest.

The real subverter, however, was a fiery agitator called Higgins, who came to Jamaica before the earthquake. Dixon again offered a description.

Higgins is a tall African man. Is him first come here and make people know that black people have a home in Africa. Even before Bedward start preaching, is him first come here. I remember I did little, but mi mother used to carry me every Sunday with mi little bench to hear Higgins preach about Missis Queen and to get under Missis Queen shift and drawers and cuss. Higgins! Him nose big and him face like when you woulda have marki-marki. Him a African man, like him face cut, but it don't cut, you know. That man preach about Missis Queen, and tell the people that them must turn them eyes and them heart to Africa and them must stretch forth them hand to Africa. Amen! You hear? Mi 'member that! Him tall, him wear full black, and pretty something like wrap over ya so, and black shoes with the latch over ya so, and the big red bow down to earth. Is since me into this doctrine me realize blood should greet the earth. And the white man dem and the police dem, the whole of dem, carry come and circle round him.

Here we have a clear and somewhat definite description of Warrior Higgins: tall, scarified face, large nose. Sister Dixon believes Warrior Higgins was a continental African because of his foreign credentials and the marks in his face. He was a Jamaican, of course, who had lived in London and boasted of having traveled to Africa. She correctly places him around the turn of the century, sometime before the death in 1903 of Queen Victoria, whom he virulently attacked. Being a mere child, Dixon might not have remembered that he was a Revival leader, whose band was called the Millennium Band, or that he once used to baptize alongside Bedward. What impressed her was the fiery nature of his message, his teaching about Africa (which the newspaper accounts failed to mention),[1] and his ritual paraphernalia—large red sash, which she identifies as symbolic of the blood shed for the faith, and sword—codes of dress easily understood by the ordinary Jamaican, as can be observed today from the march of members of lodges and burial societies. Garvey himself took these codes to new heights. The sword is also a Revival ritual object (Simpson 1956, 363). Elkins (1977) describes how Higgins, fully arrayed, on

1. See the Livingston Collection in the West India Collection of the University Library, University of the West Indies, Mona.

the day after he was released from prison, led a march past the police station and there gave an officer's salute with his sword to his arresting officer. He clearly had a sense of humor.

Garveyism

In 1929 Marcus Garvey held a UNIA Convention for the first time in Jamaica. It was an event of international significance and the event that most early Rastafari remember when asked about their knowledge of Garvey. The 1929 Convention is their reference point. Some, however, remember hearing of him before that, either before they migrated to Kingston or as migrants in Central America and Cuba, where important contingents of the Garvey movement were based. One man said that while living in St. Elizabeth he heard about Garvey's work and his trial in the United States, but his real knowledge of Garvey came in Panama, where black Panamanians and West Indians lived in close solidarity with one another: "They couldn't associate with the white man and it bring the black people together."

This same sort of solidarity common to minorities was felt by others in Cuba, where they believed race consciousness was higher among black Cubans than among the black Jamaican migrants.

Garvey common over Cuba. Nothing but Garvey. Any time you hear a bell there, is Salvation Army or a man talking about Africa. Even the Cubans. I remember one day a Cuban man asked a Jamaican man what him is, and the man say him is English. The Cuban man say, "You English?" "You English?" And the Cuban man laugh that day! Till I shame! Him say, "You is an African, not an English!"

Cuba, to be sure, had the largest number of UNIA Branches outside of the United States (Dominguez 1988, 303). The impact back home of experiences like that of the returned migrant from Cuba was twofold. First, these experiences served as a channel for communicating to those at home what was taking place in the outside world. Migrants gained the impression that Jamaicans lagged in race consciousness. Whether this was true or not, return migrants were wont to be given a readier ear than were nonmigrants. Second, by trying to unite blacks across continents under the inspiration of a single destiny tied to the decolonization of the

African motherland, Garvey's movement, more than any other, made Africa into a powerful symbol of unity. To be a good Garveyite meant to be a keen analyst of events and conditions that affected the lives of Africans, at home and abroad.

This international perspective was reinforced in the 1929 convention. There is none who migrated to Kingston in the 1920s who did not remember it. It was the first real taste of Garvey's presence, the first glimpse of the scope of his movement. "Is that I start get my inspiration from," said one. Another heard the procession while selling coconut oil on the streets in Fletchers Land, so she hastened to Manchester Square, where she watched, impressed. One even took part in the convention as a member of a delegation from a lodge.

In the five years that followed, Garvey's main activities were concentrated in Kingston, although they did not exclude the rural towns. One informant, for instance, remembered him addressing a crowd from the steps of the Savanna-la-Mar courthouse in 1929. But in Kingston every informant remembers Edelweiss Park, or "Eloise" or "Eldawees Park" (as it was variously called by the people), where he held his open-air meetings, and Liberty Hall. His activities were varied, covering a wide spectrum designed to attract and hold the masses.

His own personal characteristics made him stand out. Informants describe him as "short, black and thick." He dressed and carried himself like a dignitary.

One day I was going to the market and I saw this gentleman with a crook stick round his hand like this. He had a bow tie, white shirt, his stout felt hat. His neck is very short and stout. I say, this must be the man. He had a jacket and a cloak over his hand, too. And I pass him and stop and I bow to him. And he gone and I gone and I never ask him any question. The spirit in me teach me that he is a great man. From the moment the people said he is a prophet, I know he is an honorable man from God and you must have a great respect for persons like these.

Veneration for Garvey was clearly not reserved for the generation after his death. Even as he walked the streets "everybody say, Mr. Garvey!."

Baia describes his first experience of Garvey and gives us a picture of one technique Garvey used to use in conducting street meetings.

I saw this short man at Bond Street and North Street, where they build the school. They have a step was there before they build the school. Well, he was on the step, but when I went there the people never carry more than four to five persons. I saw a stick in the ground standing up, a crooked stick with a black hat on top of the stick. And he was on the pavement as if he was talking to the stick and not to the people. So I stand by and I see one, two, three begin to come and it was there for a long time till a crowd.

Garvey apparently would not wait for a crowd to arrive. The meeting would have been announced beforehand so that people knew when and where to go. Garvey would come along at the appointed time, and whether or not a crowd was there, he would begin the meeting, even if he had to speak to his own cane and hat. But the technique was not only an idiosyncracy, it also served to teach the value of punctuality. Another point to note is that he did not carry around an entourage. He simply came and spoke, and people listened. This was in fact more the sort of tradition at the time, especially in and around the heart of downtown Kingston, by the Parade, where in bygone days several meetings used to take place simultaneously. Some of Garvey's meetings were held on Bond, Regent, and Dumfries streets in the heart of what was then, and still is, one of the poorest areas of the city, an area that received migrants from the country. The great Back-o-Wall slum was within a short walk away.

Not all Garvey's meetings were successful, as we hear from this account of a meeting at the corner of Dumfries and Regent Streets.

I believe it was a Thursday. I saw him, short, black and thick. And I stand up watching him. Him face turn eastward and him back west, and I stand up at northeast. And I hear him was talking and no one there. I stand up there about half hour and I listening. And I leave him and I go away, and when I come back, him same place, standing, and no one was there. And I stand up there again around half hour and no one come and I leave.

We get the impression here that Garvey had been speaking for a long time, and that unless he had persevered until well into the evening, he would likely not have received a good turnout.

In addition to his political agitation, Garvey held religious services. On Sundays, according to my informants, young boys sent to church would instead go to Garvey's services at Edelweiss Park.

Although the UNIA was closely association with the African Orthodox Church whose Primate Archbishop George McGuire was the UNIA's honorary chaplain, "Garvey was concerned that the UNIA be a forum for all blacks of religious faith sharing the same aims as the UNIA" (Potter 1988, 157). His Edelweiss services were therefore probably nonsectarian, geared more toward teaching an understanding of God suitable for the black people, as enunciated in his *Universal Negro Catechism*:

> Q. *It is true that the Ethiopian or Black Group of the human family is the lowest group of all?*
> A. It is a base falsehood which is taught in books written by white men. All races were created equal.
>
> Q. *What, then, is the chief reason for the differences observed among the various groups of men?*
> A. Environment; that is, conditions connected with climate, opportunity, necessity, and association with others.
>
> Q. *What is the color of God?*
> A. A spirit has neither color, nor other natural parts, nor qualities.
> Q. *If then, you had to think or speak of the color of God, how would you describe it?*
> A. As black; since we are created in His image and likeness.
> Q. *On what would you base your assumption that God is black?*
> A. On the same basis as that taken by white people when they assume that God is of their color.

(Quoted in Potter 1988, 148–49)

Culturally, he organized his own scouts, of which one or two informants were members. He also wrote and staged plays, one of them entitled *The Coronation of the King and Queen of Africa*.

The last day of the coronation in a market place. A girl named Pearl Campbell and a fellow come from Mexico named Sagwa Jones—him used to dance rumba dancing, dis girl named Pearl Campbell she crown him the King and he crown her the Queen (The two of them did married, you know, and him took her to Mexico). Mr. Garvey say he has to present the King and Queen in Africa. So one day we have the King and Queen crowned in Africa. That's 1929 and they were crowned 1930.

According to Hamilton (1988, 97), this play, one of seven so far identified, "is said to be a dramatization of the work of the UNIA. The plot centers on attempts by European leaders to destroy a worldwide black organization. They fail and eventually an African king is crowned." We can now see why the prophecy "Look to Africa when a King is crowned, for your redemption is at hand" is attributed to Garvey. In his publicization of *the performance,* we can well imagine Garvey saying he would present the king and queen of Africa; the play itself might even have contained those very words. And because the plot took off from real events, it is easy to see why Brother Duggie along with countless others interpreted the last scene of the play as a rehearsal for what did take place in real life on November 11, 1930, the coronation of Selassie. "The last day" in his testimony refers to the events in the play itself that culminated in the coronation ceremony. He did so retrospectively, attaching some significance to the fact that the difference between the prophecy and its fulfillment was a matter of only one year.

Through cultural, religious, political, and other means, Garvey conveyed his message to the masses of Jamaica. We can broadly identify four distinct points he made, four broad themes, as gleaned from the accounts of our informants. His first theme was Africa for the Africans at home and abroad. "Well, black people have a land, like the white man have a land, like the Chinese have a land that is called his home and the Syrian also. The white man feel that he is good, so the black man can feel alike, that he is not inferior to the white man. Is that kind of a topic his argument is on." Garvey linked the dignity and equality of blacks to their ability to claim a land they could call their own, one in which they could be their own master. His message, therefore, called for the decolonization of Africa, that is, freedom from political and military control, as well as freedom from institutional, such as religious, control.

As a juvenile scout in the UNIA, Brother Biini understood the concept of political control to be a major issue of Garvey's who "used to instruct us and let us know that it was important, it was the Negro's concern, speaking about a Negro government and a Negro empire." But he also saw that this concept inevitably implied other things we well, and so his own experience led him to conclude that black people should have their own church.

I were what you'd call endowed with certain amount of church movements. I go to various churches but I always like to know that the Negro government have a way of functioning, in the sense that you would say, well, just like how the Chinese build a temple and call it the Chinese temple, I would like to know that the Negro people could demonstrate a church or a society named after the empire or country of the said people. For like say I'm a part of a race and I am one among the group of suffering humanity, I love to comprehend the appreciation of being a member there.

In other words, as the Chinese are respected for their cultural form of worship, the black man should be too for his. Every other race, Biini felt, can practice its own distinctive praising of God except the Negro race. Until the Negro race can have its own, so Biini argued, we shall fail to achieve equality. Biini learned this as a lesson, and apart from seeing the Rastafari religion as the way forward to achieving this equality, he saw himself as a member of a government in exile, one equal to any other exiled government. Not being ashamed of the black race or the black government, or the black king or the black empire, inspires a show of confidence "in the face of the Black man," such that "a few white men shake mi hand when I talk to them" (Biini). It is this feeling of equality, then, that led him to a practice other Rastafari would have spurned.

I respect every government and every flag. Sometime in last year, I have on one of the same uniform with the Rasta braid, red, yellow and green braids, and with the red, yellow and green cord and the cape, and I still use the Jamaica flag, the color of the Jamaica flag, as a matter of respect to the Jamaica Government. Well, as I came right at the Denham Town Station I saw a Inspector and some constables stand up, and I gave them a salute, which they responded. And as I turned up Albert Street I saw some soldiers in a car. They look towards me, and some did stand up out by the station gate. Well, I gave them a salute too. And when them look and them see the Jamaica flag on the uniform, they gave me a salute and I pay them a certain amount of military redress and I gone my ways.

A precondition to gaining equality, Biini reasoned, was being prepared to treat the other as equal, which meant honoring the Jamaican government in order that the latter, through its representatives, the military and police, might honor the African government-in-exile. The pathos in such acts of deference lies in the total indifference of the state, not just indifference but disrespect. Some Rastafari have sought to have their "theocratic government" incorporated as a legitimate religion. Groups like the Mormons, which up until recent years denied that blacks went to the same heaven, have been incorporated, but the main carriers of Garvey's torch, the Rastafari, have been denied incorporation. Incorporation exempts a religious group from certain civil obligations such as paying taxes.

Garvey's second theme was the theme of unity. This principle guided the formation and presence of the UNIA in North, Central, and South America, and in the Caribbean. One man saw and heard Garvey only once, but the principle of unity was imprinted on his mind: "He was talking about the race and how we must unite ourselves in one single body, because we are all black people."

Self-reliance, the third theme, was a quality Garvey impressed upon his followers. "One Sunday night, he was having a discussion at Edelweiss Park, and him say, Look here, my people, I going to tell you something, but me mouth too long. If I put a book here and I put a five pound here and go away, you going take up the five pound and leave the book. And the five pound is empty and the book would enrich a man or woman." "Mi mouth too long," is an expression meaning that whatever I say always comes true. Knowledge is of greater value than money was his lesson and to reinforce it, he continued:

And him say, "Look here, who can read. Piece of newspaper run fly to you, take it and read it because something you might see there you never see before. And when you can read, help the other one and read, teach him, tell him things, yes, teach him." And him say to us, "Remember again, you following Garvey, but they going oppress you because they want you to leave Garvey to stick with them, to leave Garvey teaching. But remember this, that you not going to go to University and you can't get a job. You pass all the exams, you can't get a job. Open your little private school for youself." Mr. Garvey speak that word. You see how many private secondary open in the island now? From that come out, them say they won't employ you but employ yourself. All Buxton and the whole of them start up. Some of the men couldn't get a job. Why? Because some of them like Garveyism: some of them wear the button and some of them talk about Garvey.

Garvey's point, according to this informant, was that for blacks, education was not a guarantee of a job, but educated blacks who found themselves unemployed should seek a livelihood in opening up schools, and through these schools perform a service to their fellow black brothers and sisters. The counsel was a criticism of the racial discrimination both in the area of employment and in the area of education. The opening of new schools for blacks was necessary because a black boy or girl stood little chance of getting past the elementary level of education. In the two-tiered system of education in Jamaica, the grammar schools run by the major establishment religious groups in the country—qualification for which was attained by attending preparatory schools or by private tuition—served the middle class. After this schooling, middle-class children went on to professional careers. Peasant and working-class children, on the other hand, started elementary school at age seven and ended at age fifteen, after which they entered the labor market. Those, however, who showed exceptional ability and aspired to some sort of career had the chance of sitting the Jamaica Local Examination, which qualified them for entry into the teacher training colleges and seminaries, or for the lower rungs of the civil service. Small private secondary schools like Buxton High School and Grantham College performed invaluable service for thousands of peasant and working-class children.

As a philosophy, or a principle, self-reliance is today best identified with socialist ideology among Third World political parties and movements such as Ujamaa in Tanzania and the PNP in Jamaica. Its driving force is nationalism. But Garvey, though admiring the achievements of the socialists and communists in the Bolshevik Revolution in Russia, was far from accepting that the destinies of the African peoples could in any way be tied to that historic development. Thus although several people, including a worker by the name of Beckford, used to borrow materials on the Bolsheviks from the Institute of Jamaica and pass them on to Duggie—Duggie even bought a booklet once for a penny— Brother Duggie soon learned from Garvey the full meaning of self-reliance. "I was in favor of them, but Mr. Garvey actually change my mind in this way. Him said, 'The white man have his "ism", you must find your "isms." The white man "ism" for himself. "Socialism," "Communism," "Democratism" is the white man own. But make your own "ism." ' It sound good, but is just for the white man. You must find your 'ism.'"

Finally, Garvey's fourth teaching, which left a firm impression on many, was his words on deportment in the presence of whites.

Once him said, "Look here, when you speaking to the people, don't hold down your head, look them in the face. You must respect them, but make them respect you. Because when you hold down your face, you come like a little schoolboy to them, so that when you thank some of them they stomp them feet after you." And him give you that impetus, you must fight for your right.

In the previous Chapter, I showed the abuse to which some domestics were subject, and the subservient and patronizing relations that were normative in both amicable and not so amicable employment to whites and mulattoes. Lowering the eyes or head, or turning the face away at an angle is, according to Herskovits, an African form of deference to people in authority. Under slavery and colonialism deference is transformed into subservience to whites. Garvey denounced the practice as inconsistent with the self-conscious pride of a liberated African.

The Garvey Myths

In a country where recollection of history is largely dominated by oral rather than written tradition, mythology plays a major role in the development of national consciousness. The world of reality becomes transformed into the world of symbols, and when mortal men become heroes, they are seen to acquire divine characteristics. In this sense, Marcus Garvey was already one of the heroes long before he was accorded that title by an official act of government in 1964.

It is fairly certain that very few of the prophecies and feats attributed to Garvey originated with him. Garvey, whatever his shortcomings, did not regard himself as divine or visionary. Nevertheless, the people regarded him as such. To the Bedwardites of his day, Garvey was the reincarnation of Moses, as Bedward was the reincarnation of Aaron—the two brothers, one prophet, the other high priest, on whom God had bestowed the responsibility of leading his chosen people out of bondage. Garvey was not yet dead before the people were making divine claims for him. But if we bear in mind the Revivalist worldview of the people whom he addressed, this remarkable process of deification can be understood. The significance, therefore, of the Garvey myths lies not in what they tell or do not tell us about the man himself, but in what they indeed tell us about the Jamaican people.

In my fieldwork among the Rastafari, which included many informants other than the founding members, I came across many myths, some dealing with ganja, others dealing with Haile Selassie (Chevannes 1976; Yawney 1976), but the largest number were about Marcus Garvey. Those myths dealing with Garvey are not confined to the Rastafari—indeed I have heard them on the outside—but as the largest and most influenctial movement to derive inspiration from his work, the Rastafari are today the myths' main transmitters. I found seventeen different myths, twelve of which keep recurring (this is to indicate the strength of their influence throughout the movement) and five of which I heard only once. I have grouped all but one of them into four broad categories: (a) those attributing heroic or divine characteristics to Marcus Garvey himself; (b) those confirming the messianic role of Haile Selassie; (c) prophetic utterances addressed to the struggles of the people; and (d) curses.

Garvey as Divine. In this category are three myths. The first is a prison myth. In 1933 Garvey was sentenced to the Spanish Town prison for publishing a campaign manifesto judged to be seditious. According to one version of the prison myth, he placed a seal on the door of the cell he occupied, and to this day it has never been opened or occupied by another man; he also placed a seal on the door by which he left the prison, and it too has remained closed every since. The myth also speaks of the table in his cell, which mysteriously broke up after he left it and has remained broken up ever since, no matter how many times they patch it up.

The common motif running through the prison myth is the exclusiveness of everything touched by Garvey. The object became sacred by his use, and therefore taboo to all others. I am told that Garvey was in truth spirited out of prison the night before his release and through a back door, for fear of a demonstration.[2]

The prison myth is embellished even further:

I was told that Marcus Garvey was a kind of mysterious man. You couldn't do him anything. He was a mysterious man like a superman. They set up all kind of various different traps to destroy him because them didn't want him to preach and turn the people heart back to Africa. But dem couldn't catch him. One time they sent him to Spanish Town, so I learnt, and they

2. Personal communication from Richard Hart.

set him a bath, but they poison the bath to let him go in there and bathe and to kill him. And when him go, him say, "No, not this one!"

A "mysterious" man is one whose movements are unfathomable—a superman. The traps laid for Garvey were laid by the enemies of black people, those who saw the danger of his nationalism. An identical story about a poison bath was related by another informant, but this time the hero was Leonard Howell. This motif has wide currency in folk beliefs. We know that ritual baths are employed as a form a healing. Naturally, if baths can heal, they also can destroy.

The second myth in this category and undoubtedly the most widely current in the entire body of myths, is one that says that Marcus Garvey is alive, that he did not die. It became all the more popular when, in collaboration with the British government, the Jamaican government had Garvey's remains brought to Jamaica and entombed in National Heroes Park in 1964. "I was at the send-off preaching for him. And him say that him have some friends in Jamaica, but him not coming back. And you will hear him dead and him ashes will be comong to Jamaica to rest, but when the ashes come, test it to see if it is an animal ashes or a mortal ashes. And him preach the farewell sermon and him go away." The event being described in this excerpt was Garvey's departure for England upon his self-imposed exile in 1935. According to this account he did not feel that everybody was against him, but that he still had friends in Jamaica. Nevertheless, he was not coming back, not even his ashes. According to one variation his enemies will three times present ashes as his. Some informants went as far as to name the animals, such as the cow, whose remains the establishment would try to pass for Garvey's.

If Garvey, then, cannot die, where is he? When President Tubman of Liberia paid an official visit to Jamaica in 1954, he was thought of by many to be Garvey himself. To those who remembered Garvey's aborted attempt to set up a colony of blacks in Liberia, the mention of that country would evoke special sentiments. At any rate, Tubman was, if not stocky, certainly short and black. Missis remembers seeing a picture of Marcus Garvey printed in the *Daily Gleaner* in 1953, so how, she asks herself, could he have died in 1940?

On the front page of the *Gleaner* one part, I see Marcus Garvey, the half of him as usual, for him never take the full photograph, only the half of him with his big stout, hefty felt hat on top of his head, stick around his hand like this, black tie with shirt. And I see mark under him, "Marcus Garvey." Marcus Garvey in Congo, civilizing the Congolese them! In nineteen fifty and three and I saw that! Under the heavens and earth I could a never let go that! You see this country here? Whatever effects that is in this country is very bitter. I must need tell you the truth. They are very bitter.

A search in *The Daily Gleaner* failed to turn up any picture that might even remotely resemble Garvey. But Missis's belief in Garvey's continued existence is linked to the suffering of his people in Jamaica: the "effects is very bitter." We should take note of the role she assigned Garvey in the Congo: civilizing the Congolese. She clearly had internalized missionary attitudes toward Africa.

The third myth in this group is one that attributes to Garvey the saying "he will return riding on the winds of a storm." Actually, this myth is based on words Garvey in typical oratorical flight uttered as he bade farewell to his followers on being deported from the United States. According to one informant these words were fulfilled in 1951 when hurricane "Charles" struck Jamaica. It is the only myth that places Garvey in a role of mass destruction, but as we have seen he left Jamaica apparently feeling a sense of being let down by his people. The storm was punishment for betrayal.

Garvey as John the Baptist. In the second category we find four myths that seek to establish the messianic role of Selassie. In the first one, Garvey prophesied the arrival of Haile Selassie in the same way that John the Baptist prophesied the arrival of Jesus. None of my informants who recounted this myth claimed to have actually heard Garvey himself prophesy Selassie's arrival, but that is not as important as the fact that it is widely believed. "I never hear him speak, but people told me who listen to him that there was a man coming after Marcus Garvey, that he was not worthy to loose the shoelace at his feet. And we consider Marcus Garvey a very high man, in other words the highest man on this land. And if he tell us that word, now, the man must be very much higher than him." Others were even clearer that one did not need to hear

Garvey say it or read it in his *Philosophy and Opinions,* for by reading the Bible one could see that it was the same work John did. "It was only a rehearsal." The real task, therefore, was to find the worthier one. Some informants stated clearly that they at first thought it might have been Bustamante but decided against it because Bustamante was a mulatto and his outlook was pro-colonial.

Well, when this man Bustamante come, we wanted was to lay hold of the man, saying it was him. But when we look at the man eye, and see them red, white and blue at his office, we say, "No, this couldn't be the man!" Then we turn away from him and we seek it on the saying of the Honorable Marcus Garvey, saying "Africa by Africans, those at home and those abroad!"

The "red, white and blue" colors hanging in the office of Bustamante were an indication of Bustamante's political leanings toward the defense of the British Empire. His British sympathies, coupled with the racial factor and the recollection of Garvey's slogan "Africa for the Africans, at home and abroad," prompted the Rastafari's rejection of Bustamante as a messianic figure. The later attitude of Bustamante toward the Rastafari, especially his suppression of them following an incident near Montego Bay in 1963 when a Rastafari allegedly went berserk and killed several people, merited him the aponym "Busta*men*te." To the later Dreadlocks who became dominant from the 1960s, "man" indicates a genuine person, "men" an insincere person and a member or defender of the establishment. Bustamante was a "men."

I have already referred to Garvey's play *The Coronation of the King and Queen of Africa,* which some took to be the enactment of a real event especially because one of Garvey's dreams was to establish an African empire equal to that of the British or to any other empire. The idea, therefore, of an African king was one many could relate to, and was the core of the second myth in this category.

He always pass sentiments informing us that there shall be a coronation of an African King, but he never gave the full details. He spoke at Edelweiss Park with an open speech that there's a prince in Africa to be crowned King for the black people of the world, and when such a King is crowned then he Garvey's work will be finished. He said so. He said, "When the King is crowned, my work will be finished." So every equipped character knows that he's the forerunner to the King, while he was on the international subject of Negroes equality and the redemption of Africa, of 468 million Negroes from the Western world.

Selassie was the only prince to be crowned king, therefore it was of him Garvey prophesied. The third myth even pinpointed the year when, and the place where, Garvey foretold the divinity of Selassie. "It was in 1928 by George VI Park, and him look up at the elements and say, 'Unu [you] say the elements blue, but let I tell unu: as black as the elements! as black as God himself!'" All that remained was to find the other side of the equation, which Howell provided by identifying Selassie. The fourth myth went further than that to attribute to Garvey a direct reference to Selassie. "Garvey had a place at Edelweiss Park, and the last meeting him have there I hear him say, 'Ride him Selassie, ride him Selassie, ride him Selassie.' But we never did know what him a say about that." The reference would have to be about events leading up to but certainly not after the fascist aggression against Ethiopia, for Garvey had already left Jamaica by then. People later interpreted this reference as Garvey's saying that Selassie was the messiah, though they did not know it at the time.

Garvey as Prophet. The third category represents the single largest grouping of the Garvey myths I have collected; it contains seven in all. These myths foretell doom, hardship, and redemption, all relating to struggle. What binds them together is that they are addressed to the people. For example, one of the first told to me by informants, Rastafari and non-Rastafari, was that according to Garvey, anyone who passed through the seventies would be able to pass through anything. I heard this prediction many times, but without finding out why the seventies were singled out. Undoubtedly, conditions were extremely bad, and the country was just beginning to feel the full impact of the world economic recession with a dramatic rise in the cost of fuel early in 1974. As 1977 approached, the myth took the form of doom— "when the sevens clash"—and was even popularized in songs. Then as July 1977 approached, the refrain became "when the three sevens clash." Naturally for some, July 7, 1977 (7/7/77), was a day of particular significance (White 1983, 296–98), and some politicians even tried to secure mileage out of it by predicting the government's downfall on that day.

Another prophecy tells of Garvey's attitude toward migration.

Marcus Garvey told the people, "Black people, don't go to the white man country. Look for Africa and go in your own country. The white going to fight you, people, don't you hear?" In 1954 President Tubman came to this country and when he go back he write and he said he had seen the infirmities in Jamaica, so a lot of skilled men is to come in Liberia and find life, because life is there. He said he don't prefer brown; black people he wanted. More skilled men. And you will get a house to live in for three months furnished, until you build your own. And I have seen a lot people sell their cultivation, sell their mule and sell what ever they had and going to book for Liberia. A man, the name of Seaga, said now, "Gentlemen, 57 pounds to go to Britain, them want a lot of workers in Britain." And the people them go and take back them passport from going to Liberia and book for Britain. Some of them man them said, "Man, you don't hear? The prophet Marcus Garvey said that black man must not fight to go in the white man country. Keep out and look for your own country!" Marcus Garvey said.

The backdrop of this myth was the massive emigration to Britain that began in the very late forties and continued up to about 1962. During this time, thousands of Jamaicans sold their belongings and trekked to the United Kingdom, crossing the Atlantic in cheap banana boats. Many travel agencies sprang up, and according to this informant, inveigled the migrants away from going to Liberia, where they had been invited by Tubman, with the enticement of a low fare. As the migrants booked their passage to England, Rastafari reminded them that Garvey had prophesied that they would be lured away from Africa and to the white man's country. The interpretation this informant gave to the mass migration movement was therefore a condemnation of the migrants, who in rejecting a black country in favor of a white country provided another instance of betrayal by a people still not yet conscious of their destiny.

The theme of lack of race consciousness appears in another saying attributed to Garvey, heard rather frequently when Rastafari expound on the infidelity of the people to Garvey's ideals. "Black people, you are not going to know yourself until your back is against the wall, because you fight against one another, and when

it is too late, that time you will find your back up against the wall."
"Yes," added Sister Missis, "everything against the poor man, because everything gone against the black man, everything."

Two other prophecies, or perhaps two versions of the same one, have war as their themes, with a graphic symbol of blood. The first, told by Sister Missis, I have heard nowhere else. "Him said, King Street blood shall reach the bridle upon the horse neck, because if you steal the black man, him laugh; if you beat him, him laugh; if you kick him, him laugh; but he wouldn't like to be in this country to turn a flea when the black man them get vex. That's what he said." The myth tells why there shall be bloodshed, and who will shed it. More difficult is the second prophecy, which says simply, "Swallowfield shall be a battlefield." Who the contending sides will be, when the confrontation is to take place, and with what outcome are questions the prophecy does not attempt to answer; it is up to anyone to interpret. Some regard the prophesied action as a confrontation between the army and the police, based on the presence of a police depot alongside Swallowfield Road, the presence behind the depot of the northwest section of the military camp, and the occasional animosity between members of both organizations. Others believe it refers to an event to take place at the National Stadium nearby. Still others are content not to understand it and, instead, to await its fulfillment.

The next two myths relate to redemption. According to one Rastafari, Garvey prophesied that a set of people would rise up from the Dungle and overthrow the government. Garvey, he believes, was referring to the Rastafari, for it can be said that the Dungle and other slums of the West End that housed many a peasant youth were the strongholds of the Rastafari. But the most widely heard prophecy is that which interprets the growth of the city of Kingston to the very borders of St. Catherine as a sign that redemption is near. Garvey is credited with saying that when you see Kingston and Spanish Town joined together into one, then you will know that your redemption is at hand. Because it implies divine intervention, this prophecy is one of the more apocalyptic.

Garvey's curses. In the fourth and final group we have two curses. The first was the curse against Bag-a-wire. Bag-a-wire was a mad derelict who used to walk the streets of Kingston dressed in crocus or burlap. The name was probably "Bag-and-wire," or "Bag o' wire," to describe the burlap bags sown with wire. According to the myth Bag-a-wire, a Garveyite, betrayed Garvey and Garvey condemned him to wander through the streets dressed in sackcloth. Every child knew Bag-a-wire and many used to stone him. He died a long time ago, but Burning Spear revived the myth when he originated the Garvey trend in Jamaican reggae music of the seventies with the song, "Marcus Garvey Words Come to Pass":

> Where is Bag-a-wire?
> He's nowhere around, he cannot be found.

A different sort of curse was the one placed on Norman Manley, founder and for thirty years leader of the People's National Party. The myth is based upon a case in court, in which Manley found himself legal advocate for one of Garvey's enemies. This event took place during the period before Manley's entry into politics.

> The case [was] at King Street. The Judge ask Garvey if him don't sail a flag, and him say yes. And him ask him if is him emblem there, and him say yes. And I think the Judge ask Manley if him see a flag, and him say he see a piece of dirty cloth. And Mr. Garvey said, "That same piece of cloth, you shall use it when you roll up your shirt sleeve and fight for the same people you are fighting against. But you shall be ten years late!"

In 1937, after a period of soul-searching, Manley entered politics and threw the weight of his prestige as a famous barrister behind the nationalists from the middle strata. The People's National Party was formed on a platform of broad national unity in the struggle for independence. With backing from Bustamante, who by the end of the general strike of 1938 had established himself as the leader and organizer of labor, the party was about to move Jamaica forward into internal self-government under universal adult suffrage, when Bustamante suddenly defected and formed the Jamaica Labour Party to contest the 1944 elections. Bustamante won a landslide victory. Not until 1955 did the PNP under Manley's leadership finally come to power, "ten years late." The curse was to extend to his son, Michael, who assumed leadership of the party on his father's retirement: Independence from Britain came in 1962 under Bustamante and the JLP. In 1972 Michael

Manley came to power, again, say some interpreters of the myth, ten years late.

There is finally, one last myth, which is a prophecy of Garvey foretelling the coming to Jamaica of the Ethiopian Orthodox Church. This myth does not easily fall into any of the previous groupings. Many Rastafarians feel that one should not join any organization, for whatever "join can bruk," that is, whatever is joined together can be broken. When the Orthodox Church was first set up in the 1960s, the Rastafarians further denounced its practice of baptism. Baptism was one of the practices rejected by young turks in the movement during the 1950s as being too close to the Christian and Revival traditions. Also there was the very sensitive question of the divinity of the emperor, on which the Orthodox Church members maintained diplomatic silence. Those who were received into the church found themselves on the defensive.

Many of the foregoing are really prophecies. However, if they are taken and understood not piece by piece but in their totality as pronouncements of a man who has joined the ranks of "heroes," in the original sense of that word, then they should be treated as part of the mythology of the Jamaican people. We must allow for the fact that the myths have a basis in real life. Indeed Garvey might have said some of the things he is believed by Rastafarians to have said. But Garvey also said things that clearly did not become the subject of mythmaking. Moreover, not everyone who heard him speak was disposed to construe what he might have said as evidence either of his own or of another's divinity. The focus of our attention, therefore, remains the different manners in which the many things he said were interpreted by some of those people who heard his words. Whereas some evaluated his teachings in a political way, others evaluated them in a way that fitted more closely into their worldview. Bedwardites and Rastafari were among the latter.

An important difference between the Bedwardites and the Rastafari where Garvey was concerned was that the Rastafari abandoned the view that identified Bedward as the reincarnation of Aaron and that placed him alongside Garvey, the reincarnation of Moses. Instead Rastafari compare Garvey to John the Baptist because of their common roles as precursors.

The Bedwardites, while calling for the black "followers of Christ" to crush the white "Pharisees, Scribes, and Sadducees," retained the view that white was superior to black; so that the end of white oppression would at the same time be the transformation of black into the status of white. This conclusion was discredited by Garvey's teaching that black people's God must be black "since we are created in his image and likeness." This God the Rastafari found in Haile Selassie. Ideologically speaking, then, it was Garveyism that provided the basis to transcend the limitations in the Revival concept of nationalism, which the Bedwardites failed to do.

For a man who died only in 1940, and whose wife was an ardent defender of his cause up to her death in 1973, Garvey is remarkable in that there are so many things said about him in a manner that clearly clothe him with divine qualities. These myths are in one way or another the tales of a people formulating ideological strategies of resistance. Garvey passes to the rank of divine hero because no man who has done as much to unshackle the people's consciousness about who they are could possibly be less than a divine hero. Myths about Garvey are therefore part of the ethnic identity of Jamaica's poor, dispossessed blacks, once the object of enslavement, still the object of oppression in a society that only now is beginning to demonstrate that it values black as much as it values white. It is no accident that the main bearers of the oral tradition about Garvey—the magical works he performed, the prophetic things he said—are at the same time foremost exponents of the idealization of Africa, the Rastafari.

Garvey knew the Rastafari. His attitude toward them, however, bordered on scorn. They attended the 1934 convention of the UNIA, but he disassociated himself from them and made his position known to the convention. A delegation was led by Robert Hinds. "We the Rasses march, and when we went to Edelweiss Park he said he welcome everybody but the Rasses. Because he ignorant, of course, for him never know that Ras Tafari was God; him only say that God was black. And he made a junction between us. Him deh ya so, and we deh ya so. And him have a crowd at the back so that we couldn't come near to him." Garvey was very supportive of Selassie's struggle against the Italian invasion but at the same time critical of Haile Selassie's unprepared-ness and lack of Pan-Africanism (Lewis 1987, 168–75). He also felt strongly that Selassie ought to have remained in Ethiopia instead of fleeing to England. To hold such a man as God would have been regarded by Garvey as blasphemous. Nevertheless, the Rastafari have upheld Garvey's central role in the destiny of black people, a testimony both to the popular strength of Garveyism and to their own maturity.

Forms of Conversion

Those who became members of the various groups of Rasta-farians were the bearers of a largely peasant and fiercely national-ist outlook on life. The articulation of this outlook became a force-ful appeal that mesmerized the new migrants who were fresh from the hardships of rural life and thrown into the squalor of the most backward parts of the city. Those individuals who became converts to the cult were, most of them, drawn by the force of it. If we keep always in mind the fact that Garveyism was the leading social movement among the black masses at the time, and place it against its background of Revivalist cosmology, it is not difficult to under-stand the power of a photograph or of a dream. Howell is said to have brought with him from the United States a copy of an icon he claimed was a picture of the real Christ, a black man. By then, which was sometime in 1932, people had come to know what Selassie looked like. One look at the icon or at the picture of Selassie was enough to confirm their belief that the resemblance was not just close, it was identical. For Robert Hinds, the Bedwardite preacher, the main change in his religious outlook was the identity of Jesus Christ, black and reincarnate. Hinds drew a far greater following and membership than any other of the early preachers.

Not surprisingly, there were no "on the road to Damascus" type of conversion by skeptics and persecutors. All saw the light in a process shaped by traditional faith in the Bible and in dreams, two channels of communication from God, and by the quest for re-demption from material and racial oppression.

Dreams and visions are an integral part of traditional religious life of the Jamaican people of all strata. Of the twenty-eight founding members from whom life-history data have been collected, seventeen related having experienced visions in the course of their religious life, either leading up to the conversion or afterward. To use the distinctions made by one Rastafari, not all dreams are visions, only those of significance in revealing things yet unknown to the sleeper. Not all visions are dreams, either. Some are hallucinations, which informants describe as "seeing things naturally," in the waking hours of life. We can identify six informants for whom visions were important in their conversions, two happening before exposure to the doctrine, four after.

Brother Barnes's vision was already discussed in chapter 2. Twice while in Kingston on a visit, Brother Barnes smoked ganja and dreamed of a dwarf of a woman who prompted him to buy lottery tickets. He did not know it then, but it was through ganja that he was to come to discover his true fortune, the Rastafari doctrine. How did this happen? When he arrived for good in Kingston in 1936 he heard people talking about Ras Tafari, both on the streets and in the yard where he lived. He did not accept it, but looked to Bustamante instead, as the man prophesied by Garvey, to lift the masses out of their condition. He himself was in dire straights, a tailor reduced "to rags," and unable to find a job. But Bustamante was not a black man, and this bothered Barnes. The pressure to accept the Rastafari view was therefore greater. In desperation, he did what many of the contemporaries of Jesus were said to have done, namely, ask the claimant to prove his claim. If Ras Tafari was God, he prayed, he ought to know Barnes's conditions, to know that Barnes wanted to serve him but was unable to because of his economic state. He asked for assistance, "even to sell ganja that I can move from this stage."

I met a Ras sister. We used to live in the same yard, but she move out of the yard and I never see her for months. And one day I was walking along Spanish Town Road and I met her and ask her where she was. She have a sister she give some money round Ebeneezer Lane to sell some herbs for her, and the sister mash up her money. So I turn to her and say, "Sister, you couldn't help me?" And she say, "You would sell it?" And I say, "Yes, look at my condition!" And I turn back with her and we bought an ounce for one and six wrap it three shilling; she take one and six worth and I take one and six worth. I sell my one and six, make one and six, plus mi have fi smoke. And we go back and wrap six shilling. And it go on so that I could attend a procession, for I tell you I couldn't attend functions because I never had no clothes. And is the 8th January, 1939 that I baptize at Ferry. The way to God is not one way, straight; you have to go up and come down. Is a winding stage.

Unable at the time to decipher the meaning of his two visions of the little woman, he now realized that his salvation was the ganja that had produced them. The little woman of his vision is a recurring image among those smoking ganja for the first time (Rubin and Comitas 1975, 38). We should also note that the process in his conversion included a challenge to God to prove himself. But the main pattern is there: a vision deciphered, long after it has been forgotten, as a result of a later episode. The following example is much clearer:

Dead lonely place, and all I see was corn: corn what them a mould; corn what come up, just sending up heart fi plant; corn a tie baby; corn send out a make okro seed; corn what if you open it you see it make the seed already and the little yellow coming 'pon it; corn yellowing and corn—you have fi call it dry corn. But the whole place is nothing but pure corn. And I buck up on the big mount and I see three gentlemen sit. The one in the middle the smallest. I stop. They were talking but I couldn't tell nobody what they were saying. Meanwhile them talking, the one in the middle look 'pon me and him write. When him done, the one on the right break and pass a young corn give me just making okro seed, and the one to the left break one give me what make the corn already. And the one in the middle break one give me, you can call it dry corn and say to me, "Turn back! the time is not yet." And I jump out of mi sleep.

The main imagery here is corn, not only a symbol of fertility, but of life in all its stages, represented in the vision by the different stages of growth and maturity known only too well to the peasant. The maturest stage is that of the dry corn, and this the little man in the middle broke and gave him. The three figures, which also occur in other dreams, probably represent the Trinity. This vision was forgotten until one night in 1938 at the parade in Kingston when Hinds, reading from Revelation 19, mentioned Christ as having woolly hair and saying to the disciple, John: "I, God, shall return back to you, but I shall come back with a new name, and on my tie and on my breast the name shall be written, King of Kings and Lord of Lords." Having read it, Robert Hinds shoved his hand in his breast pocket and drew out a picture of Selassie. As the subject saw it, "mi heart stop, leap so, bup! and mi head just grow like." He recognized the little man in his vision. A woman beside him asked what was the matter. "Something that was lost from me", he said, "it come back to me!"

In these two cases, later experiences in real life bring back a recollection of the visions and serve to clinch the conversion. In the following example, the pattern is reversed in that other experiences and encounters prepare the way for the visions. A young woman *was* on her way on an errand, when she was challenged by a man.

> "Gal, who is your King?"
> "What you say, Sir?"
> "Who is your King?"
> "How you mean to ask me who is mi King? Mi no have no King, Sir."
> "Who is your King?"
> "King George." Afterwards mi say, "Rastafari."
> "Him say, 'Who tell you?'"
> "No Ras Tafari, Sir! A black man. No the man what crown a Africa."

Here, the stranger forced her to concede that her king was Selassie, not letting up on his question until she produced the right answer. This encounter was followed by an assurance from a young male friend that Tafari was in truth God. If that is so, she replied, she was begging him to manifest himself to her, for "if mi really know God, mi no think mi would suffer so!" Then came the vision: She was traveling from west to east when a man queried her and she replied, "I don't know where I am going, sir, look like I lost my way." Reassuringly, he told her to follow. He was dressed in full white, wore a bowler hat, and carried a sword with which he felled the trees as the two of them flew through the air. They came to a river. "One part of the water clean, and one part was pure blood." There he left her. Looking around she took a descent and found herself at a crossroad at which a large crowd was gathered. As if led by someone, she rejected that crossroad and proceeded to another. Then she woke up, puzzled. Some time later a young friend invited her to accompany her to a Rastafari meeting, and there she saw the picture of the black Christ. "The eye can't pop me; is the same man, but you know they give you one white and one black. . . . And one Tuesday evening, mi go back down to her yard, and mi see King Rastafari manifest himself to me, natural, like how you sit down there. Show himself 'pon the white horse. And from that day until today, mi no put him down."

The journeying, the river, and the crossroad are motifs common in the dreams of Revivalists. Legba, the Yoruba god of the crossroad, usually presents the sojourner with the challenge that faces every wanderer: which way to go? In this dream, it is the crowd through which the challenge comes. In Jamaican folklore the wanderer is instructed to break an egg at each crossroad, each egg the choice of disguised fortune or misfortune. The presence of blood in the river alongside the pure water is related to baptism rituals and also occurs in dreams. However, it is also said that to dream of blood is not a good sign. Perhaps a religious manifestation is considered different, for biblical imagery depicts the blood of the Lamb as salvific. At any rate, the gradual process toward the Rastafari movement should be noted. Several things added up to a good preparation for the final hallucination and led up to this woman's final conversion: the Garvey background, the challenge presented her by the stranger, the puzzling dream, the persuasion of her friend, the colors and the picture of the Black Christ.

The other two cases follow a similar structural pattern. The visions are preceded by conversations and discussions, whose effect is to preoccupy the subject with the most burning issue: the identity of God. In the dreams and hallucinations, the same motifs of river, blood, and vast green fields are present, and of course "the little man" also appears. Some sort of danger lurks whether for the individual or for mankind. Escape from this danger is at the same time the road to salvation.

The Black Christ

Portraits of the Black Christ and of Ras Tafari played a great role in drawing the attention of the crowds and converting many.

There were proffered like exhibits in the argument of the prosecution, incontrovertible, logical and true, brought all the way from "foreign," the great outside world where truth is not suppressed. The "photographs" figured prominently in the conversion of four of my informants. "It drive me home, you know, sir. I say that is Jesus Christ photograph. Dead stamp, dead stamp of Jesus Christ. Dead stamp of it. Christ was always white and that drive home everybody. Most of the people saw the photograph say, 'But look, Christ change! This one is black.'" And how did the subjects know what Jesus Christ looked like? For some the point of reference was the conventional European norm, including hair and facial looks, for others the hitherto undeciphered vision. From all accounts the "photographs" had a stimulating effect on the masses.

Every day I see a group of people in the Park, under a big tree. And one Thursday evening about 3 o'clock, the spirit say to me, "Go down there and hear what them saying." And I hear them saying, "Yes man, one King crown a Africa and them call him Haile Selassie, and that King there is our God and King." You see the photograph when him move out of prince to King? A man take one out of his jacket pocket and say, "See him here, is this man crown a Africa. Look 'pon this man and see if him don't favor the same white Jesus, only thing say him black!." Mi say, "Mek me see it, sah." And him show mi it. And mi look 'pon it and say, "Yes, this is the man of the hour!" And from that date, I don't let him go.

The Park is Victoria Park, where until recently, in the southern section, the street philosophers and "older heads" could be found debating political, religious, and philosophical issues. It was clearly not a formal meeting in progress. The incident also brings out more forcefully than any of the other cases the element of suggestion inherent in this process. Someone you trust, or someone in authority, presents you with a portrait and makes the *suggestion* that it is the picture of a face you have already seen. The norms determining when a man can be said to resemble another are influenced by cultural and societal factors. In the same way that "all blacks look alike," according to a white sterotype, whites are sometimes said to resemble one another. Today, some non-Dreadlocks may presume that all Dreadlocks "look alike." The nurturing of a beard in a society where beards are not normative also influences perception, as do social characteristics such as gestures, speech patterns, and lifestyles. People were used to seeing a white bearded man depicted on a cross. Change the color of the man but leave the beard and the cross and you have the "dead stamp" of the former. Such is the power of suggestion.

The Written and Spoken Word

In most cases of conversion, the Bible, the infallible written word of God, becomes the final arbiter, the source of ultimate appeal. Many Rastafari were converted by its power. The process involved a general predisposition to its influence, followed by the discovery of particular aspects of its contents, either heard at street meetings or on the road. One Rastafari, for example, an ardent reader of the Bible, was skeptical that the word *Ethiopia* was found in it, as he had heard a preacher claim, until he went home and proved it for himself.

And I say there is a great mystery in the Bible that we don't know 'cause this was there and I read the Bible a lot, and I never hear anybody read it, never know that Ethiopia name was mentioned in the Bible. I just begin to get more conscious for a nation. The Bible is really the black history, you know. They term it the "Holy Bible" but is black man's history, his present and his future recorded in there.

This discovery was the beginning. Or again, "I write down every one of those passages that I must look for in the Bible, and I look for them, and when I read them done, brother! Mi pillow was as wet as if I throw water on it! I cry, and I don't know that I am crying. And from that day I don't go back to Christ Church." Others, on the other hand, who could not read, listened. The frequently read passages included The Book of Revelation, chapters 5 and 17 and The Book of Isaiah, chapter 43.

The spoken word also had the power to convince. Some accepted the doctrine as simply as Brother Roy, who, on hearing Howell preach that God was black and that the king crowned in Africa was God, agreed immediately. Among others, however, the process was quite gradual and involved meeting after meeting until they found themselves joining— "I didn't have a great conversion. I'm going to call to you a flower. It had a bud first and then it suddenly grow old and you can't see when it pass from one stage to the other, but then all of a sudden you realize that it is already a flower." Nothing dramatic, no great visions or trauma. But the preaching on the streets as a social form of communication eroded skepticism and doubts until, without knowing when, or how, these people found themselves caught up in a current. The greater the power of that current the greater the erosion. On coming out of the Salvation Army service and hearing Hinds's group singing the song,

> Hail to the Lord's anointed,
> Great David, greater Son

Brother Hall had his name set down immediately.

Because Rastafari bases its teachings on the Bible, the same source of Christian orthodoxy, some of my informants when giving a different interpretation to its contents also accused the traditional churches of distorting or hiding the truth from the people. This outrage was not a new theme. It was very much a theme in the Sam Sharpe Rebellion and in Bedward's attack on the establishment in which he denounced the ministers of religion, and we later find the presence of this theme all through the development of the Rastafari movement. It was a favorite theme of Claudius Henry, against whom the Jamaican Government acted in 1960, and was present in the call made by some Dreadlocks in the 1970s for an open debate with the ministers of religion to be held in the National Stadium for all "God's chosen race" to hear. To the early Rastafarians, the ministers hid the true facts about Christ: "They don't give us a full understanding. They only give us the outside parts, but the inside part them don't tell you." The idea of the Bible having hidden mysteries is common. One of Dunkley's attractions was his possession of the Book of the Macabees, a part of the Bible not found in the King James version. And the belief that Macabees contains truths for the black man that the white man hides by trying to destroy that book is the theme of Max Romeo's very popular reggae song in the early 1970s, "Macabee version."

> Bring back Macabee version that God gave to black man,
> Take back King James version, it belong to the white man.

Deceptiveness is characteristic of all churches, according to Brother Baia, who, recalling how the local Moravian minister used to exploit his peasant congregation while the congregation remained poverty-stricken, attacked the church's teaching of a life after death. "No good in them telling me when I am dead I go to heaven, when I done old! Milk and honey up there, but none down here. And is not that it don't down here, but they refuse to give that which is down here!" And he again recalled how the Salvation Army used to make much of the song,

> Lion of Judah shall break every chain
> And give us the victory again and again.

until the Rastafari movement took root, when "quietly I don't hear Salvation Army sing that again. I say something is wrong on their side. Now [that] he choose a Black man come with the title, you stop singing song? Something wrong!" So, judgement will be theirs, warned Missis, "I don't know how they are going to face Almighty God, from Roman Catholic to Church of England, Baptists, Moravian, Presbyterian, Methodist—the whole of them!"

Discovery of the "truths" hidden in the Bible about black people, the awakening of the revelation of the true and Black Messiah, gave the early Rastafari a conviction that compensated for the minuscule size of the movement overall and brought the Rastafari into confrontation with the establishment almost as immediately as their doctrine began to take hold. What opponents considered so much more dangerous than the organized work of Garvey himself was the Rastafari's millenarianism, which served to place a sense of immediacy upon the affairs of black people. There was little time to waste, before redemption would take place, and before the terrible fall of Babylon prophesied in Isaiah and previewed in the mysterious Book of Revelation would descend on the oppressors. On the first day of August 1934, the hundredth anniversary of the Emancipation Proclamation, repatriation would take place. It is one thing to live in hope of returning to the land of your forefathers and so escape the great sufferings of an enslaved and despised people, but quite another seeing that hope begin to mature before your eyes—nay, before the eyes of the whole world—in the return of God, the one to whom you have always prayed for deliverance. "Israel, awaken, your deliverance is at hand! He is none other than the King of Kings, Lord of Lord, conquering Lion of the Tribe of Judah, the Elect of God."

4. Early Leaders and Organizations

One of the characteristics of Revivalism in its organizational form was its lack of centralized leadership and structure. Neither the categories of "Church" nor "Sect" as defined by Troeltsch (1950 331 ff.), could be used to describe it. Simpson (1970, 159) used the generic word *cult* mainly to focus attention on its syncretic aspects. Early observers and scholars spoke of "Revival Bands" when referring to organized Revival, and "cult" or "movement" when speaking generally (Beckwith 1929).

The proliferation of prophets, shepherds, captains, and their small bands was possible because the beliefs and rituals of Revival, Zion or Pukumina, were based on a worldview common to the population as a whole, which did not necessitate the organization of religious doctrine into a single sect or church, with a single orthodoxy. Nevertheless, everywhere a Revival group existed, the same rituals and symbols, the same beliefs about the role and function of the spiritual world were also present. And with a tradition going back centuries to the emergence of Myal, more or less the same structure of captain (or leader/leaderess), a charismatic figure noted for prophetic or healing powers, deacon, evangelist, secretary, armor bearer, and so on prevailed. There is nothing unusual about all this, for similar patterns have been observed in other societies: the Ethiopian and Zionist prophetic movements in Southern

Africa (Sundkler 1961), the *abangan* cult in Java (Geertz 1960), or even Hinduism in India.

As a derivative of Revivalism, Rastafari owed and continues to owe much of its beliefs, practices, and structure to its predecessor, notwithstanding some very significant departures from it.

To reach people, any new group must utilize the existing channels of communication. In Jamaican cities in the first half of the twentieth century, before the spread of radio among the people, street meetings were a major form of communication. Illiteracy being widespread, the printed word was entirely subordinated to what one was able to hear with one's own ears. That is not to say that spoken and printed word were exclusive of each other. To the contrary: they were intimately connected; what was written could only reach people by being read to them, and what was heard was surer to be true if it could be proved that it was written. So although people gathered to hear a speaker, the speaker's ability to back up an oral message with references from the sacred writings of the Bible, other books, pamphlets, and newspapers was well understood. Every Revival group had at least one literate secretary.

The main channel in passing on Rastafari beliefs was the street meeting, where the speakers expounded the doctrine, backed up their words with references from the Bible or from documents relating to the coronation of Ras Tafari, prayed in the name of the returned Messiah (the reincarnated Jesus), and sang choruses and hymns already familiar to the people. The message was directed mainly to the migrant peasant. There was a distinct concentration in and around the market area of Kingston, that is, the area bounded by Victoria Park on the east, the vicinity of the Coronation Market on the west, and by North Street. Favorite spots were the steps of the Coke Methodist Chapel on the east side of Victoria Park; the front of the Ward Theater and of the Salvation Army headquarters, both on the northern side of the same park; the Redemption Ground market, once a cemetery for cholera victims, along West Queen Street; the corner of Bond Street and Spanish Town Road, opposite the market which was later built there as the Coronation Market (named for the coronation of George VI); and the junction of Regent Street and Spanish Town Road, known then as "Dog Park."

Rastafari street meetings up to the 1940s took the Revival form. According to one Rastafari informant, a band of members dressed in white clothes embroidered with the red, gold, and green colors derived from the Ethiopian emblem would move forward to a pre-arranged spot. The group would set up its three-spout kerosene oil lamp, and, accompanied on the familiar musical instruments of drum, tambourine, and shaker, the members would sing familiar choruses. The meeting formally began with a prayer and the singing of the "national anthem," "Ethiopia, the Land of Our Fathers," and selections from Ira Sankey.

It will be clear that most of the data presented in this chapter come from former followers of Robert Hinds, but there were among my informants a few members of organizations led by Howell, Hibbert, or Dunkley.

Leonard Howell

Robert Hill (1981) provides the only written source of a brief sketch of the life of Leonard Howell. Born in 1898, Howell claimed to have served as a soldier in Panama and at Up Park Camp in Kingston before returning to Panama to join the U.S. Army Transport Service as a cook. In that capacity he came to New York in 1918. He was discharged in 1923. He knew Garvey but old Garveyites remembered him as a "con-man." Hill (1981, 38) thinks Howell may have come under the influence of the Trinidadian black nationalist George Padmore, who was "after 1927 the rising black star of the American Communist Party." He returned to Jamaica around 1932 in the midst of an upsurge of Revivalism.

Throughout the Rastafari movement Howell is universally credited with being one of the first if not the very first preacher of Rastafari. As recently as 1975, the time of my fieldwork, Howell was still alive with remnants of his followers living in Bushy Park, a few miles from the famous Pinnacle estate where for fourteen years (from 1940 to 1954) they had settled. Having suffered much at the hands of the colonial state, this group had grown very circumspect and wary of the presence of strangers. Howell himself was locally known to be inaccessible to interviewers, though this changed later.

From the earliest years Howell's main drive was toward the establishment of a *community* of believers. According to informants this was why he moved to St. Thomas in 1933, a parish with a proud history of anticolonial resistance. This was also his reason for later buying and settling on Pinnacle estate in St. Catherine in 1940. Between living in these parishes, he lived with a small community in Kingston, which earned its living by running a bakery.

Unquestionably, one of the main strengths of Howell was his defiant anticolonialism, which comes across even in the University *Report,* in which he is said to have encouraged or threatened peasants not to pay taxes. His very approach to organization was a criticism of colonialism. According to one of my informants the bakery was run in such a way that "when a poor man go there and buy a piece of bread you get a little sugar free and a little cornmeal." Informants also verified that while in Kingston he published another newspaper called *The People's Voice,* no extant copies of which have so far been found, but I am told that it carried news about Africa.

The Pinnacle community gave to the Rastafari movement its close association in the mind of the public with ganja. "Anywhere through the island a man want ganja fi buy is right there him come. . . . He carry the best herbs." Howell, it would appear, was the first ganja *farmer,* as opposed to the small cultivator. He produced this substance on a sufficiently large scale to meet its growing demand in Kingston. Ganja was Howell's main cash crop.   But there were others also. "Once ago we have a drought in Jamaica. The prison was short of food and that place supply the Government. Gungo peas, cow peas, red peas, sweet potato, yam, coco. You have some store houses—through how the people work hard, you know—you have some store houses full at all times with these things." Livestock included fowls, cows, goats, and beasts of burden. Pigs, ducks, and pigeons were taboo. Howell utilized the free labor of the community to stockpile food. This community might seem like a commune, but a young informant who grew up in Pinnacle said that each household provided for itself by working private plots of land granted by the "Gong" or the "Counsellor" or "Prince Regent" as Howell was variously called by residents.

The food stored away also provided entertainment for the visiting Rastafari who came to Pinnacle for celebrations or for visits. "I went to Pinnacle three to four times when them have big convention, them call it function. Plenty food to eat and Howell preach." Some of these functions were the feasts to celebrate the passover, and the anniversary of the emperor's coronation, before which there would always be fasting.

Pinnacle was not an isolated community. After leaving the community's infant school, Howellite children pursued their education in the schools of nearby villages. The community also relied on the outside for bread and other groceries. And according to one of my informants, remembering the enumeration, the 1955 general elections, which took place when he was six years old, the Howellites voted for Johnny Grant, the People's National Party candidate.

The Howellites had an internal life of their own. Although, as I have said, each family was responsible for its own upkeep, there was the practice of communal labor for the good of the organization as a whole, and the sharing of an integrated social life. On the edge of a small pond used for watering plants and livestock, the community lived in tenement flats, every three or four of which were separated by lanes with given names (e.g., Corn Lane). The tenements were typical of the homes of poor peasant houses: one room, thatched roof and earthen floor, and a yard space outside for domestic activities such as cooking, eating, washing, and talking. In front of the houses stood a parade ground where rituals took place and a playing field where children played ring games. On Sundays it was customary for Howellites who owned goats to slaughter and sell them to members who did not. And after the Sunday dinner they would gather in the parade, dancing and singing to the rhythms of the *baandu* and *funde*, the two kumina drums. "The music force you to dance. It will drop you on the ground and they have to keep the rhythm going." According to present-day Kumina dancers, failure to keep the rhythm going while a dancer is in a state of trance could result in that dancer's death.

Social organization at Pinnacle was based on Howell's charismatic leadership. At the head was the "Gong," beneath him several deacons, and below them the rest of the people. The Gong lived apart, on the hill that overlooked the estate. He alone ruled the community, and he alone gave the punishments, which could be harsh.

Him always want we the Rasta in the town to be with him, and through we don't, him think say we against him, but it wasn't that. His administration did want to be a little freer than how they were. There were certain restrictions that not even the Government was pleased about, such as punishment. Suppose you disobey him, him order you fi get lash, and if is in yu hand, you have fi take it. If is twenty, take the twenty in you hand. If you violate what him say, you get flogging, and if you refuse, you was sent out of the compound. We have some regulation up there that him say not to go and bathe until him give the order. And sometimes is a fact that him keep away the people-them too long from having a bath. That's why the people always call Rastas at those times ram goat, say you smell like ram goat, billy goat. If he say don't bathe until three month time you cannot, else you get punishment. Is just his rule of opinion within himself. You know, a man on him throne like Nebukadnezzer.

It is not clear why there was the taboo on bathing, unless it was a part of the fasting ritual. This informant makes it clear that Howell's desire was to see all Rastas united under him at Pinnacle, and equally clear that they, on the other hand, resented his autocratic leadership. And autocratic it was: not even his deacons were entrusted with administrative functions, outside of religious ritual.

Besides preaching and ruling the community, Howell also had a practice. "He had his instrument like a doctor when him perform 'pon the people, just like a doctor up at U.C." This would seem to be a stethoscope. There is some truth to this claim, for after his release from the mental asylum, Howell set up an office along East Queen Street, where he treated people coming to him for cures. Like Hibbert, he had a reputation of being a "scientist."

Teacher Hibbert

One of the cornerstones on which Hibbert built his organization was "occultism." The feeling that there were hidden secrets in the Book of Macabees or in the publications of DeLaurence, a sentiment which in other groups was subordinated to other concerns, became dominant in Hibbert's organization. He impressed the people with his breadth of knowledge:

I find that Mr. Hibbert is the more historical man and he have books and Bible and he can declare every chapter in the Bible. Tell you how much chapter, how much psalms, and he can go from before the birth of Christ until the end of Christ right up. I say, this is the man fi I draw near, for with this man I will gather more experience, even when I can't read. But with fi him instruction, mi brain will develop into something good.

Hibbert gathered around him many such men, awed by his reputed powers and desirous themselves of learning the art of magic. According to an informant, an Englishman wanting to get a true picture of what was going on back home in his domestic life visited Hibbert. Hibbert sent for his former common-law wife, and, using her as a medium, told the man the whole story. The Englishman was so impressed that in addition to paying Hibbert's fee, he gave the medium a one-pound note. Up to his death in 1985, Hibbert continued to be known for his occult powers. On one of my field visits there were one-half dozen patients, including a Jamaican whose residence was in the United States.

What brought the decline of Hibbert's organization was, according to informants, a combination of two things. First, he did not want to impart his innermost secrets to his initiates.

They call you to learn science. You are member of the science group, you pay you money. Then when you pass through certain stage, you even go from low to high, and it have a time you go higher and higher. Then when you go to the highest part now, him refuse to give the lessons to the people them. That's why plenty brothers had to leave him in the early forties.

Second, Hibbert could not take challenge to his leadership, which came about in the establishment of the first chapter of the Ethiopian World Federation (EWF). According to Brother Duggie, the EWF came to Jamaica through the initiative of Brother Paul Earlington, who saw the advertisement in a copy of the *Ethiopian News* sold on the streets by a man named "Polly." This was late in the 1930s, following the fascist invasion of Ethiopia, a period during which the Rastafari and Garveyites showed intense interest in Ethiopian affairs. The advertisement made it clear that a minimum of twenty-five dues-paying members in good standing was necessary to establish a charter. Earlington appealed to Hinds first, then to Dunkley—both of whom turned down his request for sponsorship—then finally to Hibbert. A big ceremony was held at Edelweiss Park and Bustamante was invited to unveil the charter, number 17. Hibbert's place on the executive was as far down as third vice president. Because he could not be president, so Duggie says, he ordered all his members out of the local branch. Duggie himself remained and later joined up with the Afro-West Indian Brotherhood, led by Downer, who had already broken from Hinds.

Archibald Dunkley

About Dunkley's organization, I did not find out much. He himself was very much alive, but I was unable to contact him. The only things I was able to gather about him were his use of a sword at meetings but at the same time his aversion to the Revival practice of spirit possession.

We went to Highholborn Street and the meeting was so powerful that I find myself couldn't stand up. All I try to keep down miself I was just wheeling and spinning. And I hear him say him don't want that in here, and continue talking. I feel that I want to stop to steady myself, but I couldn't control, and him say him don't want that there. I don't say anything, but I never go back. Because if you living clean, the Spirit of Almighty God lives in you and if him find a clean body him will move in you.

Spirit possession, the initial stages of which this informant was describing, was not tolerated among the Rastafari.

Robert Hinds and the King of Kings Mission

Robert Hinds was a follower of Bedward and also a Garveyite. According to Bedwardites, Bedward used to preach that Garvey and himself were reincarnations of Moses and Aaron, respectively, the one law-giver, the other high priest and that in the hands of both was the destiny of Israel, the African race. When Bedward set out to "do battle with his enemies" in 1921, on what turned out to be his final journey, Robert Hinds was one of those followers ambushed by the police and military and taken to be tried at the Half-Way-Tree Court. "The time when they apprehended Shepherd Bedward and lock him up, it was the both of them they lock up. And they send Shepherd to the asylum and send him home to Linstead where he born and grow. But he told the judge in Half-Way-Tree that he will be sending him home this evening and he will be back in Kingston tomorrow morning."

The exchange with His Lordship may be apocryphal, but Hinds was again to experience the hand of colonialism when twelve years later he accompanied Howell to prison for sedition.

Hinds was undoubtedly the most successful of all early Rastafari, in terms of membership, and one reason must surely be that his appeal to the people was that of the most experienced religious leader, a man who once defended the old but who had now seen the light of the new. And, understandably there were the visions of conversion. "Mr. Hinds say that he was a man that God call. Him say one night he went to his bed and he got a vision. He heard a voice say unto him he must feed the hog, and when him look he saw a breadfruit tree. And the voice said to him him must bend down the breadfruit tree and pick it off and feed the hog-them." At first he could not interpret the vision; then he got another, in which he saw a bundle of fire and heard a voice telling him to go and lead the people. Upon meeting Howell, he came to understand whose voice was leading him—Rastafari. On his release from prison, Hinds launched out on his own, instead of returning to St. Thomas with Howell, and set up his headquarters first at 82 North Street then at 6 Law Street, where he remained up to the early forties. His headquarters were known as the "King of Kings Mission."

At the height of his career, Hinds led an organization of over eight hundred members on roll, and a turnout at functions of a couple hundred. His problem was essentially one of organization, how to maintain so large a membership. In the end he was unable to solve this problem, and as they gained experience his lieutenants left him in order to establish their own organizations, carrying the membership with them.

The King of Kings Mission was organized along the lines of a Revival group. "Leader" or "Shepherd" was Hinds himself, whom the members regarded as a prophet. Beneath him were the secretaries, two chaplains, an armor bearer, twelve male officers, and twelve water-mothers. The secretaries were recording officers; literate, they read lessons at meetings and were responsible for correspondence, such as asking for permission from the police to hold a march. The chaplains, water-mothers, and officers were indispensable at the baptism rituals, which took place twice a year to mark the reception of candidates into full membership. The process began when a person accepted the doctrine and at the end of the street meeting gave his or her name to be entered on the register. The candidate then attended the regular weekly meetings, learned more about the religion, and received the instructions of Mr. Hinds. "You only sit and then Mr. Hinds tell you how you must walk and how you mustn't walk. And you have a different life to live; you mustn't walk in the street with a wantonness, and all like that."

Baptism used to be held at the Ferry River, on the border of St. Andrew and St. Catherine, on two important liturgical feasts, April 1, the beginning of the Ethiopian year, and August 1, Freedom or Emancipation Day. The ceremony began at the headquarters where all the participants assembled the night before for the march of seven miles to the riverside. Everyone except the candidates dressed in full white. Men wore red, gold, and green armbands, and women wore white headkerchiefs "like a head nurse." At "six o'clock," that is at sunrise, baptism would begin. With the help of an officer, one of the chaplains submerged the candidate, while the secretary read the baptismal formula from the Bible. Male candidates were attended by the male officers, female candidates by the water-mothers. At no time were the candidates unattended. "I take this candidate and give to that one and the other one, until she pass right out. That candidate don't walk by he or herself to the shed. And there is some in there to take off your clothes." Dressed in full white at last, the neophytes emerged from the shed to take their places among the faithful. The procession would then return to headquarters before breaking up. Later that evening at the ceremonial feast, each neophyte was allowed to say how he or she felt, in other words, to testify.

Feasts were usually preceded by fasting. Before the Passover, the largest feast, they would fast for up to three days, without food or water. The Passover lasted fourteen days. On the first day they killed a "lamb" (usually a goat), roasted it, and ate off the meat without breaking a bone. "And whatever you leave you have to burn it." For the next six days "all that we ate is crackers, for we don't carry no bread in our home; no bun and all those things can't go in the home. We can eat crackers and whatever food you cook." In other words, they refrained from all leavened products. On the eighth day and until the two weeks ended "you open the gate and you prepare enough so that everyone come in and eat." But every morning the leftovers had to be burned. Hinds, part East Indian, was especially fond of roti.

As Israelites they had to eat with staff in hand, "because we can move at any time."

When him say staff, you know, every man suppose to have a staff and when you eat you put it under your arm and eat, cause we don't eat with knife and fork. When you want to have meal you wash you hand, every man wash his hands and wipe it into a white towel. The 8th day is the same. All well-wishers come, just wash their hands and eat. We don't use no fork.

The passover ritual served as a reminder to the King of Kings members that they were merely sojourners exiled in Jamaica, and left them with the hope of returning to Africa one day. There was no evidence that Hinds at any time prophesied repatriation on or by such and such a date. This was to come much later with Claudius Henry, in the late 1950s (Chevannes 1976).

The armor bearer, as the term suggests, had to be a faithful and reliable orderly. In Revival, such a person had the responsibility of assisting the shepherd or leaderess, or anyone else who became possessed by the spirit. In Hinds's Rastafari mission, however, the armor bearer was like a standard bearer. As the members marched to a street meeting, the armor bearer carried the lamp on a pole, seeing to it that the rest of the people followed closely.

Anyone familiar with Revival would readily recognize the closeness of Hinds's organization and ritual practices within it. His reliance on baptism was a carryover from Revival, whose candidates are prepared and baptized in a similar fashion and who also testify upon returning from the river. Likewise, fasting has importance in Revival and is viewed as a means of achieving spiritual strength and triumph over evil. On a recent field trip a Revival bishop berated the mainstream churches for excluding Revival from their annual prayer breakfast to which national leaders are invited and join in praying for national unity and civil peace. If they want to end political violence, she declared, let Revival teach them, not through eating but through the opposite, fasting and prayer. A notable feature of Hinds's organization, and of Howell's also, was the presence of women. Women performed specific functions such as watermother. In Revival today, women outnumber men and perform high functions. There is no reason to believe this was any different in the past. One-third of the founding members who provided the base for this study were women. But as the Rastafari underwent further development, of these three aspects of Revivalism—fasting, baptism, and high female participation—only one, fasting, was retained.

As an organization grows in size, special problems also grow with it. On the one hand, there is the matter of its own internal structure; on the other hand, and in the case of an organization which poses a threat to the established order, there is the matter of defense. To meet these problems, Hinds created two new roles: he appointed a "cabinet" to look after problems within the mission, and several guards to manage all aspects of security. The cabinet comprised seven of the most faithful and promising men.

After when he find himself was so strong in the work and he became a right man and having so much members, well, he said some of us will has to help him to do the work, and he forms a Cabinet by getting out a certain amount of man, young man to hold up his arms that some of the work we can shoulder it too. He choose seven, I was one of them. They are solely responsible for the organization. In other words, some may be sergeant, you call one a sergeant and one a corporal within the rank and file. But we seven now, never call ourselves that; we a member of the Cabinet. None of us never think ourselves higher than the others, but the rest of the members hold us responsible for the house. You the members of the Cabinet you come just like members of Parliament.

The seven were not each appointed to a different portfolio, but together they held the position of responsibility and leadership, including leading different bands on the same night to different street meetings. This responsibility gave them valuable experience. The cabinet also functioned as a court. When one of the security guards, such as a corporal, brought a case forward, a week's notice of the trial by cabinet was given to the defendant and to the membership in general. One judge in the lot by agreement presided over the proceedings; the rest acted as appeal judges for cutting down sentences. Punishment ranged from fines of a shilling "to hinder him from do it again," to a period of fasting, or a period of suspension. If the case involved a common-law separation, the cabinet had the power to force the man to support his former common-law wife, unless she was found to be culpable. The more usual type of case, however, involved such charges as attending meetings with ganja or with alcohol on one's breath or indecent language or other violations of the code of ethics. Sometimes it was not possible to thrash out a case conclusively. The accused was then given "a next chance." Brother Roy remembered one case in which a member appeared before the cabinet for smoking ganja openly. The case was finally dropped because the guard lacked sufficient evidence.

It might seem a bit surprising that the early Rastafari proscribed ganja smoking in any way. Hinds was not against using ganja, but he demanded that whoever used it must do so in the privacy of his own home. The reason for this was obvious: to give the colonial authorities as few pretexts as possible for harassing the Mission.

Although it had taken root among the urbanized peasants, Rastafari had to contend with hostility from many quarters other than the police, and to meet the demand for security the "guards" were formed. Their function was to keep close watch over the crowd at meetings, to spot and disarm provocateurs, and even to inflict punishment. For this reason, the guards often did not dress ceremonially. For a long time the early Rastafari could not proceed to a meeting safely, unless they first met at headquarters and advanced in a body, or unless each hid his insignias and rosettes until he arrived at the meeting place. They were subject to abuse and assault.

Opposition to the Rastafari took several forms. First there were skeptics who passed simple remarks like "Is them print the Bible; is fi dem Bible!" or "Rasta a foolishness!" Second there were those who made every effort to dissociate themselves from the movement. In this category belonged Hinds's landlord, who gave him notice to leave from his North Street headquarters; employers who refused to employ known Rastafari; and close relatives who expressed their shock by disowning them. Thirdly, opposition came from gangs of youths, who resorted to violence from as early as the mid-1930s. Brother Baia recalls how a gang led by one Albert Angus raided Dunkley's headquarters and fired a shot at the group. Dunkley had to run for his life, and this became the subject for a song by the famous bards, Slim and Sam. And Brother Inki remembers Maudy Melhado's gang, at around the same time, which in one night broke up a feast of the Howellites at their Princess Street headquarters, did the same at Dunkley's headquarters on Oxford Street, but were stopped when they came to Hinds's only because he had once been on friendly terms with Melhado. According to other informants, Melhado was a very tough woman with a record of prison terms, and her gang included older boys and girls. Hinds's security officers often had to retaliate. They frequently armed themselves during a march, or posted themselves before the headquarters with the dreaded "cow cod," a whip made from the sexual organ of the bull. They had to be fearless men. "We were at Gold Street and Laws Street one night, and stones start to throw. We see the yard that the stones coming from, and we went to investigate it. Now, we weren't fear; we knew no fear, don't care who you is." But their fearlessness was to become, by the early forties, fearsomeness, as Rastafari, like a Rastafari character known as Gorgon, probably after the mythological figure, could intimidate police constables, forcing them to release their detainees. By the 1950s and early 1960s, when the Dreadlocks became normative, many people were actually *afraid* of the Rastafari. Guards were a necessity as long as marauding gangs threatened the young movement. Howell had guards at Pinnacle. When this was no longer necessary, when the movement had become the dominant force in the great slums such as Dungle and Back-o-Wall, the custom persisted nevertheless. Guards acted as lookouts against police agents and patrols.

There was, to be sure, police opposition. It was aimed at suppressing the spread of movements devoted to the propagation of anticolonial and antiwhite feelings. The police carried out its task by keeping close surveillance of Rastafari street meetings, taking shorthand notes, and seizing literature, and by sometimes breaking up meetings and marches. The following pages furnish insight into the dynamics of the relationship between the early Rastafari, who were bent on reformulating prevailing ideas about the status quo, and the main agents appointed to defend it. Also, Homiak (forthcoming) argues an important point when he notes the reliance by the Dreadlocks on other sources of authority than the Bible. Here, as we will observe, it was a tradition of the early Rastas as well, twenty years before the era of the Dreadlocks.

The fascist invasion of Ethiopia by Mussolini to establish Italy as a colonial power and to avenge its defeat some forty years before, stirred great anger among the early Rastafari. According to Baia many declared themselves ready to sail to Ethiopia to join the resistance there, and at least one informant mentions the impact the invasion had in drawing him into the Rastafari movement. Interest was not confined to Rastafari only, but was fairly widespread (Weisbord 1970; Lewis 1987). I get the impression that from about 1935 on, a relatively great quantity of literature began to reach Jamaica. Among my informants the most frequently mentioned newspapers were the *Ethiopian Observer* and the *Pittsburgh Courier*, which could both be ordered from the United States through a local agent.

The *Courier* was especially popular in Hinds's King of Kings Mission. Hinds would order between twenty and twenty-five copies for his members. At the time a very influential mouthpiece of the black American middle class, the paper carried a strong black nationalist and at times democratic position. For example, an editorial comment on November 28, 1936, strongly criticized Haile Selassie for his trust in the League of Nations and expressed the view that he ought to be learning from the big powers' betrayal of republican Spain. As he watched the big powers surrender the Spanish people to fascism, "the little emperor must be wondering why he ever thought that a group of big white nations would come to the aid of a struggling black nation." The *Courier* not only reported regularly on the progress of the Ethiopian war but also carried feature columns and cartoons that tried to reconstruct black people's history. "I read in the *Pittsburgh Courier* that in time past the English people-them used to boil people in a big pot and eat them before the pot even boil. Kill people and eat them. You see them pot 'pon the fire. Him draw it, you know, and give you the reading underneath it." Cannibalism was therefore not only African, as the white man had tried to make out.

In the October 3 issue of 1936, there was an article by a minister from Ohio that made claims such as the following:

The Jews at the time of Christ and before in the Old Testament were yellow, brown, reddish and black in complexion, not white as pictured in our text books and writings.

Moses, according to the Coptic or Ethiopian Bible, was the illegitimate son of one of the Princes of Egypt, the cause for Pharaoh to issue an edict placing all Hebrew children in the water. He was a brown man and put his hand in his bosom and it became white or leprous. (Read *Exodus* 4:6). And you can prove from the context he was brown.

Hyram of Tyre, a black king who had a navy and worked with King Solomon was black, and a descendant of Ham—*Genesis* 18:19. The black people of Tyre and Sidon were among the first to sail the seas. Black seamen from Africa were in America and discovered it long before the Norsemen or Christopher Columbus came here. They introduced tobacco, yams and corn here and traded with the Indians.

Goliath was a black giant, not a white one as pictured . . . *Genesis* 10:19.

With their strong religious outlook readers would undoubtedly study such claims as convincing proof of the destiny of black people as God's chosen people, of the black complexion of the messiah, God himself, and of the white man's Babylonian intent in suppressing an Israel that one day would again be free.

Another aspect of the *Pittsburgh Courier* that reinforced certain aspects of the Revival worldview of the early Rastafari and their idealization of Africa was the serialized adventure story of "Dr. Belsidus and the Liberation of Africa." Samuel I. Brooks, the name of the author, was probably the pseudonym for a black nationalist who obviously was impressed with the high organizational discipline of the International Communist movement and its firm leadership, and whose message through the story was therefore that the decolonization of Africa along the lines proposed by the Garvey movement required a "Black International" of all the black countries in Africa and the Western Hemisphere, under wise but ruthless leadership.

Dr. Henry Belsidus and his black brain must conspire to overthrow white imperialism and free Africa. After building up a remarkable international organization through modern scientific and unscrupulous methods, he secretly trains a black army and transports it to West Africa. The capital of Liberia and all the principal towns are quietly captured in the dead of night. The President and leading officials are in prison. The Liberian army surrendered and all radio and cable stations are taken over. Crates loaded with technical equipment are rushed from New York to the Black International headquarters. Meanwhile, assassinations and activities perpetuated in Europe keep the news of the Liberian conquest out of the newspapers, thus giving Belsidus time to consolidate his gains.

As he gathers his delegates from all over the world, Belsidus outlines the four hundred years of misery imposed by white men, concluding that it is the duty of the Black International to end this oppression.

All revolutions are started by minorities who use majorities to do their bidding. All successful revolutions must be conducted along dictatorial lines by a minority obedient to one man. I am the man.

I have the responsibility of directing this revolution. To direct it successfully I must be obeyed implicitly.

But, of course there are traitors among the lot, and those include the *Jamaican* delegate, who is ruthlessly exterminated. Belsidus, using bombs and germ warfare, exterminates the whites and gains a position of advantage over the colonial powers. In comes the message: "Mussolini conciliatory . . . British and French may postpone war. We must strike now." Strike he does, spreading death over Ethiopia and eventually succeeding in completely liberating the continent and asserting black supremacy.

Brooks's intermingling of fantasy with the political situation at the time completely convinced the Rastafari that the mad genius, Belsidus, was none other than Haile Selassie. And so, Hinds had his secretaries transcribe each episode into large log books, one of which survived in the possession of Brother Anton. The installments were read out at each meeting, like a war news bulletin, in fact. "1935 when the Italian and the world gwine make war with the King, when him drive in him boat, him de 'pon the battle field same way. And him answer to that call here so, and him answer to that call there so." The reference here was to Belsidus issuing orders from the headquarters of the "Internationale" as news of the progress of battle flow in on his many telephone lines. Selassie, alias Belsidus, had tremendous gadgets he put to the service of conquering the whites. He had, said one informant, "a radio station on the mount of Fez and by the whisper of a man's voice he heard and knew what was going on." Another, however, remembers it as a television, and in addition "it have the glass what him looking in the world, I Majesty Selassie I, invisible, immortal and wise."

It may come as surprise to some that such science fiction fantasies could be thus interpreted, but one should not lose sight of the people's desire to be rid of colonialism and its racist subjugation. That was the main and positive side to the painstaking efforts of transcribing to the letter all thirty-three chapters of Samuel Brooks's creation. But the *Courier,* and other literature in addition, gave the Rastafari material with which to buttress their strong, anticolonial, antiwhite nationalism. This was the main worry of the British, who, since they could not ban such publications outright for being subversive tried to strike a compromise with the Rastafari, as Hinds's secretary tells us.

When I read the magazine to the public, the Government send shorthand writers to take jottings of what we speak and even books that we read. Them complain in English and tell we: "Listen, it is not that we feel that unu [you] is so ignorant or illiterate, but we were not expecting unu to carry all these subjects and read it so plain to the public. Unu take it as a duty to preach upon those subjects and to read, that every Tom, Dick and Harry can be what you call instructive of these definitions. We feel that unu should only read book in the mission, don't bring it on the street."

Suppose we have a book that we get from Times Store, entitled *Coronation Commentary,* they say that is politics, for it show us the position of every empire. I read a book by the name of *The Destiny of the Jews* and that book shows us when the Negro people were brought from different sections of the African countries to the Western hemisphere and their bodies were going in machines and their bones, blood, flesh, brain were mixed with the manure and thrown into the roots of trees to give manure. And I read those books to the public. When the constables from Sutton Street come, they give us warning to keep such books indoors. There was a book entitled *The Black Supremacy.* We used to read those books in public, but we were warned not to keep it up.

The Rastafari did not comply. According to Brother Biini, Hinds used to tell the police that "What I'm doing is not any unselfish [sic] movement, more than carrying out a certain amount of duty." It was therefore inevitable that Hinds would run into serious confrontation with the police.

The first kind of confrontation I would like to discuss is that which took place at meetings. In carrying out its work on behalf of the colonial state, the police used to attend the gatherings of the Rastafari, far more, it would appear, than those of other groups. It must be borne in mind that street meetings, religious as well as political, were very common, but the police seemed to pay very careful attention to the new sect, listening keenly and making notebook jottings the Rastafarians referred to as "shorthand." This in itself was a form of intimidation that Howell and Hinds knew only too well. But at times, deliberate attempts used to be made to break up meetings, as in this case with Hinds.

I remember one Sunday we were having a meeting by West Queen Street and Luke Lane corner, and Sergeant Lee comes in the meeting, you know, and having an argument. And I look at him and say, "Well, Sergeant, I am surprised at a big officer like you coming in this meeting when the Bible is reading and having a conversation; that's not proper, you had no decency that way." And he says, "Move off, and keep moving." Well, me and him really—I grab him and hold him, and him hold me and we is there wrestling. Well, one more was in West Queen Street and Princess Street and see the incident. Him run and come join the fight. Well, him come behind me and lick, me duck and it take the Sergeant.

Another form of breaking up a meeting was to declare a 9 P.M. limit on them. Whenever they met resistance, the police would move in with the batons. According to Brother Faulkner "if them come and is just a few minutes after nine, they would say is time. And some of them don't come in a peaceful way; them want to force you out; but some of the people would want to fuss about it." In fact, said Brother Roy, the police created many fights with this kind of approach. It is not clear from my informants whether the riot that took place when police moved against Hinds at a meeting at the Coronation Market sometime in 1937 or 1938 was motivated by an attempt to break up the meeting on the pretext that it had passed 9 P.M., or an attempt to seize the book he was having read. One version had it that the police first went to Hinds and demanded the book. From this version comes the myth that Hinds had received the *Coronation Commentary* from the duke of Windsor. The other version, however, was simply that the police moved in because 9 P.M. had passed. Whatever the motive, Hinds *was* reading a book about the coronation of George VI and highlighting religious and political points from it.

According to Bible, in Revelation 17, it say that him shall be a bulled king, meaning he shall reign one hour, that mean one year. He will proclaim King but him never crown King, for after him father died he was proclaimed and it was near to the coronation, but through Mrs. Simpson he abdicate and his brother now take charge. You have a Jamaican, Simpson, he is a lawyer, and Sir William Morrison. They went to the coronation of George VI but they never come back and report. So the Rastafari got news over that they have him flying and say there was no coronation. But no coronation carry on. Well, make it more stronger, Sir Hugh Whiteford wrote a book. I remember that Sunday night, the very week Coronation market was open, Hinds was having a meeting there and him was reading that book and say: "The King is dead, long live the King!" I remember that part, "The King is dead, long live the King!" And we tell him, he don't crown at all, that was like a bogus coronation.

Hinds was making two points. The first was that Selassie was the King of Kings, the one destined to overthrow the power of England and all other colonial powers. As it was always necessary to draw from the authority of the Bible, through which Selassie's true identity had been revealed, Revelation 17:10–14 provided him with the key to understand the recent events in England and their impact upon the oppressed. In this messianic vision John sees a woman sitting upon a scarlet-colored beast, with seven heads and ten horns, which as the author himself explains, "is that great city which reigneth over the kings of the earth," that is, Rome, built upon its seven hills.

And there are seven kings: five are fallen, and one is *and* the other is not yet come; and when he cometh he must continue a short space. . . . And the ten horns which thou sawest are ten kings, which have received no kingdom as yet; but received power as kings one hour with the beast. These have one mind, and shall give their power and their strength unto the beast. These shall make war with the Lamb, and the Lamb shall overcome them: for he is Lord of Lords, and King of Kings.

It was a fact that Edward, the duke of Windsor, was proclaimed but not crowned king. This fact, Hinds interpreted, must mean he was a king without a kingdom. In addition, Mussolini had already invaded Ethiopia, with the tacit permission of the other great powers, as the *Pittsburgh Courier* had already pointed out. Thus, it could be said that the beast, to whose power was added the power of the kingdomless kings, was at war with the King of Kings and Lord of Lords, Selassie. But, as the prophecy or vision continued, the latter shall overcome them. This array of political events fitted in marvelously with religious beliefs must have glued the ears of the hundreds who turned out that Sunday night to the reading of Whiteford's book and Revelation 17.

Hinds's second point is reflected in the chorus of protest that greeted the announcement, "the King is dead, Long live the King." There was no king at all because he was not crowned, George VI, that is. Here the authority is not the Bible but news that George was a *flyer* in the Royal Air Force, therefore not a king at all. Now, if George VI was not properly installed as king, then not only was he just like his brother, a "bulled king," but he had no authority and could command no allegiance from his so-called subjects. Although the argument had all the deviousness of some theological reasonings, the political message was clear enough. It was subversive.

The second version of the cause of the riot, represents the police, a fairly large detachment of them, as coming to demand an end to the meeting. "The police came and say we must over the meeting now. And we say, is not nine o'clock yet. Them say, "Don't mind, over it now: we don't want hear no Rasta meeting out ya!" Both versions could have been correct; they may have tried to seize the book being read at the same time as demanding an end to the meeting. The two versions are not contradictory, but reflect what the various eyewitnesses and participants saw. After ripping up the flag, the police began to wield their batons right and left. Hinds found himself locked in combat with one of the policemen, rolling all over the ground. In the end, however, "when you look 'pon Hinds, him was washed in bare blood." And even the women played their part: "Is the same time I get to lick the man there, for it was a fight and who can lick, lick!" Fewer than twenty men and women were arrested and held under guard in the market until the arrival of the Black Maria police van. The incident became well known throughout the Rastafari movement—no less than ten informants mentioned it, not all of them Hinds's followers.

Confrontation with the police also occurred in marches. All mass actions sooner or later take the form of marches. Bedward and his followers, including Hinds, marched against the government in 1921. The return of Garvey in 1927 was also the occasion for a triumphant march of Jamaicans through the city of Kingston. Garvey himself organized ceremonial marches as a means of showing strength and inspiring confidence in his followers. Hinds used marches in the manner of Garvey, great ceremonial affairs, several hundred strong.

We march these days right through the whole city. Sometimes we march from headquarters, go right down Three Miles and come Half-Way-Tree. March in uniform with the red, gold and green. Prettiest thing in the world! Sometimes all three hundred people line up. I remember a round banner, which mark something pon it: "Them put the Black man on Top of the World and Keep him There Forever." And the people them? Lord have mercy, man! Them would tear down the whole place to look 'pon we when we marching, you know.

A drum corps headed the procession, among them a flutist. They were followed by the officers who carried long staffs, with which, every so often when they came upon large crowds, they formed an arch for those following to march through. Marches of this sort took place on the major ritual holidays celebrated by the movement. Even in the 1930s permits were necessary from the government, but they were not always forthcoming.

The King of Kings Mission began to decline as a result of internal conflicts. Informants could not give any detailed or consistent picture of what actually happened. "Brother Hinds start to carry on with some things, because you have to say him fall. Him take away all the brother-them wife and live with them, and the Lord vex with him." There was some truth to this accusation, for a son and a daughter were born to Hinds within a month of each other. As this was in 1938 and the organization showed the signs of breaking up in the mid-1940s, one can infer that the decline was gradual. Others, like Brother Sanggi, lay the blame on Hinds's meddling with politics, at least the sort of politics he disapproved of. Others simply explained that Hinds departed from the path set by Garvey by attacking the latter. "Hear what him say, if him go to heaven, that is Ethiopia, and see Garvey there, him take him hat and walk out." As a result God struck the shepherd and scattered the sheep. Why Hinds would have adopted an anti-Garvey position was never explained.

Downer, who led one of the breakaway factions, said that he had a vision in the early 1940s in which a man who was about to fell a tree warned Downer to leave the vicinity of the tree trunk. He barely missed being struck by one of the branches. The tree he interpreted as Hinds, and the ax-man as God. So he left and formed the Afro-West Indian Brotherhood.

It is Brother Biini, however, who throws the brightest light on what was taking place. A man who thought highly of himself, being quite literate, Biini felt on the one hand that many members were jealous of his own rise from armor bearer, up through the chaplaincy, to general secretary of the organization and Hinds's right-hand man; on the other hand, he felt he was not awarded sufficient compensation for all his sacrifices on behalf of the leader and of the mission.

The teachings that people got under the instructions of my administration and the instruction of the administration of the leader bring them up to a certain stage that some of them feel to themselves that them know as much as we now, them can do without we. So some wanted my post and carry jealousy at it and a certain amount of feelings to say that is not me one can preach, and is not me one can write and is not me one can do this. I actually had was to draw one-side and let them, you know.

Biini associated himself very closely with the leader, Hinds, and claimed that together they raised the level of leadership, making it possible for some of the dissatisfied to grumble. The cabinet members, as we have seen, were empowered to lead bands of members into the streets to preach. They did not, apparently, even have to require the particular permission of Hinds, though Hinds generally approved of the practice. In this way, they gained training, established a name for themselves, as well as following. Being secretary, Biini saw the mission through an intensive period of growth, in which, he said, membership grew from a mere 100 to about 250 in a matter of eight months, and over the next few years to some 800. Many were jealous of his ability and position, whereas others were sympathetic. "Many a time them decide say them going make a purse to give me—plan a big collection that will assist me to eat something good or even buy a few good piece of clothes that I could appear in public with. But some believe that it was too good fi me and some criticize it and cry it down."

It is clear that division and conflict in the organization between the young men in leading positions, and among the membership led to the breakup of the King of Kings Mission. Hinds had devolved some of his authority over to his most trusted lieutenants, but not enough to suit them. By mid-1940s a group of them elected Morris to set up a new organization, carrying off a portion of Hinds's membership. When he took sick in 1950, Hinds had not one single faithful left to attend him. He died in the Kingston Public Hospital on May 12, 1950, and was given a pauper's funeral. There was only one mourner, his own sister. Few people knew about the funeral, and those people who did know, like Sister Hall, were too busy to attend.

All four leaders—Howell, Hinds, Hibbert and Dunkley—ruled over their organizations with charismatic authority. Hinds was the only one to share authority with his lieutenants, and rather than subvert the King of Kings Mission they broke away to form independent bodies. Charismatic leadership does not preclude factionalism, as Sundkler illustrates with the nationalist movements among the Bantu.

An aspect of charismatic leadership is the belief in the supernatural powers of the prophet or leader. Mention has been made of Hibbert's alleged power to practice in the occult. A similar claim was made for Howell.

In the asylum now, they give him a dangerous drugs fi kill him. And when him drink it and them say well, we sure that him dead now, and them put im 'pon the stretcher—that time him stretch out stiff, you know, them call two man fi go carry him away. The two man hold the thing a lift him. That time him gut swell big so, and him just jump up and blow something and say, "Yes, boy, what happen now?" And the big gut just take time and come right down.

To justify his belief in the possibility of something like that really happening, Brother Cyril explained the philosophy behind such powers.

A man have a spiritual life to live, that if you really can live it, I tell you what you could do. If you can live a spiritual life with food, you can take the life and put one side there so, and just lay down there so, and when you done you take it back. You never hear them have a little story say the witch can take off im skin and left it and go away and come and put it on back?

The story of the witch might be just a story, he added, a joke, but it is really possible "to invoke yourself to death and bring back yourself. All things is possible to God." As he saw it, God gave certain men those powers. Dunkley did not do anything quite as dramatic as that, but according to Baia, he had the power of disappearing. The night Dunkley was fired at, the police descended on the headquarters. Dunkley hid in a little room, but when the police entered it, using torches, they still could not find him, "and him still in there." Later he got up and walked through the gate leaving them looking for him in and around the yard, "and them still don't see him."

Dunkley also prophesied the burning down of the Roman Catholic convent on Duke Street, which took place in October 1937. Hinds was also reputed to have done something similar: "Him tell them him coming with a sledge hammer and him going bust up all the busts of Mary and what them have there." That was why they called him "Prophet." Several of Hinds's followers also claimed that while in jail one of the twelve times he was arrested, he sent a letter to Edward, duke of Windsor, warning him not to ascend the British throne if he wished to escape assassination. According to the story, Edward abdicated and in gratitude sent Hinds the *Coronation Commentary*. In reality, this book, written by Geoffery Dennis, then chief of the Document Section of the League of Nations, and published by Heinemann, was most offensive to the former king and the subject of a libel suit.

The men who went with Morris set up a committee to run the new organization. But it seemed to have been too closely patterned after the King of Kings, with leader, chaplain, secretary and so on. Rather than oust Morris, the dissidents broke off once more, under the leadership of Downer, and established with another Brother the United Afro–West Indian Brotherhood. Morris claims that his organization continued until 1960, under the name of the

Ethiopian United Body, when it simply went out of existence. The brotherhood attracted many of those people who had broken off from other leaders. Sensing that a new mood was gaining momentum throughout the movement, the deepening desire for repatriation, Downer got the brotherhood to apply for membership in the Ethiopian World Federation in 1955. When the Ethiopian Orthodox Church was established in Jamaica in the 1960s, the Afro–West Indian Brotherhood was dissolved. In the meantime, however, a different trend had taken hold of the movement, steering it further away from the traditional leadership and organization than Downer or Morris had done. I refer to the Dreadlocks.

5. Enter the Dreadlocks

The most outstanding characteristic of the Dreadlocks is, of course, his hair, a sacred and inalienable part of his identity. It defines his status. The longer his locks the greater his standing as a professor of the faith. He affectionately calls his hair his crown, comparing it to the real crown of his king, Selassie, and sometimes to the mane of the lion, a symbol of male strength.

The Dreadlocks reform trend within the Rastafari movement set out to purge the movement of many of the Revivalisms that had been retained in ritual and organizational life, and in doing so to challenge many of the social and religious norms taken for granted. Their matted hair was a symbol of this.[1] What will emerge from the analysis of this process of reform, however, is that the Dreadlocks only went halfway in their elimination of Revival retentions, impelled though they were by their hatred for any form of accommodation with society. The result of their reformation was a mixture of innovations and traditional elements from Revivalism.

The early preachers of the new religion concentrated on the question of the identity of God. All informants confirm that this

---

1. The meaning of hair in Jamaican culture with particular reference to the dreadlocks phenomenon is treated in my forthcoming essay entitled "The Phallus and the Outcast" in Barry Chevannes, *Rastafari and Other African-Caribbean World Views* (forthcoming).

was so. The early preachers of the new religion concentrated on the question of the identity of God. All informants confirm that this was so. This thrust accomplished at least one objective: it undermined the racial values of the colonial status quo, which to a significant extent had gripped the poor peasant into compliance. Regardless of the nuisance Bedward was thought to be to the status quo, he never challenged the identity of the colonial Christian God. The Rastafari did. God was none other than the little black man ruling over Ethiopia. What was more, God had always been black. He was King, and all true believers were to serve him.

To claim allegiance to a foreign ruler was incompatible with paying allegiance to the ruler of one's own country. Relations between Rastafari and the state were antagonistic for this reason. The charge brought against Howell and Hinds was "sedition and blasphemy." As Rastafari grew in the overcrowded city the antagonism was expressed in police harassment, as sketched in the last chapter.

However, Rastafari's anticolonial stance has to be seen in the context of that wider awakening that culminated in the 1938 uprising. A single opposition comprising the brown middle class and the peasant and working masses confronted British colonialism in a display of unity that lasted only a few years before splitting into the two major political parties, the Jamaica Labor Party led by Alexander Bustamante and the People's National Party led by Norman Manley—the JLP and the PNP.

The Rastafari were themselves part of the larger struggle at that time. Two of my informants were working in bakeries at the time of the general strike. One was intimidated by more militant workers into supporting the strike. The other played an active role in forcing the stoppage.

The Chinaman say if we can't come to work, him gwine shut down the bakery. We tell him we don't mind if him want shut it down. Him never directly say him would fire us, but we tell him we naa work because seaside gone off.

I was the only one Rasta there. I make a lot of noise. Them have some guard in the store room. Mi tell them 'Unu [you] come out, mek we lock it up!' We see tram car a go along, we stop him tell him come out and lef' it, an him have fi left it same place in the road there. Him have fi do what we say, for is better we a look.

Another informant carried news of the strike to his fellow workers, thus playing a direct role in getting them to shut down the public works on Mountain View. "Unity," he counseled, "is strength. You mustn't try to divide yourself. You cannot be working while man strike all over the island an say you naa stop. You must stop work!" And he saw the hand of God in the wonderful solidarity that everyone displayed. But he would have nothing of the violence.

I don't tek part in wrongdoing. I will see them doing it but I won't do it. But you know, it was for the fulfillment. God will make a person for a purpose. I am here like a kind of watchman to watch what they are doing, but me don't indulge in no kind of evilness, like see the car stop and go in there and rob people. I can't do that. I will watch them and come away and have a little joke, like.

He was cautious in his support because he associated the rioting with actions contrary to the commandments of God, even at the same time as he saw it as the fulfillment of God's designs.

Although only a few of my informants actively participated in this watershed in Jamaican history, the events as a whole did not fail to receive the overall attention and study by the Rastafari who were determining their position of involvement in the ensuing political struggles.

The emergence of Bustamante as a national figure caught the fancy of Robert Hinds. "Our leader, Brother Hinds, tell us him pray to God for somebody to assist us with food, and when Busta rise up him say, 'This is the man.'" Hinds then sought biblical justification for this conclusion, which he found in the story of Baalam, "the only gentile prophet we have in the world."

Baalaf was a Babylonian king, and this man Baalam was chosen by God that anything him bless it bless, and anything him curse it curse. Baalaf called Baalam to curse Israel, like how you see them have birth control now to curse us so that we would decrease instead of increase. And Baalam said to Baalaf him going to get orders from the Lord what to do. The Lord tell him to tell Baalaf, who him bless no man curse. And Baalam disobey. Him tell Baalaf, "Tek these oxen and go to the mountain and have them cursed." But anywhere food is, is blessing, for after Israel get food him bless black people. So instead of cursing them, Baalam bless them. And when Busta first win the election in 1944, him kill 11 head of cow at Union Hall and give it to poor people free.

Bustamante came to help the poor, Hinds taught, but Bustamante was not "one of Israel," that is not a black man, hence a gentile. By identifying Bustamante as Baalam, Hinds found a way to bridge the gap between Bustamante's racial origins (a brown mulatto) and his role as a leader of the black masses.

With this interpretation, Hinds encouraged his mission to vote for Bustamante in the 1944 general elections. Not everyone, however, was disposed to do so. By then some Rastafari had become anti-Bustamante for two reasons: his negative attitude toward the racial question, and the attractiveness of the socialist platform of the PNP.

Setting himself on an all-out campaign for national leadership of the labor movement, Bustamante is alleged to have turned his back on some of the other leaders who had fought alongside him. St. William Grant became his first casualty. According to one informant, it began when Bustamante insisted on prefixing his name to the Union. "Grant say that Busta should never say is 'Bustamante' Industrial Trade Union. He should call it something that belongs to the people. But like how him have it, it come in like a one-man thing." And to show that it was a one-man thing, Bustamante expelled Grant. "Is not Grant himself left, is Busta fling him out. Him become big man after the people dem say 'we wi follow Busta till we dead!'" Grant was a democrat, Bustamante an autocrat. When the election campaign began, Grant and Busta found themselves in opposing camps. "Him go run election 'gainst Busta. Busta look 'pon him and say, 'Look at that snotty-nosed, knotty-head, thick negro like that coming to run against me in election!' So in those days now I look into myself and I have seen where those men is a traitor to the black race." Another informant said she heard Bustamante deny having any African blood. "I know that God Almighty choose up man to do his work, but from the moment you change your attitude from the poor people you don't mean them good. And we hear him say he don't have a drop of black blood in him. That's what he said: his father is an Irish man. He said it out of his mouth." Bustamante father's name was Clarke. If that informant's claim accurately reflected his attitude toward the racial question, it was unlikely that he would have been sympathetic toward the Rastafari.

In the same way that some Rastafarians were repelled by Bustamante, others were drawn to the PNP, which in 1940 had put out a manifesto calling for far-reaching changes, through a policy of broad nationalization of sections of the economy and sweeping land reform. The program caught the imagination of many Rastafari. To organize the masses around the program, Ken Hill set up a group on the Dungle, according to Brother Sanggi. They named the group "Western Cosmic." The group would meet and study the literature passed on by Ken Hill, as well as pray and read the Bible and chant like any other Rastafari group, or, as he put it, they preached "the two doctrine." There was also he said, another group from Back-o-Wall called "The Underprivileged," from which were also drawn many of the men who helped build the Coronation Market. The social democratic program was the most promising in terms of changes in society, and on this basis several of my informants voted PNP. Whereas Bustamante alienated Baia because of his racial slurs against blacks, Ken Hill, because of his association with the black masses, drew him in.

I vote for Ken Hill because he was a good fighter. He fight our cause because him talk the African way. Like him tell us now that his mother was poor black woman selling in the market, foreparents came from Africa like mine. And we know that quality brown people come out of the line of our black sister to make themselves white and forget where them coming from. So when he speak those ways I look into him and say something must be in him.

Duggie, who could read, studied and believed in the PNP's program. That he switched his vote at the last minute was due to the hold that his religious beliefs had over him.

First time I vote with Bustamante. I will tell you the reason why. Now, when the PNP start them have a little book called *The Plan for Progress*. Penny for it. When I read the book really I don't have nothing. My children could starve and naked and dem going socialist, I say that would be good. I really go for them. But brother! One month before the election I go to bed one night and a voice come to me and say, "Don't vote PNP, PNP is no good!" I didn't consider the voice to know enough knowledge. Like tomorrow the elections, tonight I go back to my bed and the voice come back to me in a rough manner and say, "Don't vote for PNP, is no good!" I get 'fraid and vote for Busta.

He did not say that the voice was that of Selassie, but rather a voice from the unknown. The vision aptly symbolized the confusion that must have been in the minds of many people at the time. The planters had lost no time in spreading anticommunist hysteria. Bustamante, anticommunist that he was, undoubtedly could not have failed to make anticommunism one of his campaign issues. In 1942 he had used it to reaffirm his autocratic control over the BITU and to break with the nationalists (Munroe 1977, 4). According to Sanggi he was an opportunist.

The Bustamante split naturally weakened the nationalists. The failure of the PNP in the elections led to the demoralization of those Rastafari who had voted for them. The two-party system, they had begun to argue, could not work in the best interest of the masses. Speaking of nationalist Ken Hill, Baia said:

I prefer to give him a X, not because X is right, for I know X is wrong. I don't have education but I know that you go to school and you get you sum wrong and is X you get. So since you become big now, you find out say X and that mean that when them hold you in a corner and cut you backside you must decide to say if it down the bottom it couldn't be right up at the top. But according to the policy of the European system where them coming from them push before the black people and give you the wrong part and hold the right for themselves. And this is the down plan of slave. And if you try to get away you come like a bundle of crab inside a barrel: while one trying to creep up the other one drawing him down back. All a wi must stay till hot water come.

Baia's cynicism came from his disillusionment. Voting, so say the hundreds of Rastafari who voiced this sentiment, is the system the white man uses to keep the modern slave down on the bottom while he stays on the top. Anyone can see that it is wrong: all incorrect arithmetic problems are marked with an X. Therefore when the system requires of you an X beside the candidate of your choice, it is committing you to a wrong.

Even followers of Bustamante, although they had emerged victorious, were beginning to turn from him. One informant, who during the campaign used to sing on the JLP platforms, tells of confronting Bustamante for having raised cigarettes from three farthings each to a penny.

"How the blasted hell you tell the people you will decrease the thing and you increase it?"

"Oh," replied Bustamante, "you are a damn PNP."

"Romans 8 says neither you nor PNP is any good. I am a servant of God."

Whereupon Bustamante drew his gun. "Chief, Chief," intervened Lindel Newland, one of Bustamante's lieutenants, "Him belong to us!" Bustamante calmed down, "You are a brave boy, brave boy," he commended my informant and dismissed the police who had rushed to the scene. That informant's decisive break with Bustamante and party politics came when in defending a PNP friend from a JLP gang, he was beaten up.

Turning away from politics, Rastafari stepped up their agitation for repatriation. That repatriation was an ideal from the beginning was evident when Leonard Howell mobilized for it on the centenary of Emancipation, the first of August 1934. As followers of Marcus Garvey, it was only natural that they would seek to implement this form of the idealization of Africa, but the Rastafari also had other items on the agenda. They had to sow the notion of a Black God and this became their focus of attention in the decade of the 1930s. By the 1940s, however, following further disillusionment with the new politics led by the brown middle class, repatriation was given a major thrust. According to Baia, a group of Rastafari went to see Bustamante and demanded that his government send them to Africa. Bustamante replied that they were Jamaicans, not Africans, and sent them instead to build a lane in Cross Roads. This would have taken place after 1944, for that was the year Bustamante came to power. Some time later, Baia and twelve others were arrested for leading a march through Kingston.

We had seen something in *The Daily Gleaner* and *The Star* which said that men with whiskers and beards should march to BITU Headquarters. There we would see a spokesman on the Back to Africa movement. We used to say we want Repatriation. I was going to market the Friday morning to sell some shoes. I saw a meeting; it was Hinds, who called us and told us about this Back to Africa meeting for bearded and whiskered men. So seeing that the idea was one close to my heart I joined. Then, we had our drum and thing. Five to six hundred well-wishers made up that amount but there were around three hundred Rastafari.

Baia made a clear distinction between Rastafari and non-Rastafari, and through this distinction we understand that the Back to Africa sentiment had support beyond the small circles of Rastafari.

Baia's is the first account of mass action by the Rastafari around repatriation after Howell's 1934 call. It does appear from all my other informants that the main activity of the early preachers was centered on establishing the theological claim that Selassie was the returned Messiah, the King of Kings. Repatriation as a teaching was always present in the movement from the earliest days, but it was not the main focus; it became such only after the hopes generated by 1938 and 1944 events began to evaporate. Baia placed the march in the late 1940s.

Undoubtedly, the process of withdrawal from national politics was a gradual rather than an abrupt one. As late as 1949, according to Sanggi, Hinds was campaigning for Bustamante. "When I hear and went and look I get down and says, 'I'm surprised at you, Mr. Hinds, how you gone, you're a politician!'" The revolt that had set in against the traditional leadership of the founders was being crystallized around the issue of involvement in versus withdrawal from society. This was the climate in which the Dreadlocks emerged.

The Youth Black Faith

The Dreadlocks trend had its beginnings late in the 1940s. There were several young Rastafari converts who held their own on the streets, among them Brother Taf, Pete, Brother Firsop, Badaman, and Watson. They were guided by their love for the doctrine.

Although there was a proliferation of preachers, there was no dearth of an audience, for Kingston was expanding rapidly as peasants gave up rustic for urban poverty. Back-o-Wall had already burgeoned into Ackee Walk, adjacent to the large May Pen Cemetery, and had stretched farther south all the way to the seaside but for an intervening portion occupied by the Water Commission. Up Trench Town, also, the poor settled on all available pieces of land. Each slum was a network of yards fenced off for privacy and connected by footpaths and alleyways.

It was in one of the slums on Ninth Street in Trench Town that Brother Taf and Pete lived when Brother Watson, or Wato, met them and decided to pool resources with them. Their preaching encompassed places as far away as St. Ann and Clarendon, but the fact that they operated out of Trench Town meant that their yard became a "camp," a place where brethren simply came and stayed to listen to the reasoning and discussion.

Watson's was not the only camp. According to another inform-ant, there were several around, their main purpose being ganja sale and smoking. This is an indication that ganja smoking and mar-keting were still somewhat centralized. People like Barnes used to peddle it in the streets from as early as the 1930s, but got their supply from centralized outlets. As late as 1957, when Prince Emmanuel called his all-island Rastafari convention, all the ganja in the city, informants insist, was consumed and they had to use tea leaves instead. This could not have been possible unless the known sources were at the time few, or, and this cannot be ruled out, pro-duction had dropped after the destruction of Pinnacle in 1954.

The idea of an herbs yard was not new. A very old non-Rastafari informant remembered taking part in ganja smoking contests in the yard of an East Indian who used to peddle it around the time of the First World War. What seemed to be new was its rapid spread among the African population and the sub-culture that began to grow up around it. Informants remember "Kencot" as having a big camp in the Dungle and that in the mid-1940s he was tried for murder, a crime generally attributed to ganja, although at the time you could be arrested for smoking "ram goat rationale," or periwinkle. The camps developed certain codes of conduct, among them (1) denying one the chance to leave camp before the herbs was consumed; (2) passing the "Kutchie" or cup from left to right; (3) gracing the cup before taking one's draw; (4) emptying the cup when all the herbs was burnt out and not before; and (5) good behavior while in camp. Some rules, such as the last, served the function of avoiding unnecessary attention from the police. The manner of passing the cup was a transferral of ritual patterns of collective movement common to Revival and other African-Jamaican religions. The rest of the codes were probably passed on by the East Indians, including gracing the cup before smoking.

By the time he joined up with Pete and the others, Wato would alredy have been familiar with camp practices because he had spent several years under the influence of another camp run by a Rastafari by the name of Gorgon. He would have been familiar too with the strictness of the codes, which when violated could fetch fines and other punishment, including suspension, from the other brethren who acted as judges. Wato's camp was different in that he turned it into an organization, the Youth Black Faith.

The Youth Black Faith was founded in 1949 by what we may call activists. They were young, and they were on fire with the doctrine. They were for the most part the young men who entered adolescence in the late 1930s, left the country for Kingston, and embraced the faith in the following decade. As one of the most influential members of the Youth Black Faith, Wato describes the leadership of the new group as being born out of their contempt for the waywardness of the older leaders.

I remember I and Brother Anton used to go among Hibbert and them brethren and hear how them administrate. We walk among them many days and see them movements. And it always impress my spirit so much that I say, of a truth, those men who carry the doctrine of Rastafari them really preach and teach. But there was something in the midst. For I know one named Hibbert who have some other scientific ways to deal with, such as burning candles and we condemn those things. Man like Hibbert them have other powers that them use and the prophecy preach against those things. For those man used to burn candles. I wouldn't say directly about the drug store oils, but I know that if you go to the drug store to buy candles to burn for a purpose, peradventure you could want to buy oil too. And seeing that them do these things over and over in our presence we say that these things are not necessary.

This was clearly a revolt against the Revival tradition. Revival leaders and obeahmen generally used candles of various colors in their rituals and special oils to which are attributed special powers—"oil o' look-but-don't-see," "oil o' forget-me-not," and so on. Burning candles was unnecessary, the young men felt, because the Apostle John had declared Christ "the only golden candlestick."

And we always verse up these things to the elders. If you have any candle let you oneself, you temple, be the candle; we will look at you, we will listen to you when you talking to you administration. We will lift you up for your good organization and your good principle that you have to all the faith. But to any other supernatural thing or suspicious thing you would bring in that is not corresponding to the spirit of truth, we will condemn that.

"Putting it on the line," one might say. The young men did not reject the old leaders outright; in fact they paid them their due as teachers of the faith and even promised to strengthen their organizations, providing they reformed the Rastafari movement to get rid of such practices identified as having Revival character. But this was not the only thing they wanted reformed.

And Downer. Brother Downer now used to lick out against man who carry beard, for him don't carry beard—him shave clean. So in fi him house him never like to see much of the beard man come in. Him call we ram goat. So it always fiery to I how you teaching about His Majesty Haile Selassie, and is a man who carry beard, yet among the brethren you just on the brethren about his beard.

Beards were being worn from the mid-1930s, according to informants, but they were not made much of until they became identified with the Rastafari a decade later. Slim and Sam in one of their compositions referred to the fear bearded men inspired in others:

> Run, man-without-beard,
> Beard man back o' you!

Downer's attack occurred clearly during the 1940s or later, and if in objecting to beards he was objecting to the kind of impact the movement was having on the non-Rastafari society, his position was tantamount to compromise with the society.

At any rate, there were two things for which the Youth Black Faith stood up: the denunciation of traditional practices of superstition, identified with earlier Revival beliefs, and upholding the right or desirability of members to wear beards. That the new trend was one of reform was indicated by Wato who declared that their intention was "to step more deeper in the whole security than the principles and the actions that we see many other brethren, even man who was older than us, administrate. And when we step within the prophecy, we find that most of those actions is condemned by the prophecy." The Book of Revelation had condemned the older practices.

As the Youth Black Faith grew, a new structure evolved. Offices such as leader, chaplain, and even the designation secretary were dispensed with. A simpler structure comprising chairman and tableman replaced the previous offices. The chairman's function was that of chief spokesman, to "make statement as to whatsoever aim and office we have, to administrate to the congregation," in other words, the convener and guide of all meetings of the organization. The tableman was necessary because literacy was not high; he was called tableman because his place was at the table that held all the books to be read. Membership was at first open to all those whose names appeared on the register, but the practice was discontinued because "We say that every man have free access to the tree of life." The Rastafari concept of being free to come and go solely on the basis of one's conviction became institutionalized through Youth Black Faith. Under the conditions of urban slum life the new thrust gathered momentum.

As resistance to the backward traditions of organizations led by the elders stiffened, and the younger members purged their own organizations of Revivalist traits, the title "Warrior" or "Dreadful" was conferred on those who distinguished themselves with ascetic discipline. Wato was one such person.

They used to say I was very "dreadful." I was very strict to my duties to see that a man don't come anytime him want to come. Him come whenever the time is appointed. If we say the house is to meet tomorrow morning to discuss something, I always stand up to see that him don't come 10 o'clock or 12 o'clock and all that time. I am always strict to them things.

The "duty" was an obligation. The group had only one duty as a regular weekly feature and that was the prayer meeting they held every Wednesday night. Other duties were such as the House decided should be arranged at other times. These were the formal meetings of the Youth Black Faith, and Watson and Firsop demanded of other members strict discipline both in punctuality and conduct. In earning the name "warrior," members were motivated not by a sense of office, for warrior was not an office as such but by a sense of deep religious conviction. In time, the designation gave way to a more appropriate biblical one, "Bonogee" [Boanerges], or "Sons of thunder," the name Jesus gave to the brothers James and John. One who earned that name inspired dread in other brethren by the forthrightness and frankness of his critical remarks and the defense of the principles essential to the Youth Black Faith. "Dreadful" or "Dread" was therefore synonymous with "upright."

Outside of formal duties, the Youth Black Faith met in a continuous stream of reasoning, for as I already mentioned the group was also a camp. This meant that ganja was smoked. The increase of police activity against ganja in the period after the Second World War made trafficking and possession highly dangerous. Moreover, Rastafari were known to be anticolonial, and it had not taken the colonial authorities long to realize that ganja offered a good pretext for imprisoning Rastafari. This had been the rationale behind the strict codes enforced by Hinds. The Youth Black Faith went a step further. It institutionalized ganja as an integral part of the Rastafari reform movement. The reasoning behind this was simple: there was nothing wrong with ganja, so if the government attacked the people because of it, such an attack must be motivated by the desire to suppress the people.

We don't count ganja as a criminal offence. We show the policeman at all times that we rather if you destroy us. For God says, "The evil things 'pon this earth is the hand-made things." These are the things that brought up falsehood 'pon the people, those is the things that destroy the people. So, this is not the things that hand-made, this is God natural creation, and it always virtuous to show the man the Bible and Revelation 22: "the herb that bear the various fruits, the leaf of it shall be the healing of the nation" and in Psalms 104 him says, "All the herbs that bearing seeds upon the land is made for man." So this is the chief argument we always confront them whenever we have an attack by the police. Yet, them never listen to it.

And to make sure that they used ganja specifically as part of their religious practices and beliefs, the Youth Black Faith instructed its members not to carry ganja on their persons. "If policeman intervene in our congregation, him couldn't find no other charge. The father say, 'when they persecute you fi other things it is not; but when them persecute you fi the word, I Jehovah God is with you.'" Such reasonings as the house had were reflected in the decisions it made. As Brother Barnes had noted, selling herbs in 1937 was an economic necessity. Sanctifying it now was a way of reconciling that necessity with the existing law against it.

Another important innovation of the Youth Black Faith was the institutionalization of the locks. At the time of the founding of the Youth Black Faith, locks were not in vogue. That is not to say that there were not Rastafari who did not trim. It had not taken long after the movement was founded, in fact, for some to wear beards in the manner of Selassie (and of course of Jesus). It was believed that only those who wore beards would be repatriated on August

1, 1934. From the 1930s, therefore, beards became a practice, and a biblical reference was found to justify it, namely, the Nazarite vow of Samson. What the Youth Black Faith debated now, however, was whether to comb. The issue was largely a social one at first because society simply did not accept unkempt hair. Not to comb one's hair was to declare onself not merely antisocial but extrasocial, like mad derelicts and outcasts such as Bag-a-wire. It was precisely this concern that was the issue. The side that won was the side of the Dreadful, the Warriors, the Bonogees. "It appears to I many a times that things that the man comb would go out and do, the man with the locks wouldn't think of doing. The appearance to the people when you step out of the form is a outcast. When you are Dreadlocks you come like a outcast." Locks had a shock value, but they were also a way of witnessing to faith with the same kind of fanaticism for which the prophets and saints of old were famous, men gone mad with religion.

Wato claims that the warriors were the first to start the trend, and as their hair grew they became even more dreadful. According to a non-Dread Rastafari informant, the debates were hot. The Warriors, or Dreadfuls, were so vociferous and quarrlesome that a split developed in which those who could not take the new order "shif up," departed their various ways. The two houses that separated in the 1950s were the "House of Dreadlocks" and the "House of Combsomes." In 1961 when an unofficial government mission was sent to Africa to examine the possibilities of migration for Rastafari brethren, the leader of the three Rastafari members of the delegation was a Dreadlocks. Less than a decade later, the Combsomes had all but vanished, as was revealed in fieldwork as early as Barrett's (Barrett 1968).

The leadership that emerged as a result of the new trend in the Rastafari movement did so within a more open and democratic structure. These leaders defended the principles of the organization and expounded the doctrine of the faith more forcefully and with greater commitment than had leaders of the past. The Bonogees had a new kind of charisma, based not on mysticism like Hinds's and Howell's, but on moral authority.

Another important difference between Dreadlocks and their antecedents lay in their approach to the society. Whereas Hinds and Howell encountered police harassment in the course of their missionary activities, the Dreadlocks seemed bent on *inviting* confrontation. Whereas Howell and Hinds were not afraid to stage pitched combat with the enforcers of the law, the Dreadlocks were contemptuous of the law itself and seemed to delight in demonstrating it.

In 1954 three members of the Youth Black Faith were arrested in Trench Town for indecent language and refusing to give the constable their names. The case was called up at the Half-Way-Tree Court. The full membership of the camp was on hand in solidarity.

We never go there to make no upsturbance. Each and everyone of us who left that habitation, left with this conversation that each man's meditation today is that them free the brethren. So we was there from court call, till court adjourned in the afternoon. Go back to court again, after lunch time, then court call around 2 o'clock. And when these brethren was called upon before the court, the judge remand them until such time. One bredda in the lot, called Derminite, he have a spirit that say, "Hoooop! Back them up!" Him never do any other much talking, that was just him sound: "Hoooop! Back them up!" And him make the sound. A little after, you find that we were surrounded with a lot of police. And while Breda Derminite give a hoot, I really gave a sound, "Fire!" because them time I was a hot fire man. While him say, "Hoooop! Back them up!" I say "Burn them! Fire! Burn!" That give the Government them strong words, and them was on us. From there now, we were hold up by the police and beaten, and locked down and charged three months for contempt of court before the final case try. That show the judge was ignorant and illiterate. For him say, "What is your name?" "Rastafari!" Him say, "Thirty days for contempt of court; take him away." And in the same time, you have fi try the same man with the same name and sentence him to twelve months in prison. So I look into those things and say that is ignorant. I come like a child you just send to school.

According to the account given in *The Star* (Sept. 15, 1954), eighteen Beards were arrested in an attempt to free their three colleagues. When called on, they "refused to give any other name but 'Ras Rasses.'" They were detained for medical observation. The following week when they appeared each gave his name as "Ras Tafari" and were again remanded in custody for another eight days. The third week, however, they were each cited for contempt of court and fined 10 pounds or thirty days in prison.

The group, which included two women, "went cheerfully off to the lockup when the sentence was announced" (*The Star*, Oct. 6, 1954).

From that period, "sounds" became an institutionalized characteristic of the Rastafari movement. Derminite's sound "Hoooop! Back them up!" did not mean anything in the literal sense, but in context was a threatening sound of disapproval. So also was Wato's sound, "Fire! Burn!" which today is commonly heard among youths. Fire itself became one of the symbols of defiance in the Youth Black Faith, and played a central role in a ritual death dance. To call down fire was to declare hostility. Summoned to give their names, each of those so accused said his or her name was "Rastafari!" and each received thirty days for contempt. The ritual was repeated three times over the course of three months before the magistrate decided to try each "Rastafari" and sentence him or her to a year for creating the disturbance. The court was "illiterate" according to Wato because any sensible person would know that the Rastafari were not going to yield. A moral victory was won, but the price was heavy, an extra three months in prison and a possibly harsher sentence in the long run.

The Youth Black Faith went on a march on April 14, 1954, a full year after Kenyatta was sentenced. Brother Anton got the vision that they should do so. There was no other purpose to the march, but in a general sort of way the Youth Black Faith felt it was a way of carrying on the struggle against the state; they expected a confrontation. Everyone was advised to carry a Bible. They set out from Wato's camp on Ninth Street in Trench Town, led by two men carrying the red, gold, and green banner and a woman carrying a photograph of Selassie and proceeded along West Road, east along Spanish Town Road, and on to North Street. Crossing Duke Street they saw the police Black Maria speeding to overtake them. Anton ran in front to warn the standard bearers, one of whom was Brother Saasi. "Do you have a permit?" asked the police. "Yes," replied Saasi and produced his Bible. At first the police attempted to break up the march, but when the marchers insisted on continuing, the police moved toward them. According to Saasi, "before them touch anyone of us, we just run down and go full up the van." There were thirty of them, including eight women.

At this time, you have a policeman name Ras Jackson. He come off duty this morning and he was with us in the march the said morning. When they take us inside now, them line us up. Them feel now is block-up we block-up, but we of ourself didn't have no control over that—just the Spirit, you know, manifest him that way. When they line us up, them grab one of them; the first one was the policeman, and when him look him say, "But raas, no Jackson!" And there goes police from all the place. Them send for this priest, this black priest, Gladstone Wilson, through him is a spiritual man and is spiritual warfare we is on. Them send call him to see what he could do or what him could say. The most thing him could say to the Government [was] if they can get out what is in us they can stop us, but if them can't get it out, them can't stop us. And him gone. They sent for a doctor now to test Jackson to see if is mad him mad, but him sow 'way the doctor and them had to send call another one. Then him curse the Government, from the Queen come right down, call them all kind of Sodomite.

"To sow 'way" someone is to drive him away insultingly by behavior characteristic of a hog. Saasi was admitting that Jackson, and the rest of them too, behaved terribly, in a way designed to alienate everyone, especially Monsignor Wilson, whom they must have been especially glad to see. For the Roman Catholic Church has always been a special and favorite target for the Rastafari, and for several reasons. First, the secrecy of their rituals and reliance on an abundance of external symbols seem to people of a Protestant tradition close to the practices of magic. The Duke Street convent was commonly regarded as housing many secrets, no doubt because outsiders, especially males, were forbidden to enter it, according to the rules of the cloistered followers of St. Francis. This practice of cloistering, though a common tradition in Catholic countries, was not widely understood in Jamaica. Both Dunkley and Hinds are said to have warned of the convent's destruction by fire. Gladstone Wilson himself, as a brilliant scholar, was generally regarded by many Jamaicans as the only black man privy to the "secrets" of the Roman Catholic Church, having served as one of the pope's secretaries in the Roman Curia. That is the meaning of Saasi's description of him as "a spiritual man." Second, the siting of the headquarters of the church in Rome has always stimulated anti-Roman Catholic and millenarian movements in the Christian tradition to identify it as the harlot mentioned in the Book of Revelation. Third, to make matters worse, Pope Pius XII had given his blessing to the fascist troops of Mussolini as they set out to conquer Ethiopia.

If we read Saasi's account correctly, it would mean that the police had a slightly more tolerant attitude toward the brethren. They did not proceed to arrest the brethren, but instead to break up the demonstration. Also, sending for Monsignor Wilson first, indicates that the police preferred to deal with the Youth Black Faith primarily as religious fanatics preaching a new doctrine than as political agitators. They were obviously not regarded at that time as subversive. It should be pointed out that Jamaica's journey to political independence had already begun, and limited self-government had been instituted in 1954. Nevertheless, Wilson's doctorate in psychology, one of his many qualifications, did not seem to advance any understanding of the movement.

The presence of a police constable among the members of the Youth Black Faith comes as a surprise, revealing that joining the constabulary force was not regarded at that time by Rastafari as incompatible with upholding the faith. From the 1960s on, the Dreadlocks' conferral of the name "Babylon" first on the society and derivatively on its protectors is the cause of the virtually absolute polarization of the Rastafari and the police.

The case finally came up for hearing. "Three times they carry we over to the court, and we shut down the courthouse." The thirty brothers and sisters went wild; they filled the halls of the Resident Magistrate's Court with their terrible sounds of "Blood!" "Fire!" and passages of judgment drawn from the Scriptures. Some of the Dreadlocks had to be gagged and straitjacketed. According to Anton,

The last morning we go to court, the whole of us sit down in the cell. We chant, read wi Bible and we pray. And when we finish, the Clerk of Court greet us and we greet him back. Him say to us if we go over court house today and behave weself. We say, yes, while we get justice. And the same time we there in the yard in the sun, we get another paper which say them hold up Kenyatta. Same time we here 'pon the work, same time Kenyatta there 'pon the work in Kenya. So this Youth Black Faith is the first throughout the whole world march for freedom!

They "behaved" themselves and Judge Duffus bound them over to be on good behavior.

Saasi's oral testimony accords closely with the written newspaper reports. Picked up at the corner of North and East streets, the thirty "made sounds of rejoicing and sang merrily all along the street and into the station proper" (*The Star*, Apr. 14, 1954). They refused to give any names, and only Jackson was identified by his police colleagues. He was attached to the Police Training School and Depot as a mechanic (*The Star*, Apr. 15, 1954). We learn that by April 22 they had created an uproar in the court for the third time; their actions included quoting from the Bible and speaking in an "unknown tongue." Ras Jackson was later reported dismissed from the force. (*The Star*, May 19, 1954).

The experience taught the Youth Black Faith that they could create chaos in court by the use of words. Brother Saasi related a number of anecdotes, probably real, about brethren up before the court. One person set the courtroom in fits of laughter when, to the usual question of guilty or not guilty, he answered, "Everybody guilty!" Another was arrested for taunting a policeman with the words, "Babylon gone!" When the judge asked, "Guilty or not guilty?" the accused responded, "I don't know 'bout it, I stand! From Babylon gone, I must stand!" Saasi himself spent six months in prison for ganja, under the name, "Blood-and-fire Rastafari!" In recounting tales such as these, the older Rastafarians conveyed a feeling of pride for having defied the police and the judiciary, proving their fearlessness in the face of armed might.

The excerpt conveys this informant's pride in linking their version of the Jamaican struggle with the national liberation struggle of Kenya. This identification is all the more remarkable when we recall the colonialists' vilification of the Kenyan patriots. The news media, keenly scrutinized by the Rastafari, painted the patriots as "terrorists" who murdered innocent whites, rather than as liberation fighters. In 1956 when Ghana won its independence, the Dreadlocks joined workers and other forces in a march and have followed ever since with great zeal the process of national liberation on the African continent.

Impelled by strong religious conviction, the Dreadlocks' militancy was the militancy, nevertheless, of zealots. It was not always measured by the pursuit of concrete goals nor by judgment of what was possible to be achieved, with the result that the Dreadlocks often ended up paying unnecessarily the exacting price demanded by the colonial state of those who dared to threaten or ruffle its stability. But it was a militancy, as I have tried to show, born out of the political developments of the 1940s and characterized by innovative departures in personal conduct, style, and organization from the traditional leadership, as well as by an exorcism of Revivalist retentions in ritual life. With calculated fervor they chose the role of outcasts from society. A young informant who grew up in Western Kingston remembers many of the Dreadlocks as people who, during the early 1950s, sometimes dressed in burlap, the local variant of sackcloth.

I would like to return to an observation made by Brother Saasi: "Them send for this priest, this black priest, Gladstone Wilson, through him is a spiritual man and is a spiritual warfare we is on." Wilson was regarded as a "spiritual" man in somewhat the same way as Hibbert: a man learned in the spirit, a "four-eye" (with eyes seeing into the past and into the future) man in fact. The Dreadlocks themselves believed in the existence of such secrets and the possibility of mastery over them. But the main point I wish to bring out is their conception of their own action. They were fighting a battle, but on a spiritual and mystical plane. The march itself had no known motive, apart from the obvious defiance of colonial rule. A vision was all that was necessary to set it in motion, and they armed themselves each with a Bible. In 1921 the Revivalist Bedward with eight hundred followers set out on a march to Kingston. They had no weapons, yet the purpose of the march was to "do battle with his enemies." In 1952 the march of the Youth Black Faith members was no different in kind.

The obsession with "spiritual battle" resulted in the creation of a ritual dance called "nyabinghi," which, as mentioned in chapter 1, was supposed to be the name of a secret order sworn to "death to white oppressors." Now by the 1960s, according to the University *Report*, Nyabinghi meant "Death to black *and* white oppressors" (Smith et al. 1960, 7; my emphasis). The ritual dance was introduced into the Youth Black Faith mainly through the instrumentality of Badaman (himself one of the Combsomes), who claimed that he had derived the practice from a book lent him by a mentor. The nyabinghi was a death-by-magic ritual in which an effigy representing the intended victim is consumed by fire while all the participants dance under a spell of *burru* drumming called "tuokin [stoking?] the drum." This development took place around the time of the 1952 march. The ritual was performed in the presence of Rastafari only.

One important difference from the destructive machinations of the obeahman was the political aim of the nyabinghi dance, in the sense that the intended victims were never private but rather public individuals, those defined as oppressors, whether they were black or white. I imagine that such dances as were held were performed against figures like the colonial governor or government officials. Shortly after I began my field trips in 1974 there was strong talk among one group of Rastafari of dancing the nyabinghi for the prime minister, owing, so they said, to his failure to fulfill certain promises made to them. Here, again, we have another instance of the Revivalism among the Rastafari but under a different formula, so to speak.

The same process might be observed in Rastafari institution-alization in their outlook of certain attitudes toward women. One aspect of the Revival outlook toward women is the perception of them as necessary evils. Revival leaders (and evangelical preachers among the poor) have a reputation for stressing the "necessary" side. Orlando Patterson provides a rather true-to-life sketch of this in what has been called a sociological novel, *Children of Sisyphus*, or *Dinah* (1964). The early Rastafari did not much object to this side of women. Howell was said to have had several wives (thirteen, according to apocryphal stories) and, as I said earlier, Hinds became the father of two children born within weeks of each other. The Dreadlocks rejected this kind of behavior. But in their rejection of promiscuity they seized upon the other side of the tradition: the "evil" aspect of women. According to one of my combsome informants, the Dreadlocks instituted celibacy. The Youth Black Faith had women, as should be apparent from the anecdotes, but as the Warriors gained the upper hand, women disappeared from the House. Many of my younger informants were celibates of up to ten years vintage. Those who, "rather than burn," sleep with their women themselves observe certain sexual taboos. Women may never cook their meals or participate in ritual smoking (although I have seen both these taboos broken). Avoidance reaches a peak during the women's menstruation.

The Dreadlocks also built on a Jamaican tradition of fascination with words. Beckwith (1929, 199) made the following observation: "Among a people to whom a pun in a name or the utterance of a pithy saying carries almost the determining character of Fate, the proverb or familiar sayings attain a rich and distinctive development." She drew references to the proverbs, riddles, and lies; to the repetitive character of the songs; and to the "easy loquacity of the Jamaican and his picturesque phrasing."

A quick pun born of the moment is not uncommon. An old story is often repeated of the Negro slave who, hearing of the efforts made for emancipation by its great advocate in England, expressed his confidence that if Wilberforce could not gain from Parliament freedom for the slave he "will by force." When Lord Burnham visited the island a few years ago he was greatly amused to hear a lad on the street say on the occasion of a bad fire in Kingston "If dem bring Bu'n'em come heah, what mus' expect but bu'n'em?" (Beckwith 1929, 199)

The rum bar of every peasant village is the silent witness of this "easy loquacity," this "picturesque" and proverbial wisdom.

The circle of the Youth Black Faith, however, carried this tradition further, bequeathing to the contemporary Rastafari movement on a whole, a tendency to place intrinsic value on the spoken word itself. According to Wato, the jargon presently attributed to the Rastafari as a whole had its beginnings with the Youth Black Faith.

It just arises in conversation, describing many things. Or several times you have several different types of reasoning and you step up with the words. Now that you have seen that the Chinaman in this country, if him want to destroy you, him can destroy you, and you can stand in his presence and speaking something to destroy you and you can't know. You can stand in the presence of the Indian man and him speaking something to destroy you and you don't know. And you have other people here who speak different language and you can be in the midst of them and them speaking something to destroy you and you don't know. So we, the Rasses, supposed to speak, that here, there and anywhere we find ourselves, we suppose to speak and no one know what we speak beside ourself. That's how we get to start.

Words like "seen" for "yes" and "overstand" for "understand" developed in the course of the intense reasonings in the camp. The guiding force was nationalism, expressed in the nostalgia for the lost African languages from which the white colonialists and slave owners robbed their slaves.

Jamaican is the combination of mostly English words put into a modified African structure (Cassidy 1961). Standard English is therefore not natural to the peasant or worker, and his own efforts at expressing himself in it are often quite tortuous. Undaunted, he strives for mastery nonetheless, for Standard English represents the formal, the official language of even religious ritual. The Dreadlocks have taken the language they inherited, and, beginning with the Youth Black Faith, have made a deliberate attempt to develop a subdialect. Certain words and phrases have become popular modes of speech, among the urban youths in particular. Indeed, the most important of them all carry religious or moral implications. The most important is "I," the personal pronoun. To the Rastafari this is the same as the Roman numeral *I*, which follows the name "Selassie." "I" substitutes for "me" and for "mine." The religious meaning behind this substitution is that the Rastafari is also part of God, and if God is a visible, living man, it must mean that the Rastafari is another Selassie, another "I." Because everyone is an "I," one does not say "we" for plurality, but says "I and I." As the most central word in Rastafari speech, "I" transforms other words as well. "Brethren" pronounced in the dialect as "bredrin," becomes "Idrin"; "eternal," "Iternal"; "hour," "Iowa"; "times," "Iimes"; "creator," "Ireator"; and so forth. The word *Iri* is of doubtful derivation. It could mean "high," and is often used thus—"feeling Iri"—but it is also used to mean "yes," "good," and similar exclamations. Once this process of dropping or changing prefixing sounds is set in motion, other interesting things follow. The *f* of "food" is substituted by *y,* and thus "food" becomes "yood"; "thanks" becomes "yanks."

If everyone is an "I," then there is no place for the second person either. If one were to say "I see I with I rod," theoretically one could mean (1) I see you with my rod, (2) I see you with your rod, (3) You see me with my rod, or (4) You see me with your rod. Therefore the Rastafari use "the I" for "you," so that "I see the I with the I rod" takes care of possibility (2), and they rely for clarification, as all language speakers do, on the context.

Other colorful changes were also made. "Oppression" becomes "downpression," and "holy," rejected because "anything holey runs a leak," is replaced by "hola," "because it whole." The word *man* like "the I" implies more than simple preference; it has a moral meaning. It implies integrity; its opposite is "men." And so innocent words like "judgment" become "judgemant," and pronunciation of "many" changes to "mani." Sometimes "the man" is used for "you," and "this man" is used for "you," or for "I." Referring to Michael Manley as "Menlai" or "Menlow" indicates opposition to his politics.

Some words are not changed but are given special meanings: "sound" means speech, or words, and to "block a sound," or "block a yound" means to speak, but it implies words of serious import as does the word *chant*, used to denote the reasoning of the brethren. Exclamations such as "Blood! Fire!" and the like express disapproval of another's behavior and are used frequently to restore order at meetings.

The play on words knows no limits. When it was a college of London University, the University College of the West Indies was referred to by Jamaicans simply as "U.C." Dreadlocks who, for whatever reason, had a grouse against the university or its staff created the name *U Blind*. Similarly, those who thought little of Bustamante, or more recently of Seaga, both politicians, styled them "Bustamente" and "Blin'aga," respectively. Even the country Jamaica has become "Jah-make-ya." In truth, when Dreadlocks decide to reason in this argot it requires some aural experience to be able to follow.

Building upon a basically peasant tradition, the Dreadlocks have used the language to express their rejection of society. However, in doing so a fetish is sometimes made of the power of the word to develop and to convey nationalistic spirit. For example, it is generally accepted that the word *backward* is synonymous with "reactionary," as in the phrase *backward views*. The word *back* both spatially and temporally implies a retrogression. Viewing themselves as a movement dealing with the progress of black people, the Dreadlocks rule out the use of this word. How then does one say,

"I will soon come back"? In dreadtalk one would say, "I man soon step *forward!*" or "I man soon *forward!*" The fetishism was displayed at a 1975 youth conference, which included Dreadlocks and other youths influenced by the Rastafari, when a senior official of the government in addressing a Plenary Session used the phrase "go back to our history." Interrupted with reproving shouts of "forward," he repeated the phrase. Again came the correction. This time he simply ignored them and continued. And the point he was making was one they were in agreement with.

I have characterized the Youth Black Faith as a reform trend inside the Rastafari movement because its main aim was not to reject the main articles of Rastafari creed as preached by the founding preachers and passed on by the lesser lights who first began to break away, but to purge the cult of manifest traces of Revivalism. The main targets were the use of ritual objects such as candles and the encouragement of occultism. They felt that Rastafari was, in spite of its teachings about a black God and his reincarnation in the person of the emperor of Ethiopia, insufficiently distinguishable from mainstream Revivalism as the radical nature of Rastafari teachings warranted. And so outward changes began to take shape first in the organizational form, by dispensing with the Revival structure, and then in personal appearance and discipline by the gradual ascendancy of the Dreadlocks.

In an exciting recent discovery, John Homiak (forthcoming) has marshaled oral evidence that disputes the claim that dreadlocks started among the Dreadlocks or Warriors in the Youth Black Faith. In the version he presents the responsibility lies with a group of ascetics known as Higes Knots who introduced a new "livity" into the movement, that is, a code of relationships with God, nature, and society. Thus along with dreadlocks came the "ital" (natural foodways), lifestyle, dreadtalk, retreat from women, and other practices. Homiak titles his essay "Dub History," in recognition of the fact that "oral narratives . . . are rendered in many versions as they circulate among members of a speech community." In Jamaica's reggae culture the rhythm track of a popular tune may be taken by other artists and their own words dubbed onto it, producing various dub versions. Higes Knots may not be the final word on dreadlocks, any more than the Youth Black Faith. Both may be dub versions of the same Dreadlocks rhythm. Three things, though, are beyond dispute: the groups emerged around the same time; they were part of a revolt against inherited traditions; and they retained in the new order traces of the old.

It is curious, however, that despite this desire for a radical break with the past, despite their attempts to rise above the Revival worldview, the Rastafari still remained very much a part of those traditions they sought to dispel. Engels, speaking of Thomas Muntzer, remarked that the worst fate that could possibly befall any great leader of a revolutionary party was to find himself at the head of a government that represented a class whose time for state power was historically premature. What such a leader *ought* to do is historically impossible; what he *can* do runs counter to his principles (Engels 1967). In a way this was the dilemma of the Dreadlocks: determined to break with the peasant worldview, but forced to remain within the mainstream of that tradition.

6. The Bobo Dread

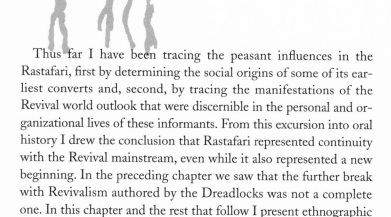

Thus far I have been tracing the peasant influences in the Rastafari, first by determining the social origins of some of its earliest converts and, second, by tracing the manifestations of the Revival world outlook that were discernible in the personal and organizational lives of these informants. From this excursion into oral history I drew the conclusion that Rastafari represented continuity with the Revival mainstream, even while it also represented a new beginning. In the preceding chapter we saw that the further break with Revivalism authored by the Dreadlocks was not a complete one. In this chapter and the rest that follow I present ethnographic data that show that the general argument may be sustained with respect to the present.

Of all the contemporary autonomous groups that together make up what we know as the Rastafari movement, the Bobo exhibit the highest intensity of Revivalism. They are Dreadlocks, but because they differ from the mainstream organizationally and in other respects, I treat them separately in this chapter. Unlike other Dreadlocks, most Bobo live together in a commune, organized in the tradition of Howell, and circumscribed by rituals. Outwardly, their separation from the rest of the Dreadlocks is marked by the wearing of tightly wrapped turbans, sometimes long, flowing black or white robes, and attractively handmade sandals. Even their form of greeting is different from that of other Dreadlocks.

The Bobo strike a compromise with the existing society by accentuating respect for certain values flaunted by the Dreadlocks in the Youth Black Faith tradition. All the agressiveness characteristic of the Dreadlocks is alien to the Bobo, who go out of their way to cultivate excellent relations with their surrounding community.

The Commune

Nine miles to the east of Kingston in Bull Bay live the Bobo in a small utopian community. The community is situated on a hillside, below a small promontory. The sight it presents a mile from the main road justifiably merits the name the Bobo give it, "City on a Hill." Large buildings are painted in red, gold, and green colors and bordered by flags flying. From the commune itself the view out to sea is a beautiful one: a vast, receding expanse of water with slightly changing colors moving away from two hills, on either side of the commune. To reach the commune, one travels between a river bed on the left, and on the right a series of settlements, one or two of them under government sponsorhsip. Farther up the road, where the gradient suddenly steepens, and immediately below the Bobo, are squatters whose numbers steadily increase day after day. The Bobo themselves are squatters on the vast crown lands.

The compound is entered through an arched gateway under which every Bobo, on leaving and entering utters a prayer, sometimes in his heart, sometimes aloud. Above the arch in bold characters is painted the name *Ethiopian International Congress*. On the gate itself is written a warning against bringing weapons of violence into the compound. Inside, and to the right, stands the guardhouse where all material things, such as knives and guns and money are deposited. Then in a very steep ascent one passes the house of Queen Rachel, the young and beautiful wife of Prince Emmanuel, and her four-year-old son Jesus. Directly above her on a terrace is the temple, and stretching out from it the large spacious dwelling house of Prince Emmanuel Edwards, or Dada, as he is called by the Bobo. Next up the hill lie the kitchen and generating plant on the right and the storeroom on the left. Where the slope becomes gentle, beside the kitchen, is the meeting yard where all services are conducted except on sabbaths and days of fast. On the edge of the meeting yard is the guest hut, a small circular shed with a table and several benches. A towel hangs from one of its posts. In front of it is raised a basin of water above a patch of basil mint. This gives the distinct impression of being a Revival seal, or sacred spot. No one uses the basin of water or towel, neither Bobo nor guests. The last structure on the right of the path is a sick bay where the women seeing their menses are confined until their two weeks of defilement (calculated by adding twelve days to the duration of the menstrual flow) are over. The other structures throughout the compound are houses. With the exception of the houses and other buildings, the entire compound is a fairly extensive field of gungu peas, covering more than half of the compound's two hectares. There are no other cultivated plants, but during the rainy season calalu is planted. Gungu peas are rich in protein, and do not require much watering. Over the temple fly four flags: a black, red, and green flag with seven stars, representing the state; a red, gold and, green flag with seven stars, representing the church that rules the earth, "as every traffic light show you"; a blue and white flag, representing the United Nations; and a green and white flag with seven stars and the word *NIGERIA* written across it, representing Nigeria.

Prince Emmanuel emerged as a Rastafari leader during the 1950s by spearheading an islandwide convention of the brethren at Ackee Walk where his camp was first set up. At the end of the weeklong meeting, the participants marched on Victoria Park and there planted the red, gold, and green flag in a symbolic capture of the city. The convention was to deal with the question of repatriation, and when this had been announced, many of those people who came in from the country had allegedly done so expecting to depart for Africa. Following the convention, Prince's followers became more sectarian. They began to attribute divinity to him and separated themselves from other Rastafarians by wearing the turbans and the robes. The Bobo remained at Ackee Walk until 1968 when they were finally bulldozed. They then settled at Harris Street in Rose Town, were again forced out to Eighth Street in Trench Town, then to Ninth Street, and finally, to Bull Bay where they have remained ever since on the rocky government lands over-looking the town. Because they regarded Prince Emmanuel as God, they believed each of their stopping places to have been recorded in the Bible. Ackee Walk was Nazareth, where Jesus came from; Harris Street was Galilee, where Jesus went after leaving his native home; Eighth Street, Capernaum; and Ninth Street, Bethlehem, for it was there that Jesus, Queen Rachel's son, was born. The settlement in Bull Bay they named Mount Temon, where God is supposed to have come from, according to a passage from Genesis.

The compound is organized simply: at the head is Prince Emmanuel, or Jesus himself, and beneath him his followers. Generally speaking, all male Bobo are either "prophets" or "priests." The function of prophets is to reason, the function of priests to "move around the altar," that is, to conduct the services. Apart from these rules are the other social functions that keep the camp going: a guard at the gate to ensure the ritual purity of all visitors who enter, the keeper of the stores, the cooks, the manager of the delco plant, and the comptroller whose main task is to purchase supplies. Finally come the women and the children whose places are subordinate to those of the men.

Socialization of Children

A relaxed atmosphere prevails in the commune. The children attend a basic school called Jerusalem School Room, where they are taught to read and write by one of the priests and receive basic instructions in the faith. The children observed are all young, below the age of puberty, and have nothing to do otherwise, unlike the children of the neighboring community. They enjoyed snatching off one another's turban. I once observed a girl of about nine pull off the turban of a boy younger than herself, and when he objected she, more in play than with real intent, threatened to "bust" his head. They were quarreling when the manager of the generator came upon them. It was interesting to note both the gentle way in which he reproved the children and that he took the explanations of the boy and his friend, another boy, as the truth without asking the girl her side of the story. His explanation went like this: they could not have told a lie on her; therefore, she must have done something to them to start their quarreling. In other words, his approach was based not on an unprejudiced sifting of the facts but on a grasp of the moral context of communal life: the boys must have been provoked for them to be angry. But the little girl insisted that they, not she, were to be blamed, and without further ado the prophet threatened to tell Dada, that is, Prince Emmanuel. Only then did she back down, confessed, promised she was no longer going to "bust" their heads, and countercharged them with having first pulled off her turban. The prophet was quite firm that he was going to tell Dada anyway, indicating to the children that once the word had been spoken it could not be taken back.

The incident further illustrates two things. First, it emphasizes the supreme moral authority of Dada, which acts as a sort of social control, even over the children. The commune is like a large family over which he presides as father. In fact the term *Dada* does mean father. Prince Emmanuel is the father of all in the commune, young and old alike. I have witnessed the manager of the generator come to Dada just to say that he was on his way to buy gasoline for the plant, as if requesting permission to leave, or a priest come to say he was now going to start the evening's service. But "Dada" also has deeper connections with the Revival tradition as a variant of the name "Daddy" (as in "Daddy Sharpe"), which highlights the *spiritual* relationship between charismatic leaders and their followers.

Second, we may note that adults feel responsible for the upbringing of children not their own. A feature of peasant morality, which one sometimes hears older people lamenting the breakdown of, was the preservation of certain codes of conduct that defined what children might not do. "Children must be seen and not heard" and "Don't spare the rod and spoil the child" were aphorisms that reflected this outlook. According to the old folk, every adult was responsible for the enforcement of this code. Children doing what might be considered wrong could be reprimanded by their elders, regardless of who they were or even by strangers. Complaints registered by an adult often resulted in parents' punishing their children without attempting to substantiate the claims. Urban life, however, seems to be undermining these values. People are more mobile, so ties to communities are not as strong, one's new neighbor today is gone tomorrow, and so forth. Even in the Bull Bay community I came across two boys whose delinquency did not seem to bother the adults, providing they were not at the receiving end. What the Bobo have done, therefore, is to restore some of the diminishing values of rural life that pertain to the socialization of children. With respect to adults in this community, children do not appear to have rights. Life on Mount Temon is like a bit of country within a semiurban setting.

There was one other example I saw of children being disciplined. These children were being particularly noisy while playing in the guest hut in the presence of a service in progress on the meeting ground. No one seemed disturbed by this behavior, until the noise level threatened the service. Then, one of the prophets quietly walked over and in a soft-spoken, nonreproving voice asked them to be quiet, calling each by name. The children, aged between five and seven, cooperated immediately. Other than in cases like these, children seemed quite free. The young Jesus, however, seemed especially free. He is the only male allowed to flaunt the convention of "covering the crown," that is to say, wearing the turban at all times.

Quite noticeable is that the overwhelming majority of children fall below ten years old. This reflected the youthfulness of the Bobo. Apart from Dada himself, I encountered only one Bobo over forty years old. If after twenty years from the founding of the Bobo in the 1950s the bulk of the community are young men in their twenties and thirties, and most of them interviewed had already passed through the mainstream Dreadlocks life before their Bobo phase, it tells us that the commune has a high rate of turnover.

The Female Taboo

The place of all females is below that of all males, regardless of age. As a "King-man" or "God-man," the male child is held up as being superior to all females even though the latter are often referred to as "empresses." The subordination of women to men is characteristic of the Dreadlocks in general, only the Bobo carry it to a greater length. In the commune all females must cover their legs and arms. Women are confined to looking after the children and performing other household chores such as cleaning and washing. They, too, are all relatively young people. The most I counted on any one occasion was twelve, but the total figure was something like twenty, the rest being "sick" (in menstrual recluse). None of those I saw appeared to exceed thirty five years of age.

Women give deference to men. A young Bobo was engaged in discussion in the round guest hut when his little daughter came running up and snuggled into his lap. Without interrupting his reasoning, he caressed her. The child was really running away from her mother who, following close on her heels, asked the prophet to hand her over to be put to bed. He ignored her totally and continued talking. Sensing that she had stepped outside her bounds, she physically retreated two steps without any show of resentment or annoyance and waited for five minutes before the child was released.

A woman may serve guests, but may never serve Bobo males. Traditionally, among the peasantry it is the woman who cooks and serves, but among the Bobo it is the men who cook and the men who serve. The women may eat sitting on a bench outside the kitchen or take the meal back to their private quarters. Of course if they so wish they may cook for themselves after their days of purification from the menstrual flow are over.

Prophet Stanley and his wife, Gladys, live a short distance below the compound, an arrangement that allow his entrepreneurial activity as a shoemaker and manufacturer of wood-roots beverages to avoid being stifled by the demands of communal life. He is thirty-seven and has been a Bobo for seven years. During this period he has not slept in the same room as his wife. Whenever he wants, he has sexual intercourse with her and then leaves. Women, he says, distract from meditation.

If a Bobo is faithful to his marital union, his sexual activities are limited to twelve days out of a twenty-eight day cycle. The other sixteen days, his wife must remain hidden from the view of all men. This is where the "sick house" comes in. Sometimes her period of defilement lasts longer than sixteen days. During this time, other women acting as nurses administer to her needs and take care of her domestic chores. I reckon that continence in such a situation is not always easy for the Bobo male. From time to time, around the winding bends in the road leading up to Mount

Temon, one comes upon a Bobo engaging a local woman in what would appear to be less than divine reasoning.

Bobo women are allowed to give birth in the hospital. There is no taboo about that, but they remain unclean for three months after, during which time only nurses attend to them. In Stanley's case, living independently outside the commune, he is required to give up the house and live elsewhere for the three months after his wife returns from the maternity hopsital.

I was unable to find out how Bobo women perceived their subordinate status. Once my assistant reported the case of a young girl who sought refuge in the commune after being turned out of her parental home in Trench Town. The Bobo she sought out duly made her his empress. Upon hearing this story, two of our informants from Hannah Town related what they said was a commonly held opinion, that women preferred Bobo as lovers, I imagine over Dreadlocks. On my way up to the commune one fasting day, I was asked by a young woman named Violet to tell Priest Samuel she was waiting by Prophet Stanley's yard to see him. She mentioned having been beaten by another man for living with a Bobo, who I presumed was Samuel. She could not approach the commune in her condition—legs uncovered and clothes soiled. Violet, it should be noted, was obviously conversant with commune regulations governing the conduct of women. That she was no longer cohabiting with Samuel, though still in need of him, or that she failed to observe the conduct on dress, could be interpreted to mean that she did not find camp life entirely to her liking.

Prophet Stanley warned Violet that she had to wait several hours for Samuel's fast to be broken before being able to see him, indicating thereby the observance of regulations governing fasting. Nevertheless, as soon as the message was delivered, Samuel's look of asceticism gave way to a look of much pleasure. He disappeared from the temple at once, not to return for the rest of the day.

I do not know what steps if any Samuel took on Violet's behalf. The view that women are a source of distraction could only lead one to imagine that in subsequent grips of religious fervor Priest Samuel would put the blame for having broken commune regulations and his own meditation on a woman. Women become scapegoats. When God asked Adam why he picked and ate the forbidden fruit, his answer was not that he himself wanted to taste it but that the woman gave it to him to eat.

Bobo treatment of their women does not differ essentially from the treatment most Dreadlocks accord their women. The main difference lies in the Bobo's greater ritualization of woman's "evil" nature. She is regarded as contaminating. Those prophets and priests who can contain themselves do so. Those men who cannot be sure to resist observe avoidance taboos.

Earlier, I implied that some Bobo might compensate for the ritual curtailment of their licit sexual activity by illicit relations with local women. Behind my impression is the assumption that the severe limitation on access to their women is a great strain. This of course is speculative. What is certain, however, is that religious fervor can make continence possible. Thus for example, Prophet Tommy, a young peasant convert from the Bito district near Bull Bay, had not, so he said, had intercourse for the last seven months because his girlfriend, also a peasant girl, "would not bow"; that is, she would not become a Bobo. He made it clear to me that this was the precondition he fixed on cohabitation. For him, therefore, religious fervor is placed above the personal need for sex. He also observed that he did not suffer from wet dreams as a consequence, for these he said came as a result of having rather than refraining from sex.

Beliefs and Rituals

According to Prince Emmanuel, the Holy Trinity comprises the three spirits: Prophet, Priest, and King. The King, of course, is Selassie. The Prophet is Garvey, and the Priest is Prince Emmanuel himself. In one of his discourses, without naming any specific country Prince Emmanuel said that Garvey was active in the liberation movement in Africa. One of the Bobo prophets later revealed that Idi Amin, at that time the controversial president of Uganda hounded by the West, was Garvey. Prince went on to point out that Africa was the name the white man gave to Ethiopia or to Jerusalem. Black supremacy was a must, for this was one race none other could produce. The white man was evil, for any book you picked up depicted Lucifer as white. The true

Israelite was the black man, not the Israelis who are white impostors. White philosophy could carry the black man nowhere, neither Christianity nor "religion," only righteousness. He ended the discourse by denouncing migration as another form of slavery, by which he meant using one's money to buy a passage to Africa, and declared that the only way to get to Ethiopia was to await salvation, that is to say, repatriation.

One of the priests later tried to explain what was meant by no other race being able to produce black. Black, said Priest Mark, is the lowest class of people, yet they are God. "Black is God because it brings every other nation." If a Chinese cohabits with a black, the product of that union will be black, but Chinese bring forth Chinese. When pressed for further clarity he became confused and said black and Chinese did not produce black. The general point, however, was that the black man was in some genetic sense superior to the white man.

The life cycle of the Bobo is circumscribed by ritual as befits any utopia. Every man, including the outsider, is greeted by the words "Blessed my Lord" accompanied by a bow with the right hand touching the left breast. A profound bow is reserved for Dada himself, who returns the salutation with the same words and gestures. "Blessed my Lord," or sometimes just "Blessed" or "my Lord" are also used in place of "goodbye" or the conventional "excuse me," as for example when someone is about to interrupt or take leave of someone else.

At sunrise, noon, and sunset, each Bobo prostrates himself and prays with his head turned toward the east. If a priest is present in the company of one or more prophets, he alone prays for all.

The evening services are conducted in the open yard before an altar facing east. They begin with drumming and singing under the leadership of three priests. Everyone attending must dress in a black robe, and those not so attired must remain outside of the meeting ground. The songs are, many of them, familiar sankeys. At the end of the singing comes a series of ovations or tributes, first always to Emmanuel, the High Priest, then to Marcus Garvey, the Prophet and next to Selassie the King. Then tributes are made to the "international guests," that is, "official" people such as myself. Each tribute ends with "Holy Emmanuel I Selassie I Jah

Rastafari," with everyone's joining in the "Jah Rastafari" and hands clapping in applause. Readings from the Bible come next, and these are interspersed with singing until Emmanuel arrives. Following is a descriptive summary of one of his sermons.

He began by saying that man is God and God is man. The man who was talking here now represented Jesus Christ here on earth. God could not be spirit; he must be flesh. This was he. These words won the acclaim of all the prophets and priests, who with one accord shouted, "Jesus of Nazareth Holy Emmanuel I Selassie I Rastafari." The next fifteen minutes were taken up singing the chorus:

> I want to get ready,
> I want to get ready
> I want to get ready
> Move round Jerusalem just like this.

The last line, "Move round Jerusalem . . . ," was repeated on and on for as long as the conducting priest desired. A noticeable feature of all singing is that it begins pianissimo and very low on the scale, then rises steadily in both pitch and volume. When "I want to get ready" ended it was exactly one octave higher than at the beginning. The drumming did not stop however, and over its throbbing the priests took turns praying. They then broke into another favorite song:

> Working for a mansion and a robe and a crown
> Working for a mansion and a robe and a crown,
> Working for a mansion and a robe and a crown,
> That is a glory for I.
>
> That is a glory by and by,
> That is a glory by and by,
> That is a glory by and by,
> That is a glory for I.

At this stage the dancing and participation became very enthusiastic. A Bobo not in the congregation, because he was not attired in his robes, fell into a near trance state. His movements became rapid and out of tempo, attracting the attention of a circle of guests and noninvolved Bobo. Occasionally he would shout out "Black supremacy!" or "Revolution!" A member of the congregation came over and said something to him but it produced no change either in his movements or utterances. Everyone was feeling quite high and at the end of the drumming Emmanuel asked, somewhat rhetorically, "Who is there that can't own God in the flesh?" whereupon the semipossessed shouted "I." Peals of laughter ran through the congregation and the onlooking crowd.

Emmanuel then called for chapter 4 of the First Epistle of John to be read. All faced the east and recited "Glory to the Father, Glory to the Son, Glory to the Holy One of Creation." Then as the passage was read, Prince Emmanuel developed on its theme, in the manner of the Revivalists, verse by verse: Esau and Jacob represent black and white. The black man is God, my Lord. "So you see only we is savior of the world. Only one man could redeem you and that man shed him blood. Him send a true prophet. That Comforter don't charge none. Free! Free Salvation! Most High God, Jahoovyaah!" All shouted: "Jaah! Rastafari!"

At the end of the reading, the doxology was again recited facing the east and after this the sankey "Jerusalem my Happy Home" was sung. One of the priests called out each of the verses of the song. Jeremiah chapter 8 was then read. At verse 10 of this book, Emmanuel said: "It refer to Great Britain, America, all of them. We used to leave Jerusalem and go to the Gold Coast to pick up gold just like that. When the white man came and saw it, oh my! They would kill us out!" The audience response to this was truly great. The white man, he explained as the reading continued, is Satan. Satan is able to create images but his images do not have life like God's. This was a reference to a myth later told to me by one of the prophets that Satan once stood by watching God fashion images. God sent him off to fetch some water, and before he could return, God blew the breath of life into them.[1] Verse 21 of the chapter read "For the hurt of the daughter of my people am I hurt; I am black; astonishment hath taken hold of me." When Prince Emmanuel asked of the priest reading, "Who says I am black?" the priest answered "Solomon." Prince then turned to his audience and said: "Greater than Solomon is here!" Were a standing ovation al-

1. This story parallels closely a Yoruba myth of creation in which Obatala, who had hidden to watch, was put to sleep by Olodumare. He awoke to find the breath of life already blown into the human figures he had molded for Olodumare.

lowed he would have received one, so great was the applause. The priest added, "The word of the Lord has spoken, Jesus of Nazareth Holy Emmanuel Selassie I." "Jah Rastafari!" responded the congregation. After the doxology, Prince thanked everyone: musicians, priests, guests, and "international guests." He gave instruction to them to continue until morning if they wished, and with a profound bow to everyone, departed for his quarters.

Twice each week and on the first Saturday of every month the Bobo fast. On these days, nothing whatever passes the lips, and from noon until six o'clock a service is conducted, but this time in the temple. Outside the entrance on either side stand two standard bearers, waving their flags. Pictures of the Three Persons of the Bobo Godhead and texts of various sorts adorn the interior walls of the temple. All worshippers are robed in white, males on the right, women and children on the left. The service consists of hour after hour of singing to the beat of the drums, followed by Scripture reading without preaching, followed again by singing. Then at three o'clock, the three-hour ritual to end fasting begins with Prince Emmanuel emerging from his quarters. A priest leads the congregation in the singing of a hymn, each line of which is followed by the word *Adonai*, sung on the same note as the final word. At six o'clock Dada enters the room to the left of the altar, washes out his mouth, and upon returning breaks his fast with a morsel of bread and goes back to his house. One by one the priests follow the same procedure and resume their places; this procedure is repeated by the prophets and last of all the women and children. During these three hours, the same hymn is sung over and over. Those who, for whatever reasons, do not participate in the service enter the temple at this time and go through the ablutions and breaking of the fast. When all have eaten, Dada once more appears through the doorway. All turn to the east, in which position they remain, reciting several prayers, and end by singing a doxology. One by one, again beginning with the priests and ending with the women and children, the members of the congregation pay their living God a special act of reverence: bowing profoundly and at the same time saying a word of greeting. And each act of reverence he returns in kind, before retiring to eat his supper. Outside, his worshippers feast on bananas and other fruits.

Relations with the Outside

Through their tremendous hospitality, the Bobo have built up a special relationship with the local community. They make a special effort to invite people to attend their services and can count on a few adults and younger children. I noticed a tendency for more teenage girls than boys to respond to the invitation. A visit to the Bobo during their celebrations has the quality of going to a fair and must be seen in light of the relative lack of entertainment and diversion in this semirural community. The nearest cinema is over two miles in the direction of Kingston, reached by an unreliable bus service. On reaching the commune, visitors are seated in the round hut and feted with fruits or, at nights, with supper. Sometimes one is offered a choice of "ital" or "non-ital" food. Flour dumplings, rice and peas, oranges, and ripe bananas are the food offered, and for drink there are bush teas, beer, and soft drinks. These last two beverages are specifically for the guests, for the Bobo do not themselves drink from bottles. I once overheard several teenagers complaining among themselves that they did not get any supper from the Bobo, possibly because the Bobo had nothing to offer.

At the time of my fieldwork, to get from this commune to the main road leading to Kingston, a Bobo must first pass by a group of displaced squatters from Kingston, a lower-middle-income housing scheme, and a settlement of leaseholders, tenants and settlers—in all a community of approximately 140 households. These were the people the Bobo went out of their way to invite and to fete.

To understand the importance of these relations, two things should be borne in mind. First, the Bobo depended upon the community's goodwill to get water, which is scarce in Bull Bay. The spring that normally flowed into the riverbed had dried up, and the only source of water for the residents came from a water tank situated in a catchment area further back in the hills. The housing scheme had water piped into the homes, but the rest of the community had access to a standpipe located midway between the main road and the foot of the hill. By cultivating the friendship of residents in the housing scheme, the Bobo (along with some of the squatters) were able to avoid the long trek.

The second thing to bear in mind is that for many years, long before the Bobo settled on the hill, some Dreadlocks inhabited the beach at Nine Miles. They were by and large fishermen. Being Dreadlocks, they related to the surrounding peoples as did Dreadlocks everywhere else, aggressive in two respects: their hair and their words. They valued their tremendous locks and thought nothing of reproaching women for what they would consider an abomination, namely the "burning" of their hair. Many of them also, in their devotion to the power of words, were not above the use of "bad words," or indecent expressions. Among a small section of the community, mainly among the settlers, I found that the beach Rastas had a bad reputation. They were all lumped together as "Rascal" (a play on the word "Rasta"), "nasty," "wicked," and accused because "they interfere with people" or "they curse women." Most people, however, did not seem to mind them. The general outlook was "some good some bad," "Just people like miself," "Nothing to it if my daughter become a Rasta," and so on. One policeman remarked, "I have no feelings against them for environment fashion behavior." These neutral sentiments seem to reflect the greater acceptance of the Rastafari, who have been integrated into important spheres of national life, particularly music and the arts. All three sections of the community had stable Rastafari households in them.

Whereas attitudes toward the beach Rastas, or the Dreadlocks, were on the whole neutral, those toward the Bobo were definitely positive. Almost universally the Bobo were described as "peaceful" and "nice" because "they trouble no one," and "they have manners." Bobo gentleness was contrasted with the obstreperousness and aggression of the awesome Dreadlocks. Some respondents called the Bobo "decent." In the main they referred to Bobo meticulousness in appearing neat and clean at all times with shirts tucked in, feet washed, sandals wiped or polished, and hair concealed beneath a tightly wrapped turban. This approval corresponds with the fact that many of those people who disliked the Dreadlocks and even some of those who did not, singled out not their doctrine but their hair as the main cause of their aversion. Uncombed locks did not make one appear "decent."

Out of an entire sample of ninety-one households there was not a single head of household or spouse living in the area for more than six months who had not been invited to visit the commune.

In short, the relations cultivated by the Bobo served to differentiate them further from the mainstream Rastafari. Their observance of the norms of "decency" and "good manners," which by and large referred to neatness in appearance and gentleness and affability in speech was in direct contrast to the Dreadlocks display of their hair and predilection for "sounds."

How does the commune support itself? How can the Bobo afford such generosity? I have found no evidence that the Bobo have any other source of income than that of broom manufacture. According to Prophet Stanley and others, those who live apart from the commune and engage in their own enterprises contribute of their own independent resources, but this does not appear to be either consistent or obligatory. It would be naïve to think that the Bobo, living in the country, do not plant ganja, if only for their own consumption. But that is speculation.

To make brooms, straw is bought in the market unless it can be obtained in the nearby hills. Usually, however, it is for the sticks that the surrounding hills are combed. There are four types of brooms for which sticks are necessary. First is the small hand broom, its stick approximately 45 centimeters long and 5 centimeters in circumference; second is the house broom of shoulder length or between 1 and 1.5 meters; third the yard broom, which is slightly shorter than the house broom; and fourth the cobweb broom 2.5 meters long. The Bobo obtain hand-broom sticks from the thickets around the commune, but for the rest they must search the forests. The best sapling to make broomsticks is the "panchalan," or Spanish elm, whose branches shoot straight up, tall and slender. The sticks are then placed in the broom-making area of the commune where the brethren are free to come and make brooms. The finished products are then taken onto the streets of Kingston, especially the affluent suburbs, and sold aggressively for whatever price they can fetch. The Bobo are quite clever at this. They fix prices according to their perception of the class position of their prospective buyer. In this way they may fetch up to ten or twelve dollars for a broom worth no more than three or four.

Why do the Bobo engage only in broom manufacture? Why not diversify the source of income? Many of the members of the commune are very skilled artisans, shoemakers and tailors. The Bobo regard themselves as Israel, and when Israel was in captivity in Egypt its sole occupation consisted in procuring straw to manufacture bricks. Today it is cement that holds the sand together, but this development is incidental to the Bobo. What matters is the straw: straw work identified Israel. This explanation given by one of the prophets does not account for the fact that the Bobo do not make mats, bags, or hats, other obvious straw products for which a ready market is available. The cash derived from brooms is supplemented by gungu and calalu, which grow freely throughout the commune.

As a utopia the City on the Hill depends on rituals and fixed statuses for well-ordered organization and stability. Everyone has a place, whether prophet, priest, or woman, and *everyone* accepts that place. The prophet does not disagree with his appointment by Dada, nor does he envy the role of priest. Prince is at the head of the commune, and to enter into the apparent joy and serenity of it one must accept him and accept also the place assigned by him.

But it would be a serious mistake to believe that it is Prince himself, his own charisma, which alone draws young men and women into renouncing the outside world. I mentioned before that all the Bobo observed were young. Every one of them that I spoke to had already been a Dreadlocks before turning to the Bobo. In light of what we have so far seen regarding the differences between the Dreadlocks and the Bobo, this course of events could only mean one thing, namely, that they find the persistent tension between Dreadlocks and the society intolerable and, therefore, reject the aggressive posture of the Dreadlocks because they regard it as the prime contributor to that tension. But if the Bobo are to retain the belief in Selassie, then their simultaneous accentuation of the Revivalisms inherent in the Rastafari movement and the creation of a utopia take on the character of necessities.

One householder in the housing scheme referred to the Bobo as "pure old criminal up there." This was one of only five people out of a hundred who did not like some aspect of the Bobo. While conducting research among a youth gang in West Kingston

(Chevannes 1981), I came to understand the reference to criminals was based on the fact that a number of the Bobo had been gunmen. Bent on laying aside the pressure of politics and crime, they placed themselves out of reach of rival gangs in a way that was not possible had they remained conventional Dreadlocks. For Dreadlock membership required the continued adoption of a critical and aggressive stance at least against certain, if not all, politicians. In fact, being Bobo seemed to place them out of reach of the police. In spite of pressure by the police on the Rastafari for ganja and other alleged offenses, I have not come across a single instance of a Bobo being arrested or detained. As Bobo, they retreated further away from the world of the profane, cutting themselves off and maintaining the separation by a ritual distance. Prophet Richard, a former gunman, sang the praises of Prince Emmanuel, who he said not only saved him physically by curing his gunshot wounds through his knowledge of herbs and roots, but opened his eyes to truth. The world of the Bobo is as close as any Rastafari can come to that mental state the fundamental Christian sects call "being saved." It made complete sense when one of my Bull Bay informants remarked that 95 percent of Bobo practices and beliefs were hers too. She was a regular member of the nearby Seventh Day Adventist Church.

7. The Era of the Dreadlocks

Many of the leading exponents of Rastafari throughout the 1960s were schooled in the tradition of the Youth Black Faith. The breakup of the Youth Black Faith was due to factors such as the imprisonment of some of its leading figures and demographic pressures that began to force many people to other areas of the city, such as Tower Hill and Majesty Pen, also known as "Back To." The organization taking its place was a loose one, known in the 1970s as the Coptics, or Jah Rastafari Hola Coptic Church.[1] It differed from the Youth Black Faith in its new leadership, in that only Dreadlocks belonged to it, where initially Dreadlocks were only one part of the Youth Black Faith, and in the virtual absence of women except as spouses of some Dreads. In all other essentials they were the same: militant separatists, dreadful, nyabinghi, inclined toward celibacy, acephalous, and more democratic in organization than those groups that united under a single leader.

The organization of the Coptics is called a "house," a concept originally used during the life of the Youth Black Faith to describe the reform movement. The concept of house, as used today, reflects more than a matter of tradition. It is indicative of the open form of Dreadlocks organization. As long as one cultivates dreadlocks, one

1. Not to be confused with the Miami-based sect discussed in chapter 10.

may be called a member of the house, no matter what other organization one may be a member of. The main function of this kind of quasi-organization is that it makes possible broad solidarity among the mainstream Rastafari. Membership is based not on baptism into a church or sect, but on the visible sign of uncombed locks, of course along with upholding three other dogma also shared by other Rastafari: the divine nature and authority of Selassie, the special place of the herbs, and the principle of repatriation. At the same time, social, economic, and even political relations remain individualistic and personal rather than communitarian as in the case of the Bobo. Thus most Rastafari are allowed to lead their own lives as members of a religion but without the risk of violating collective discipline. They have a sense of identity but without ritual obligation.

The early Rastafari derived from the uprooted peasantry, who were displaced from the countryside by a variety of social and economic factors. Based on this circumstance, the movement had retained much of the worldview of the poor peasantry, and this we saw in section on conversion in chapter 3 and in the subsequent discussions of the organization of the movement. But the Bobo, the only contemporary group so far discussed, are not typical of the whole movement, so we need to examine to what extent Revivalism has influenced the more contemporary Dreadlocks. By way of beginning the examination, I first present a profile on the sort of Dreadlocks I encountered during fieldwork, apart from those ancients from whom life-history interviews were taken.

Occupational Profiles

A significant section of the Rastafari comprises people with one foot in the city and the other in the country. In informal reasonings with the Dreadlocks I frequently heard them express the wish for land on which they could set up a "ranch" and grow lovely food and vegetables. But I also came to realize that many of those expressing such wishes indeed had access to land. Geoffrey, for example, about twenty-eight years old, had a piece of land in Clarendon, but a greater part of his life was spent in Kingston. The same also held true for Bongo Floyd, whose father had died leaving him several acres of land adjacent to the Frome estate in Westmoreland. Floyd could be found weeks at a time in Kingston, where he also was a landlord collecting rent from tenants. And there was Stephen: I once took him to visit his parents in St. Catherine. As we neared our destination he alighted from the car, with tremendous excitement pointed out one of the pieces of land owned by his father, and began speculating where he could put up a house and what bananas he could grow. The land was idle and almost ruinate and by his own admission could be his to cultivate. Yet he preferred to live in Kingston, though it meant living in a slum where he kept his wife and himself alive by working as a tiler, when he could, and by knitting woolen tams.

Ras Congo and his family left Kingston and squatted on land belonging to a rich St. Mary coconut grower. A few months after the one and one-half acres had been cleared and planted, the owners sent a team of eleven policemen and a bulldozer to evict him. Congo argued with the police and won the bid for time. A death in the landowner's family eased the pressure for some time. Two and one-half years later, in October 1976, the police again came. This time they could not be talked off, and the family was faced with losing several years of its labor. Congo's family was quite large, ten siblings in all. The oldest males helped their father plant out the land in vegetables, sweet potatoes, corn, and peas, and burn charcoal out of the saplings. The girls helped their mother in and around the kitchen and the house. For cash the family learned the art of knitting, and every week or two, the mother, father, and eldest daughter spent four or five days in Kingston selling the woolen caps, sweaters, and handbags. Congo was on one of these trips when I first met him. I failed to appreciate how he could run a farm yet move in and out of Kingston with such frequency and for such long durations until I met his eldest son, a young man, to whom was entrusted the entire operation. This young man not surprisingly, displayed a greater knowledge of the crops than did his father. Congo himself, I might add, had been a peasant boy in northern St. Catherine and used to be sent by others to steal coconuts from a large plantation until he was caught. He migrated to Kingston as a boy in the late 1930s and became a Rastafari in the mid-1940s.

Zed-I, aged about forty-five, rented an acre of farmland deep in the heart of fertile north Clarendon. On it were planted ground provisions such as yams and several roots of sugarcane. Zed-I also had sown a plot of approximately twenty-five square meters of onions after reaping a crop of several hundred kilograms of cabbage, which were stashed away in a nearby cave. One of the great surprises about the farm was Zed-I's use of fertilizer. Rastafari, on a whole, feel that artificially fertilized food is not a good thing. They profess great faith in nonfertilized, or *ital* (in this case naturally produced), food. Nevertheless, Zed-I justified the use of fertilizers because his onions and cabbages were for cash; he made sure to add that he did not use fertilizers on the "food," that is, the yams, which he said he had no intention of marketing. I should add, though, that he did save some of the vegetables for his own consumption and to give a few to his brethren.

Ideology notwithstanding, Zed-I maximized his investment through the use of modern techniques, even if they had to be rationalized in the face of his ideological convictions. All the other farmers around used fertilizers, so there was an element of competition behind Zed-I's conformity.

In Kingston, Zed-I already had his own marketing outlet. This was a Chinese retail shopkeeper on Maxfield Avenue with whom he had excellent relations, so good in fact that he could obtain nearly ten dollars worth of gasoline completely free of cost. Not even the sensitive problem of race was allowed to stand in the way. Zed-I said he found this Chinese man much better to get along with than many so-called "black people." This attitude toward other races is not uncommon among Rastafari. It represents an evolution away from the aggression for which the Dreadlocks were noted during the fifties and sixties.

The friendship between Zed-I and the Chinese trader had been forged over many years. And this brings me to the main point I wish to make: in spite of making a go at rural cultivating eighty kilometers away in the country, Zed-I was an urban dweller. He recalled taking M. G. Smith off Maxfield Avenue and enriching him with six foolscap folios of notes during the 1960 University study of the Rastafari. He therefore lived in Kingston for many years. During this research he had his own house near

Duhaney Park, a suburb of Kingston, where he could be found when not on his rent land in Clarendon.

In all the cases so far there was a clear unwillingness or inability to break with city life and return to the countryside. Those Rastafari like Zed-I who made the attempt, and who showed it was possible to do so with some degree of success, provided they rejected traditional methods of farming, still retained a foothold in Kingston. It would be a gross distortion to claim that the Rastafari movement does not include rural-based members who do nothing for a living but cultivate land, but they do not form a part of the movement's center of gravity.

Most of my encounters in the Hola Coptic House were with men who professed some skill: tilers (Stephen), painters (Paul and Leslie), masons (Tigo), and other tradesmen and entrepreneurs. Paul boasted to me that the brethren had no need to go outside the House to find any skill they needed, and in proof he pointed to Geoff's house. Naturally, opportunities for putting their skills to work are greater in the city than in the country. Little wonder, then, that the House turned down a generous offer of land from the government.

According to descriptions later provided to me by informants, Prime Minister Manley visited the headquarters of the church in January of 1973 to reason with church members. The meeting, it would appear, had been set up by aides of the prime minister in an attempt to reach out to the unemployed youths, who, as I shall explain later, were also closely drawn to the movement. Manley, so they said, hoped that they might be able to assist in getting the youth back into agriculture and so find a way of curbing the tendency among them to crime and violence. He proposed that as a start he would give the church "seven thousand acres" of land to farm. Floyd, one of the elders, later claimed that he insisted during the meeting that the land must be made available in all areas of the country, rather than in any single place, because the brethren were scattered all over. The meeting ended without resolution, but Manley promised to return, and to show that he meant to make good the offer, he sent on an inspection tour with the Dreads the member of Parliament for that area of Westmoreland encompassing nationalized lands of the West Indies Sugar Company.

The Dreads, however, turned down the offer. Criticism from other quarters of the Rastafari movement were being leveled at the Hola Coptics for "selling out" by meeting with the government. Cooperation per se with the government had never been regarded by Rastafari as betrayal, unless the matter was thought of as not being in the interest of the movement. For example, the 1961 Mission to Africa had support among the Rastafari because many saw in it an opportunity to realize the long-desired goal of returning to the land of their forefathers. Similarly, support for initiatives to solve the vexing question of ganja smoking, which to the Dreadlocks is a matter of religious principle, has not been regarded as a "sellout." But the receipt of lands from the government was seen as contrary to the interest of the movement. It would have implied sinking roots even deeper in a country that Rastafari are ideologically committed to leave.

In the light of this background information, Floyd's suggestion that the land should be available in various pieces all over the country could not have been a very serious one, although it contained an important recognition of the dominance of individualism among Rastafari. As I have already discussed, those with access to land show no great eagerness to give up the city in return for the life of a small farmer. Therefore, even if the government had agreed to the proposal, there would have been, in my opinion, no exodus to the country. It is interesting that Floyd himself commented to me that they had to reject Manley's offer because as Rastafari they preferred self-reliance to handouts. Although this comment seemed born of afterthought, it nevertheless represented a true and frank acknowledgement that for the majority of Rastafari reduction to family alone was not an encouraging prospect.

A second type of Rastafari engaged in entrepreneurial activities within the informal sector. Maria and Jose, for example, produced cocoa, or chocolate balls, as their main source of income. Most days of the week they were involved in the painstaking work. First, the dried beans which they bought from higglers in the market were parched over a slow wood fire to release the outer coating from the kernel. The beans are then pounded in a mortar along with spices, such as cinnamon, into a soft mixture and flattened into small cakes. When all the moisture had dried out, the cakes were grated for refinement and reshaped into oval balls ready for sale. Thirty-six liters of cocoa beans were manufactured into between thirty and forty dozen balls, each one fetching five cents. Apart from Jose's specific task of providing firewood, and Maria's of marketing, the other aspects of production were shared. Dreads who came in and out of the yard from time to time also gave a hand.

According to Maria, their main difficulty lay in finding stable outlets for the chocolate balls. The large supermarkets were the most desirable locations, but which of them was going to purchase from a Rastafari, she remarked, especially one producing under conditions they might even object to?

A third type of Rastafari I encountered was the urban, unemployed youth. In west Kingston I found many of them either involved in gang warfare or having such a past. But they differed from older Rastafari in other characteristics as well, as the following episode illustrates.

I once gave five of these youths a ride to a celebration in the country. One posed as a truck driver whose "transport brok down," another as a worker in a dry-cleaning establishment who got "laid off" for a week without explanation; the others were hustlers out to make quick easy money: one carried several long-playing albums of the popular Big Youth, and the other two carried belts and watch bands woven with red, gold, and green wire threads.

Events during the course of the following twleve hours help to give a good picture of the kind of hustlers these youths were. The first happened shortly after midday when we made a stop to buy something to eat, and one of them snatched my change. The second happened late that night as we were about to leave for home. We passed a few girls and boys from the local community who were giggling and making jokes in the moonlight. One of the Rastafari youths from Kingston began to berate them because he had not got "even a bunch of bananas to take back" with him. He called them cheap and mean, in a manner suggesting that he meant not only them but all country folk. This incident was quite revealing, for one would have thought that the youths' main interest had been in the celebration.

The final event took place when they alighted in Kingston at the end of the return trip. In gratitude for the trip, the "dry cleaner" indicated to me that he was leaving two pieces of the sugarcane they had raided from the Frome estate lands through which we had passed. My thanks were hardly expressed when the "driver" began to unload them. The "dry cleaner" reproved him, but the sugarcane disappeared nonetheless.

Another interesting point about these youths was that they never once used names, despite the exuberant and high-spirited nature of the journey, despite a deliberate attempt on my part to find out, and despite their avowal that I was sent by Selassie to provide them with transportation.

These three types of Rastafari are apparently quite different, the first two even more so than the third. Dreadlocks like Stephen and Floyd or like Jose have little in common with hustlers, who even guard their very names as if they were wanted men. The selfishness of the last group cut a stark contrast to the proverbial sharing of the impoverished Dreadlocks. These youths represent an entire stratum of the urban populace for which the Rastafari, during the 1960s and 1970s, became an influential socializing agent that passed on to them a critical posture towards society. They adopted and made fashionable many of the outward symbols of Rastafari, such as the dreadlocks and the language, but made little of Rastafari ethos (Chevannes 1980, 1992). American law enforcers and media failed to grasp this distinction on their first encounter with these youths in New York during the 1970s. Unable to distinguish them from mainstream Rastafari, they formed and disseminated a very negative impression of the movement. The point is discussed further in chapter 10. What common link there is between these youths and the artisans and small traders may be found in their class position at the bottom of the society. Now thoroughly urbanized, all three types nonetheless represented more up-to-date versions of the people who resisted impoverishment with their feet and made the Rastafari into a movement. Then, as now, Rastafari gave them hope.

Beliefs and Ritual

Revivalism, or what I have called the Revival complex, is an integrated part of Rastafari beliefs and practices. This is the main burden of the rest of this chapter. I shall begin with a list of folk remedies I got on a visit to Stephen's household early one morning. The discussion arose when one of his boys was sick with stomach-ache.

1. Stephen's wife, Sister Nancy, recalled the story of a child who drank a bottle of Lysol and was rushed to an old man, who quickly prepared and gave the child some arrowroot to drink. "If he vomits," the man said, "he will die." The child did not vomit and lived.

2. A woman, said Stephen, was taken ill with cancer of the womb and was given up on by the doctors at the university hospital. She went home and for three months, every day and as often as she wanted, she squeezed and drank the juice of the *serasi*. She was cured. The doctors were completely baffled.

3. For colds, boil and drink "shame-me-maka," guinea grass root, and Spanish needles.

4. For deep lacerations: Beat up the plant called "fresh-cut" and mix it with finely shredded salt fish (cod). Place the mixture in the wound, bring the edges of the wound together, and tie very tightly. Stephen's own father once gave himself such a nasty machete wound on his leg that the veins and the bone could be seen. Stephen's mother applied the remedy, but also added white rum. The wound was nearly better two weeks later.

5. For "blue bos'n," or swelling of the groin, Stephen said, "pick two *susumba* berries, swallow the first one whole like a pill and throw the other over the shoulder taking care not to look behind." This was told to him by "a man." Sister Nancy said she believed such a remedy possible, for in Haiti the *susumba* is not eaten, unlike in Jamaica, for in Haiti it is a sacred plant of voodoo.

6. Brother Saasi, a member of Stephen's household, but no blood relation to them, gave his own cure for "leakings," or gonorrhea: mix a thick paste of counter flour, Alan's Gin, and laxative salts.

7. Fifteen years later Brother Saasi got another attack. This time he boiled together the heart of the female logwood tree, sarsaparilla, and "devil's horse whip" root. Into this mixture he poured a red lotion obtainable at the "doctor shop" and applied the medicine every morning until the symptoms cleared. He has never contracted the disease since.

8. For hay fever, Stephen prescribed the following: Soak the green ganja in white rum, add one-half dozen pimento seeds, and steep for nine days. Take at least one teaspoon before bed.

9. The same prescription is good to stop colds brought on from overexposure, only the application is different: Steam the mixture over a pot of hot water, strip naked, and inhale the fumes under a sheet; then anoint oneself with the mixture.

10. On another occasion Stephen told this story: There is a mixture at the drugstore for gas. Once, very sick with his stomach, he was told in a vision by a woman to get this mixture. The friend he sent to buy it reported that the druggist was amazed because nobody had ever bought the mixture for that, yet he, the druggist, knew it was good for gas. The medicine cured him, and he afterwards used it quite successfully for bleeding gums, applying it with a toothbrush. "Sweet spirit of anointer," another drugstore oil, did even more wonders: A woman to whom he had recommended it for her sore foot did not believe him because he was a Rastafari, and she went to a "voodoo man" instead. When she next saw Stephen she confessed that it was the same thing the obeahman had recommended.

These potions, lotions, and brews form part of the common store of folk medicine, part of the Revival complex. Some of them, like the cancer cure, may have a basis in fact. Serasi (*Mormordia charantia*) has been found to have growth-arresting properties. The point, however, is not whether these remedies are scientifically reliable but that belief in the divinity of Selassie, affronting society with Dreadlocks, renouncing Jamaican society as Babylon, rejecting obeah and "poco-ism," in short the very things by which Rastafari are known to be different, have not served to cut them off from the people from whom they come. Yet such tactics are expected to effect separation. This expectation provided the element of surprise on the part of the woman mentioned in remedy number 10. Because Stephen was a Rastafari, he was not expected to believe in the potency of drugstore oils and powders. More than that, Stephen also implied that he believed in the existence of the powers of the obeahman, at least where folk medicines were concerned.

Note, also, Stephen's use of the dream as a medium or revelation. Such use is quite common among the folk, as I have explained in discussing Revivalism. Homiak (1987) shows that dreams are also still part of visionary communication among Rastas.

Preparations for a Duty

A ritual celebration is called a "duty," though there is no compulsion to attend. The following description of the preparation for a duty and the impact the celebration itself had on the community in which it took place is drawn from my field notes.

In mid-February 1974, six of us set out from Kingston to a district in upper Clarendon where Geoffrey had a small house and a piece of land. The celebration of the anniversary visit to Jamaica of His Imperial Majesty was to take place there in April. The purpose of the trip was to survey the site and to make preparations. Paul, by trade a painter, and Geoff went with the intention of remaining, while the other three, Bongo, Tigo, and Ras Jose went along as senior elders of the house. This attention to detail well in advance is indicative of the importance the house attached to this and similar duties, for they not only serve to strengthen the ideological and fraternal bonds that existed between Dreadlocks but are also grand entertaining displays and sources of edification for non-Rastafari people. Consequently, they are held in different places all over the country, and according to Paul, the most senior elder, there was only one parish where the house had not held a celebration.

As is the custom among Rastafari, journeys of this sort begin with a ritual smoking and prayer in the yard of departure. The chillum pipe being prepared should not be called a "pipe," said Paul, but a cup or chalice because Deuteronomy and other sections of the Bible in speaking of sending up incense to Jah were referring to the herbs. The members of the group had been smoking their own spliffs, which were either put out or laid aside when the chalice was ready to be lit. Paul had prepared the herbs, cutting it up, dampening it with a few drops of water, and mixing in the tobacco from a cigarette;[2] Geoffrey had prepared the water, judging the right amount

2. See Rubin and Comitas (1975) for the method of preparing ganja for smoking. Rastas say the tobacco cuts down on the harshness.

by testing it, and now Tigo was about to set fire to it. All caps were taken off; Paul even bowed his head and clasped his hands as Tigo made a devout prayer in a complete silence broken only by his own long, deep sucking and the popping of the ganja seeds on fire. The chalice then moved counterclockwise, and each one before taking his draw prayed while the others ceased conversation to attend. Tigo's topic of conversation was the intention of the church to make a plea before the United Nations to decriminalize herbs, because it was a part of "I and I *Ivine* [divine] worship, for I and I do not traffic in it." They had recently led a delegation to the Legal Aid Clinic in Kingston, which sent them to the Council for Human Rights where they were told to put their petition in writing to be forwarded to the United Nations. But, said Tigo, they much preferred to deal with the council in a face-to-face confrontation rather than through the written word.

All were now ready to depart. Everyone stood, including those not making the journey, and, led by Paul, recited two psalms: "I and I protect I going out and I coming in" was followed by "Let the Word of I mouth and the meditation of I heart be acceptable." The trip was uneventful. A car full of Dreadlocks attracts attention everywhere, but within ten miles of our destination the atmosphere was noticeably friendlier. Young primary school children on lunch seemed very familiar with Rastafari and greeted the passing Dreads. Only once did a little girl shout, "Rasta, dirty nayga!" but the brethren were not in the least perturbed.

Our arrival was greeted by various people who knew Geoff. One woman describing herself as his cousin vigorously shook everyone's hand as she poured out her welcome, telling us of her love for Geoff. Another described herself as his mother, and although the relationship was not one of kin, it became quite clear that her affection for him was great. She lived on the upper unfinished floor of a very large building intended as a hardware store, adjoining the district's small postal agency. Mada (as I shall refer to her) was very concerned about Geoff, saying she had been fearful he was imprisoned, or perhaps dead—at which all the Rastafari laughed knowingly, for it is a part of the doctrine of the Dreadlocks that the true Rastafari cannot die.

Because the building in which Mada lived stood on the hillside, her floor opened on to a yard in the back. A dog, a pig, and several chickens were thus able to roam about freely through the house. Paul was obviously afraid of the pig and said so. He begged Mada to have it stay clear of him, pointing out to her that according to Deuteronomy, even to touch the rope around the pig's neck made one unclean for several days. Jose pointed out that though it was quite true that the rope defiled, it would be all right for a Rastafari to raise a pig, not for consumption, obviously, but for money.

Across the road from Mada was the shell of a structure that had been a shop until a few months before. Late in the previous year when Geoffrey had been present in the district, it was broken into. The owners assumed that though Geoff did not himself commit the crime, he was in collusion with the robbers. Why did they accuse Geoff? Because the robbery was thought to have been an outside job, and he was the only one there from Kingston at the time. On hearing that he was so accused, he went up to the shop with the awful rage of the Rastafari and poured out his curse of blood and fire upon it. A few weeks after returning to Kingston, Geoff received the news that the building and stock had been gutted by fire. This, my companions pointed out to Mada, was another proof of the almighty power of Jah Rastafari. And Jose proceeded to tell of a similar case. Late one night he himself and two other Dreads happened to pass a barbershop with its red, white, and blue sign. Disgusted not only because barbering was an occupation counter to the principle of allowing one's locks to grow freely but also because the sign depicted the hateful colors of British colonialism, one of Jose's companions smote the pavement three times with his rod, uttering the word, "Fire!" The following morning the barbershop was gutted.

Two friends of Geoff came in, both of them non-Rastafari. A heavy shower of rain started, and Geoff said to them, "Look at the blessing Rasta bring!" One of them pointed out that it had rained a couple of days before, but this did not seem to make any difference to the Rastafari. Mada accepted the Rastafari talk in good humor. "Don't say 'Jiizaas,'" Paul instructed her, "say 'Jesos.'"

She treated the visitors to several dozens of oranges and a hand of ripe bananas.

The rain showed no sign of letting up, but nevertheless Paul declared his intention to make a dash for it. But before doing so, he won Mada's attention to some serious business he had to discuss. He had learned during the conversation, and also no doubt from Geoff, that Mada had several sheets of zinc roofing that shortage of money was preventing her from putting up right away. He wanted the use of them for the celebration. The manner in which he negotiated the loan marked him as a shrewd leader. First, he prefaced his remarks by quoting a passage of Scripture having to do with words, the general effect of which was to indicate that whereas all the foregoing conversation had been concerned with trifles, his words now had serious import. Next, he cautioned her about her rights to refuse, and only then made his request. For extra measure he reassured her that no nails would be driven into the roofing, and he ended by pointing out disarmingly that at the rate her building was proceeding it was unlikely that they would be used by April. Mada was herself a good match for Paul. She made clear her favorable disposition but shrewdly declined to make a firm commitment then and there. The group then departed for Geoff's house.

On touring the site, Paul expressed his disapproval of the latrine having been placed next to instead of behind the house. Geoff had negotiated the use of another more level spot for the duty farther up the road, but the church decided that because he had a spot of his own that was not at all bad, it should be used "to keep it within the Church." Paul observed that they would have to set up a fence to keep people out of the gungu peas and the other crops, for the "founder," meaning Geoffrey, should have something for himself. He obviously was well aware of the predatory nature of the urban brethren, but Geoff, much of an idealist, objected, saying that Selassie was the only founder, thereby signaling his intention to play unrestricting host for the three days.

In preparation for the return trip we were treated to gifts of sweet potatoes, gungu peas, sugarcane, and water coconuts. A prayer of psalms similar to the morning ritual was made, and the three of us departed for home.

Discussion

This episode brings out a number of relevant issues. One item for discussion is the prayer of the Rastafari performed before setting out on a journey. Although our trip was a distance of only eighty kilometers it constituted a separation from familiar surroundings and therefore involved the risk of unforeseen dangers and hazards. Calling upon God for protection in such circumstances is a natural reflex of religious persons. But also buried deep in the Revival tradition of the rural folk is the practice of arming oneself for a journey. In an earlier context I referred to the role of journeys in visionary experiences of the Jamaican folk and to the belief in the Yoruba god of the crossroads, Legba, sometimes personalized in the lore as "a man." In the nonvisionary context, the dangers are not personalized, nor are they necessarily of supernatural origin. For instance the element of chance is considered to sometimes govern one's conduct. Thus stubbing the toe of one's left foot at the start of a journey is a sign of bad luck and enough to cause one to turn back and start again. Beckwith mentioned another procedure for divining the outcome of a journey: using the stars (Beckwith 1929, 15). I am told by an informant from Four Paths in Clarendon that it is quite normal for individuals planning a journey to get up early and prepare themselves by prayer and singing. She said the "spiritual people," meaning the Revivalists, also do the same collectively, and if possible they march to where they are going with lighted candles.

Another point of interest is the Rastafari's pronounced belief about death, which surprises many people, namely, that they will never die as long as they remain true and faithful to Selassie. When death does come, it is always explained away by saying that the subject had departed from the chosen path of Rastafari, had violated some divine precept, and was therefore struck by and the mighty power of Jah. And it does not matter whether death is by accident, by sickness, or by the agency of man. A case was brought to my attention of a Rastafari, an only child, who refused to bury his mother or have anything to do with the body, until neighbors intervened. When asked to justify his attitude he quite righteously said, "I man don't deal with the dead, only with the living" and pointed out that if his mother had not transgressed the word of Jah, she would not have died. Rastafari, therefore, do not even attend funerals.

In chapter 1 it was explained that the dominant idea governing the peasant's attitude toward death is fear of contamination. Elaborate rituals are undertaken to maintain the limen between living and dead and to ensure thereby that the dead stay in their place even while acknowledging their presence and integrating them into a cognitive system of relationships. Hence the fear of contamination is by no means a novelty of the Rastafari. What they have added is this: They deny the efficacy of death rituals and regard them as basically superstitious, but having done so they still cling to the fear of contamination and so have no other choice but total separation.

The Rastafari also share in the folk belief that natural phenomena are the agents of divine action. Participants in the journey just depicted demonstrated that rain is believed to be a blessing from Selassie (despite the fact that it had rained two days before their visit), and fire his agent of retribution. They do not depart from this tradition, except in their identification of Selassie, and not "Big Maasa," as the source. In a delegation to the United States in 1989 one of the elders issued the following warning to the authorities who had been harassing Rastas:

"People must stop victimizing the spiritual virtues of creation, lest terrible things can happen. . . . Countries can suffer by earthquake, by lightning, by thundering, by rainfall, by total destruction that come upon by their own deeds not by the hands of we committing any felony against them, but by their wicked deeds, then spiritual manifestation takes place and they crumble." (*Washington, D.C. City Paper*, Sept. 15, 1989, p. 17)

The effect the gutting of the shop had on Mada and on those people inclined to believe in Geoffrey's innocence was to put the seal of divine intervention on his vindication. The event, therefore, contributed to the erosion of those attitudes that attribute to Rastafari suspicion of criminality.

The episode also brings out two important ways that the Dreadlocks reject the older tradition. Fear of contamination from the dead is extended by the Rastafari to fear of contamination from the pig. I know of nothing in the Revival complex that acts as a precedent for the beliefs and avoidance observed by Paul, which were similar to Revival beliefs about and avoidance of the dead. A probable and plausible explanation may be found in the importance of this animal in traditional life. The wild pig was for many years during slavery the only important source of food for the runaway slaves. The maroons developed a tasty way of curing pork, which used salt, pepper, and pimento spices and was known as "jerk pork" (Hurston 1939). Easily reared, the pig has always been, apart from chicken, the most readily available local source of protein for the peasant. When pork is not jerked, it is corned with salt or saltpeter, barreled, and sold in rural shops. In rejecting the pig, therefore, Rastafari reject this tradition, probably on the same basis that many of them also reject salt fish (cod) because it was one of those foods associated with slavery. Added to that reason is the fact that the habits of the pig, one of the most efficient converters of protein, if left to itself to forage, may offend one's sensibilities. For most Rastafari, the sight of pigs rummaging through uncollected garbage on the streets of the slums or at the dumps in competition with flies, is revolting. Bolstering their revulsion for pigs with Jewish food avoidance as set forth in the Bible, they make the pig taboo.

One other practice addressed in the conversation at Mada's, emphasizes Rastafari separation from the folk, and that is the insistence on a peculiar pronunciation of the name *Jesus*. They make a fetish of pronouncing it "Jes" (as in jest) "-us" (as in the personal pronoun), and they ridicule as profane the traditional pronunciation.

A Celebration

Duties attract support from a wide cross section of Rastafari, including combsomes and well-wishers. They therefore serve as a way of maintaining the broad solidarity of all Rastafari, many of whom travel long distances to attend. Usually the Hola Coptic Church arranges for transportation to leave the headquarters at midnight, following ritual smoking, dancing, and prayer. Celebrations last for three days. As entertaining intrusions into the life of the peasant folk, duties never fail to draw large audiences.

The Clarendon celebrations began on a Sunday. I cannot account for the meeting that was held that night, nor verify Paul's estimation of the crowd he said was "thousands, man, thousands." But it was clear that the celebration was having a big impact on the local community when I arrived the following day. Geoffrey's "mother" declared that this village was proud of him for bringing so many people to Fairburn. They did not know there could be so many Rastas, and it was the first time they were seeing so many in one place. What impressed them most was the fact that the Rastafari carried on in such a "Christian" manner. Expecting stereotypes of violence and crime, they saw the Bible being used and heard them preach and chant familiar sankeys. Two young girls of about eighteen or twenty years old declared they loved the Rastas, though there was still one thing they did not like: the dreadlocks.

A woman from the community also showed how impressed she was. While the drum throbbed to the stedy *kete* rhythm she closed her eyes, and pursing her lips in tense concentration, shuffled vigorously forward and back. The normal movement is from side to side with one's shoulders turning in the direction of the leg on which the body weight is to be shifted at the next beat. Here, however, was a most interesting variation: with each forward step her weight was thrust forward with the result that it brought up to her breast the opposing forearm—an almost identical replica of the secularized *ska* dance, except that in ska the body is bent much more forward from the waist up. I once saw the movment being performed at a Revival service in St. Thomas by a woman nearing her seventies. Revival and ska tempo are much faster than that of Rastafari music, but the basic rhythm allowed this woman to dance with the same movements.

Then there was Geoffrey's neighbor who must pass through Geoffrey's yard to reach the shop. She unfortunately dropped her handkerchief with fifty cents tied up in it and with such a large crowd of strangers around had given it up as lost. A Rastafari found it and after inquiries restored it to her. Profoundly impressed she walked away swearing that she could never allow him to leave Fairburn without a present.

The celebration itself followed a pattern observed at all other such duties. Throughout the day Dreads engage in informal groups of reasoning and smoking, provide their own food (except for the leading elders of the church who were provided for out of the central kitchen), or engage in informal drumming and singing. Then at nightfall after supper, the leaders conduct the evening service. Visitors come and go freely, but usually turn out in large numbers for the service, which, following the basic Revival structure, provides a source of edification and helps to break down some of the stereotypes about Rastas. For propaganda a film may be shown. One favorite being a documentary on Selassie's visit to Jamaica in 1966 produced by the Jamaica Information Service. At the Clarendon celebration the film immediately preceding the service drew a large crowd of three hundred, most of whom departed for home immediately afterward, leaving the rest as onlookers at the service.

Also present at that duty were members of the Rasta Movement Association, Ethiopian Rasses Association, and various branches of the Ethiopian World Federation. That the Hola Coptic Church of Jah Rastafari were the organizers of the celebrations made them central to the movement itself.

8. Word, Sound, and Power

A major difference between Dreadlocks and traditional Rastafari was the aggressive posture that the Dreadlocks adopted toward the wider non-Rastafari world. In theory, all non-Rastafari are a part of "Babylon," a part of the oppressive order, and are therefore on a personal level likely to be subject to verbal and other nonviolent forms of aggression such as the tense facial expression commonly referred to as "screw face." I already alluded to this aggression in chapter 6 when describing the opinion Bull Bay non-Rastafari residents had of the Dreadlocks. In the collective context, however, verbal aggression becomes a ritual drama, a performance in which the actors assume symbolic roles.

One of the main avenues through which ritualized aggression takes place is at formal duties or at formal meetings of the elders. The object is by the very nature of the ritual usually someone sympathetic enough to the Rastafari to be allowed to participate in it, but most definitely neither a Rastafari nor a Dreadlocks and hence a part of Babylon; it is a position therefore of liminal ambiguity. In the ritual context my persona was the university (where I worked), and therefore the government ("For anything the University tell the Government, the Government must do it, for it is the seat of knowledge!"). A sympathetic cleric like Father Joseph Owens (1976) would represent Rome, and a white American would represent the United States—all aspects of the same Babylon. The ritual is not an induction that one undergoes once and for all, but rather may be repeated as the Dreadlocks see fit. Dreadlocks, who outside of the ritual context of the duty are personally friendly and warm, at the Duty become hostile and cold, for they too take on the ritual personae of Jah Rastafari. The aggression therefore is a sort of confrontation between the sacred and the profane at the level of the symbolic.

Four or five days before the Clarendon celebration I met Brother Daniel of the Ethiopian Rasses Association, a group based in the parish of St. Mary. After listening to my explanation of the research I had been conducting, he extended an invitation to visit him anytime. He was the first Dreadlocks I encountered at the celebration. But there his attitude was no longer cordial. He launched an offensive: there was nothing more to get from researching, for Dr. Arthur Lewis had been sent by the government and had gotten it all ready. Government had done nothing, and the Rastas had not benefited in any way. Therefore I would get no information. The abrupt change in attitude was brought about by the ritual celebration and was not permanent. Had I taken up his earlier invitation after this attack, I would have found him to be the cordial Daniel whom I met on the corner of Ninth Street and West Road in Trench Town, in the same way that Zed-I, one of the leading aggressors at the Westmoreland celebration in January 1974, later provided me with valuable information. In these formal encounters the target of aggression is put into a role of being more than he really is, the direct agent of Babylon, and each Dreadlocks assumes the importance of an oracle of Jah.

The Ritual

The field trip on the second day of the Clarendon celebration was made with Clem, a young Jamaican photographer who, having just returned from the United Kingdom where he grew up, was quite eager to meet the Rastafari, about whom he had heard so much.

We found our way on to the veranda where one of the small groups of Rastafari was reasoning, and there we sat down to listen. The center of attention was a Dreadlocks others identified as a doctor. Legs crossed and tobacco pipe in one hand, he was in the process of making a point that education was "folly" and that what people needed was divine instruction. Carr was the person to whom this reasoning was directed, and because I knew the stress his own organization placed on education, it was obvious to me that there was a debate going on. Soon the topic of Ethiopia came up. At the time much of the turmoil in that country had been directed against the monarchy itself. The doctor proceeded to make a clever distinction: Selassie dealt with theocracy, whereas the Ethiopian government dealt with "eocracy." The point of the distinction was that come what might, whatever changes took place to strip the emperor of his constitutional powers, Selassie still had theocratic powers. So as he saw it, what was happening in Ethiopia was nothing but a little housecleaning by the emperor. Then he turned to us. Before we knew it, we were both drawn into the discussion. The ritual began. Later Clem would relate to me that these same men whom he found so hostile during the debate were afterward as individuals quite nice and friendly toward him.

The research was unjustified, the doctor began, because there was nothing the Rastas would derive from it. It was at this point that while answering I became aware that the veranda was becoming crowded. A tense encounter about the research ensued between myself, trying to say as little as possible, and the Dreadlocks. No doubt thinking that this was a favorable moment, Clem made the unfortunate mistake of taking out the camera from his bag. His intention was to be as unobtrusive as possible, but in the small and tightly crowded space it was impossible not to draw attention. Attention came not from those seated opposite but from a tall Dreadlocks leaning on the wall beside him: "I want to ask the two of you a question," he said. Neither question nor answer was of any importance to what he had on his mind, but his statement served to shift the attention of everyone in a dramatic way. He called attention to the camera, which he said was a tape recorder secretly recording the proceedings, and went so far as to declare us both spies. This was a signal for the others to join in with accusations, and for two to three hours a heated reasoning ensued. At the peak of it there were over fifty Dreadlocks on the porch itself, on the steps and close in on the inside.

One of the questions directed to Clem was why had he come seeing that his purpose was not one of research. Rather than relate his true reason, which was to find a brotherhood among the Rasses, Clem, hoping to be spared, gave a quite noncommittal answer, which in any other kind of conversation might have satisfied and been left at that. Not so in this ritual; his response was grounds for a further charge, namely, that he took the trip lightly. "So Rastafari affair not serious affair? You know Jah Rastafari could strike a man down dead for treating the affairs of I and I lightly? Did you know that his brethren here was on a research mission?" At this point quite confused, Clem answered no. "Well then," they turned toward me, "it is this man here must bear the charge!" I received the same warning that I could be struck down; someone cited Pompidou, the French President who had not too long before died unexpectedly, as an example of what Selassie could do.

One of the Dreads turned attention back to Clem, who, now completely angry, jumped to his feet and began to speak. But the Dreads would have none of it: they ridiculed him for taking their aggression personally. "Is only sounds, man! See now! Him have fi stan up! That mean him feel wronged! Siddung, man! I and I not going hurt a man—leave that to Selassie!"

Naia once again said that we were liable to be charged by the emperor under the constitution he left when he visited Jamaica in 1966. The belief that there is such a document, which the government of Jamaica guards from the people, is commonly held among the Rastafari.

NAIA: It is of a fact unu [you] take these things blind. Rastafari administration is not a blind thing, for remember in his constitution you will be charged through his royal creative principle. So that it can be earthquake, heart attack, lightening, any source of culture. So, unu must know what unu doing, for Jah has been tired and angry of unu disposition against his people now. I am asking unu, again, to go back to the Government of Jamaica and find out from the Government what about the King of Kings constitution that he leave here in 1966 to all his royal people that suffered in Babylon here. Since unu found success now, through the appearance of His Imperial Majesty, to come amongst I an I that unu don't scorn I an I anymore, show the authority that I an I has gotten to the world let them see. For it come down from Zion and come to the end of the earth, and it must leave fi go back to Zion, and must establish on the end of the earth unto Zion. Therefore, we are a people of the royal family of creation. If unu don't come under that portfolio, remember unu are legally charged through the Human right!"

VOICE 1: Anyone I an I charge, him can't get 'way, you know!

VOICE 2: I hook him!

NAIA: I pray thee, these men don't serious.

DAVID: Could never!

NAIA: That mean no one directly send them. Is just a prober for an underground system. Don't make we dash away our pearl before the swine, for they not serious. Watch them, and investigation!

The giveaway in Naia's outburst was the clause *that unu don't scorn I an I anymore*. In spite of his argument that we were spies, he was admitting that the Rastafari deserved attention from the government. In this clause should also be read the attitude of the middle class toward the movement, for a long time one of scorn.

At this point, Jubie spoke, taking as his reference point an earlier exchange in which he had expressed the view that what I should be doing instead of research was to get the Jamaica Council of Churches to meet the Rasses to decide whether or not Selassie was Jesus Christ, and he had asked me to comment. In reply I had said that if the Christian denomination could not agree with one another on important questions of dogma, how were they going to agree with the Rastafari on who God was? He gained the floor after several calls for "one voice."

JUBIE: Where I an I show the brethren that the work him sighting to do within the books, those time have already passed; and I an I have shown him that the Church Council is them supposed to meet I an I to establish this thing here—so now, and by his own admission them don't have no unity to forward to I an I. So I an I sight then that within such manner of man chanting to I an I, I an I couldn't turn them away.

Yet when I and I Dreadlocks even chant and say the man is a spy and traitor, and that the man have tape, this man here [Clem] say is not so. Now I an I Dreadlocks would have to find out the truth. Jah say I an I must test the man when them come to I an I, and know what *Irie* [truthfulness] dwell in the man. From this man here come, I an I know what work out there bald tail [non-rasta] manifesting.

This man is a Ethiopian—where Jeremiah say the leopard cannot change him spot nor the Ethiopian him skin—but him deny Ethiopian. So from you deny it, you is a traitor. Is within *Iowa* [time] now that you gwine go get knowledge what could prove whether you have honor or not.

So when you come 'mongst I an I Dreadlocks, you have fi take what sounds you get, because you have on the shape and features of a beast. But when the man dread up within certain knowledge now, then I an I can accept the man as a man who take the step towards the integrity of the King of Kings and the *I*ternal one of creation.

Within the sounds that I an I chanting about this declaration that the King make when the King was here, now this is a very serious thing. I an I chanting to the man and telling the man here that the King of Kings leave these documents here and the man [Chevannes] never hear of this before. Now when I an I chanting, the man may believe that this is not so. But hear, I an I can prove it easily to the I.

I an I wouldn't take the man to Gordon House [Parliament] and show him the paper, for all these things must happen, but I an I know that the King of Kings chant is here, and when he see the downpression of the people, how them holding the people in captivity, when him come on the plane gangway, what him do? Him wept! And after that what is the sound him block? That Ethiopians and Jamaicans are blood brothers. Right?

TIGO: That is the most "seenry!" I an I want to see anything write down. It is enough, "Ethiopian and Jamaican are blood brothers." That is a state-ical procedure.

Jubie made three points. The first was that, although he would not turn us away, we wore the mark of the beast because we were "baldhead," non-Dreadlocks which in typical Rastafari inversion he calls "bald tail," and were for that reason suspicious. Indeed, by denying we were Ethiopians, though black, we were traitors. Therefore we had to take what abuse was coming our way, until we "dread up with certain knowledge," that is, until we became Rastafari. He therefore was implying that a function of the ritual was to pressure us into belief. And this he set about doing by trying to establish that Jamaicans were Ethiopians, his second point. The address to Parliament by Selassie on his 1966 visit had been used by Rastafari to mean that Selassie was asserting his jurisdiction over Jamaicans, for whom he supposedly left a constitution setting out their rights. That was why Tigo called it a "State-ical procedure." Third, if Jamaicans are then Ethiopians, the policy of the Ethiopian government should also be the policy of the Jamaican government. This last point Jubie set about to prove.

JUBIE: Now I an I have to look now, on the international policy of the Ethiopian Government, and look on the Jamaican Government. Because you must remember that Jah say that I an I are blood brother, and the man who say that him rule here, say him got a rod from I an I father. Hear now: There is an international set of gangsters that are now holding up the land of some people known as the Palestinians. The Palestinians used to live over this land as the seed of Ishmael, for ages throughout creation, even as I an I I-thiopians live in Mount Zion. In 1948 Bruutn and some other boy get together and run out the Palestinian and give the land to the Israeli boy-dem and say, "Watch ya, unu is Israel." Now, the Bible, I an I ancient Scripture, say "Israel only hath I known and through Israel hath all nations blessed." So, I an I know nothing bout no "Israeli." I an I no know bout it. Why him no call himself Israel? I an I know. For hear what Jah say, "Woe unto these who call themselves Jews and are not." So they are all blind diggers of Satan, they are all liar! Dem boy used to call themselves Jew until Hitler slaughter six million of them and them change them name to Israeli. Hear what Haile I Selassie I say: Haile I Selassie I say in the council of OAU: "Unless Israeli boys are made to know that they must obey international accord and withdraw out of the Palestinian land to where the border was in 1967 when they first go on with things against the man them, there shall be no peace." Haile I Salassie I say that. So hear what Haile I Selassie I do, the Emperor of Ethiopia, Creator Monarch? Him sever diplomatic relationship with the Israeli and show the world that they are violent. So, OAU had chant to all the Third World members—listen *Ia* [Nya, Brethren], that they must break relationship with those pirates! *Irie!* I an I know say I an I have broken relationship, down to British Guiana broke relationship! Who no broke it yet? Menlow and Jamaica, who say them is head of Third World. Why? Because Matalon, Ashenheim and these boys are Israeli, and everyday them carry away I an I money go to support the war effort against I an I breda. So that is one thing we show clearly, that this Government not going near the declaration I an I father left here, nor even walk near to it.

But hear, even if Jah never leave the declaration, hear how him get caught: him go Africa and say him is willing to go along with whatever the OAU chant concerning negotiations with the European Common Market. Yes, I! Him say anything OAU say, him will say it. Then how come OAU say all them things here, declare Israeli as Pirate, and you still uphold Matalon now and give him Gun Court to come shot I an I down, when I an I know that before I an I start industrialization of Jamaica, no gun never grow 'pon no tree. Is since him start industrialization, gun come ya.

So the I must check upon those things, that the I can see this Government is going completely contrary to the policy that the King of Kings set. I an I know that anyone who uphold this Government must be tried and condemned as a traitor to Ethiopian sovereignty. So the ones who have some knowledge and can sight forward and reason up these things can cleanse himself and don't find himself in that judgement.

VOICE: Save yourself!

JUBIE: The man them who would want to know the things him get this man here researching, them couldn't face Dreadlocks this day. So they are hoping that this man will not get this knowledge, or find himself in a position where him have to take this judgement for them.

VOICE: Because this judgement wasn't set up for Ethiopian, you know!

JUBIE: No! Adam fallen race! So, the I mustn't make the Ethiopian reach in there because is only careless Ethiopian could fall into this.

The Rastafari are keen observers of international events, especially those taking place in or concerning Africa, which they often interpret in their religious way. Jubie brought this experience to bear upon his argument. Haile Selassie, following the line of the Organization of African Unity on the Arab-Israeli question, took measures to isolate the state of Israel. This progressive move, he argued, was consistent with the fact that the Palestinians and Ethiopians were sons of Israel. Those who today call themselves Israeli (Jubie stressed the final *i*) or Jews, were false. But the Jamaican government under Manley ("Menlow") in failing to sever diplomatic relations with Israel followed the line of the enemy, symbolized by Eli Matalon, a major Jewish industrialist who held the important post of minister of national security and justice, in which portfolio, according to Jubie, he presided over the oppression of the poor by setting up the Gun Court. So if an Ethiopian grasped this situation, he would dissociate himself from the government instead of acting as its agent.

At this point the notion of "careless Ethiopian" entered the argument. The point scored by each major speaker from here on was that we the defenders and agents of Babylon stood a chance to salvation because we were already black. "This judgement wasn't set up for Ethiopian."

VOICE 1: Where is the capital of the whole world?

VOICE 2: Ancient. . . . [*Here the tape was unclear, but the answer was one of the ancient kingdoms of Africa, probably Axum.*]

CHORUS: Jah! Blood bath and is there Black I come from!

SHAKA: Because they never tell me say in 1665 the pirate was being commanded under the influence of this English pirate, Oliver Cromwell, which commanded the pirate Admiral Penn and Venables, Cecil Rhodes, John Hawkins, Livingstone. . . .

CHORUS: Burn them! Burn them! Power!

SHAKA: . . . to come on the shores of Ethiopia and take black people and pack them as sardines in tin and them come, rob and rape. . . .

TIGO: Two feet in space!

SHAKA: . . . and the pirate kill who them want to kill on the sea, and the remnants come down here and after I an I. . . .

VOICE: Bring it forward to this day here! [*In excited agreement with Shaka's account of the history of colonialism, there followed a general free-for-all.*]

TIGO: One voice!

VOICE: Fire! [meaning Silence!]

SHAKA: They try to tell the people that Jesus is in the sky, and the people look to the sky for Jesus, whereas I an I the Dreadlocks tell the people of such time that I an I can representatively present I an I chanting as a living monarch to the world as a representative to the world that the only monarch, the only creator, is the King of Kings. And up till this time—it going into the dispensation of another two thousand years, they cannot present their god!

VOICE: Their Jesus!

SHAKA: So I an I stand here this day to stamp away Lord God Jesus Christ and all of them. And unless the whole world, internationally Black, come to the realization of one *I*cord [accord] to know and to attain themselves to the fact that the only alternative solution to suffering humanity today and for*I*ver is Black Supremacy . . .

CHORUS: Haile I Selassie I Jah Rastafari!

SHAKA: . . . out of that there is no alternative, or just like beast that must perish.

VOICE: Death!

SHAKA: Because, look now. You could be a man of such a degree, have such a diplomacy, pass through such a record in Babylon, and still emphasizing to the international world as whole and tell the people that "Humpty-Dumpty sat on a wall, Humpty-Dumpty had a great fall," "The cow jump over the moon," and all those type of things.

VOICE: Away with these facts!

SHAKA: Those are colonial celebration!

VOICE: Imperialism!

SHAKA: And the Jamaican Government under the ruling of the colonialism must consider themselves to know that these charges must take up immediately, that they are violating the constitutional law of Ethiopia. [*Another free-for-all, with Fats finally getting the floor.*]

Shaka's intervention began by attacking the colonial view of history, which upheld the pirates and explorers as heroes and bearers of civilization rather than as plunderers. He attacked their projection of Jesus as a sky god whose promised return they themselves knew would never take place, and he denounced the content of their education. Shaka's point was that a degree in this Babylonian system was useless, for as long as one upheld that system one would perish like "the beast." The "beast" is a recurrent image among the Rastafari and is synonymous for Babylon. It derives from the Book of Revelation.

FATS: Idrin [Brethren], didn't the University come among us already and show them that just as how them burn candle in their church as their ritual that I an I should free to burn I an I herb as I an I ritual? Didn't the University publish that long time?

TIGO: Irie, in 1960!

NAIA: Right. Professor Smith and those men come and say yes. It is true? Then how we still been strangled for this? For I an I know that the only charge I an I as a Rasta I-drin have is only the herb. I have no more charge.

FATS: For I an I have been still martyred. I an I know I an I don't want gun. Selassie is my gun, my weapons of war. For in 1938 when it was asked in Geneva, who will stand and represent the black race, there was no other than His Imperial Majesty, Emperor Haile Selassie I: "I will stand for the black man in war or in peace." When any man now find himself fighting against his Imperial Majesty, where that black man stand?

CHORUS: Nowhere! Utter darkness!

FATS: Selassie I is the King of Kings, right? Revelation say "Upon his vest and upon his thigh it was written King of Kings and Lord of Lords. There was none before him and there shall be none after him." Yet the same parson man within their preaching many a time every Sunday, twist Israel so much and tell them, pointing to the sky that he is the King of Kings and Lord of Lords.

DADA: I gwine tell you, too. They put "him." That mean them don't give the significance of the "him": His Imperial Majesty.

FATS: Then if you say "Praise him," is Him! Them only tell you say "Praise him," but they don't tell you is who. [*Another free-for-all.*]

TIGO: One voice in the House!

FATS: Check full within all these people who go around as Jehovah Witness. Society accept them, them look nice. Them still don't Iclare [declare] of Jah you know, yet them say they are Jehovah Witness. Kaiser William who is founder of that Jehovah Witness, Him and Mussolini join free force to go and make war with the Lamb. Him same one see the Lamb with one foot upon the river Euphrates and one foot upon the land, dancing Iacongo [Nyacongo, Nyabinghi] and him flee. Him write now that him witness Jehovah, but him no tell the people that is the King of Kings and Lord of Lords who you beat Rasta for. Him no tell the people that. Why hold the people them back within the crucifixion and don't show them of the resurrection?

VOICE: Fire and Blood!

FATS: You same one say the man resurrect, and him walk and talk with Thomas until Thomas push all him hand and feel them out. Them say that he who confess that Christ come in the flesh is of Christ, but he that say he come in the spirit is an antichrist and a deceiver.

VOICE: Irie.

FATS: So how come the Church don't confess now unto I people, and tell them say yes. . . . [*He was not allowed to finish, the point being obvious.*] Watch, if I an I alone, you know, whole heap of rich men would send us a yard [Ethiopia] long time. But is through I speaking of "our people."

CHORUS: Irie! True, true!

FATS: But we speaking of our people, we come to our black people, round and about.

CHORUS: Yes, universal!

FATS: We know that anywhere within this little western hemisphere, this "new world," according to them, when Columbus say is him did discover it, a man couldn't discover something where him come and see that people live there. That's impossible. You could never discover a place that you come and see other people living.

VOICE: You come and see all the people with them population.

FATS: Irie! So I an I did know, anywhere you see the black man in this western hemisphere, him did come a Ja-make-ya first! And is from here them sail and transfer all over the West Indies. Then how come, now, we as black people have so much name? If we born a Trinidad we Trinidadian; if we born a Jamaica, we Jamaican. You hear that man is Bermudan, him is dis and dat, yet anywhere the Chinaman is, them say him is a Chinaman; anywhere European white man, him is just a white man. Den how come we as black man . . .

JUBIE: Them deny I an I ancient nationality. You have a nationality of birth and you have a nationality of choice. Everyone know that. Haile I Selassie I give I an I that right within the Iclaration of Human Rights. The right of birth which no man can't take from you and the right of choice. That's why the Englishman can still birth ya, and still choice England! Then wha' happen to I an I who choice as an I-thiopian? All these things these men know and them only holding it down.

FATS: That is what they maltreat us for daily, only than just telling the people the truth. What else that a Rastaman do? Show me! I only want to ask the government what fault have they really found with Rasta? All the come you come to wi yard, is only one thing you ask for, where the ganja?

VOICE: A plant that grow freely!

FATS: So why you don't fight me for the calalu, too? And why don't fight me for the tobacco that plant all about?

DADA: A pure speculation.

FATS: Yes, I, for them show them can't afford to let the American man come and take the herbs that way, for it hamper the economy of the country.

DADA: So them penalize I an I through the commercial administration fleshically. Them use to take out the internal life, until the King done object, so them coming morally now. No moral slaving for Ethiopians, for the King of Kings abolish it already.

There are four themes in the argument led by Fats, connected by a progression from one to the next, as set out in this diagram beginning with ganja.

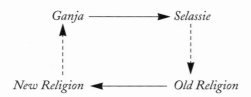

The smoking and possession of ganja are the main sources of friction between Rastafari and the police. The police have the law to uphold, the Rastafari a religion to defend. Fats's point is that the martyrdom for using ganja is in reality martyrdom for believing in Selassie, whom he therefore spends some time proving to be the true God. Defense of this core doctrine inevitably means an attack on the old religion, represented in this reasoning by Jehovah's Witnesses and the church, both of whom Fats accuses of falsifying the truth. In contrast, the new religion, which stood for "our black people," is persecuted because of the truth. And the proof of it is in police harassment for ganja. Thus the line of argument, though at first sight it appears to be rambling and enamored of big words and ponderous expressions such as "commercial administration fleshically," nonetheless has a unified structure and a purpose. The purpose, in line with one of the overall functions of the ritual, is to predispose the outsider, by the force of the argument, to cross the threshold separating the righteous and the saved from the unrighteous and the damned. The appeal at this point becomes direct, and the language at first more formal.

SHAKA: Because, remember the great war minister, the bulldog Winston Churchill, the bulldog of Ephesus. Him did say black people must consider themselves as aliens and prisoner of war, because the emblem of England, the red, white and blue, is not representative unto blacks anymore. Then tell me something, how would you look at yourself now to be an alien and prisoner of war in a ship that is lost in a storm?

FATS: But better than that. How it stand when you working for a man, and when you gwine turn your back to I-thiopia, tell me where would you really stand as a black man?

DADA: Where would you have to spend your long eternal?

JUBIE: There is no other place that black man can be!

FATS: No, for the joy of the whole earth is . . .

CHORUS: Mount Zion!

SHAKA: That's why Jeremiah 51 say I shall send famine into Babylon and it shall leave desolate—this place here, Jamaica. Little from this when you hear the blowing of the seven miles of Black Star Liners fork up to go home, they shall be leaving a hissing, without an inhabitant, a everlasting darkness, where the dust of this earth shall become brimstone. It will be a everlasting lake of furnace!

VOICE: Criminal! Burn him!

FATS: Him say here, "In this valley of Jehosophat, in the isle of Fatima, which is one of decision, where I shall judge every nation round about for the cause of I an I people!" And I an I have seen the King of Kings fulfirst up [fulfill] judgment. For I an I can remember when Kennedy send them whole heap of gun and things, the King did show that man that him plant him footstep upon the sea and rise up. And same time the King leave and go America, bam! Flora lick America. Him leave America and go Cuba, bam! Flora lick Cuba. Him come back America, bam! Flora lick America. Him say, "What have you done? Send arms against my defenseless people?"

VOICE: That's what the King of Kings ask Kennedy?

FATS: Seen [yes]. That was the same time Kennedy say to him "Thirty years ago have I seen this man, and today I see him now, the man is twelve years younger!" The King of Kings say yes, "The least you have done unto one of these, you have done unto I self, and for every one of them I shall destroy a whole nation," every nation I an I as black people have slaved for.

VOICE: And you find every nation down at Jamaica here now.

SHAKA: And up till now, no man ever seen or heard that a white man have died for a black man yet.

VOICE: Not even go to prison.

SHAKA: Remember in 1894 when Kaiser and Germany, France and all those pirates, with Mussolini, sit down and organize themself that the entire world must become a white world? Then what happen if those atrocities was to go on? What title, or what form, or what speech you would have today as a black man?

VOICE: None! [*Though the question was addressed to me. Another free-for-all followed, and Fats continued.*]

FATS: Don't care how the police. . . . You as a black man here in Babylon is only for a time.

"Your long eternal," "the joy of the whole earth," "everliving darkness," "brimstone," and so on are some of the phrases and words which, coupled with direct quotation from the Bible, gave this part of the reasoning a more mystical tone. Shaka made it clear that when the millennium comes the saved will sail away to Mount Zion (Ethiopia) in seven miles of ships leaving the utter darkness and fire of hell. Fats, on the other hand, explained that Selassie had already fulfilled the judgment prophesied against the enemies of his people through the destruction by hurricane Flora in 1961: Flora struck America because the government of that country sent arms against Selassie's people. The reference could be to American involvement against the national liberation movements. It should be noted that some of the Dreadlocks themselves were hearing of the Kennedy-Selassie exchange for the first time. The ritual was also serving as a communications medium of Rasta knowledge and interpretation.

But the main thrust of this part of the dialogue was directed at the two baldheads, particularly myself. It was aimed at convincing us that we as blacks were members of a race of people subjected to the evils of Babylon but specially loved by God and therefore to be saved by him. This in fact was the main theme of the rest of the session, except for the intervention of Brother Dada which followed.

DADA: I an I supposed to ask the brethren as a University representative towards the cause of Rasta history, what purpose and reason an emblem fly within a country?

CHEVANNES: The flag is a symbol of the unity of the people and their nationality.

DADA: Then I ask, there is an emblem of Jamaica Government flying in Ethiopia?

CHEVANNES: No.

DADA: Then what happen to the Ambassador? Don't when the Ambassador represent . . . ?

CHEVANNES: Yes, yes. That's right.

DADA: It is flying there?

CHEVANNES: Yes. I imagine that it would be flying at the Ambassador's residence.

DADA: To prove that Jamaicans are in Ethiopia to the Ethiopian Government and people, so that rights should come about those people.

CHEVANNES: Right.

DADA: Then from the time now I an I walking with I an I upon wi shoulder, and we get beating for it and all kind of sufferation and exploitation, and you the University know that it is not in the House of Parliament, outside of document, flying for the benefit of I an I who is the people of Ethiopia, and you still come here and probing again? Assassination that, you know! [*There was a wild general laughter of ridicule.*]

FATS: [Reassuringly] That don't mean we gwine assassinate you, you know.

DADA: Is not joke business! If an emblem of such a position toward the right of the people, in the universal world of any Government, what happen to I?

SHAKA: You commit a fraud against the international Government.

VOICE: Naturally.

FLOYD: But to prove what the beloved saying, Dr. Arthur Lewis, who have done make a research, know really that I an I have an emblem which we have personal right to as our own property. And from that time up till now nothing has been done. So now, what the I may showing you, that for another research among I an I, seeing that I an I have already been Isearched or researched, is not just assassination, is just temptation! [*Another round of laughter and a free-for-all.*]

DADA: Unu should hastily rectify our emblem now, to prove to the people that we are a people of Ethiopia, for I know that I an I is blood breda. No other one upon the earth has proven as near a relation of the King of Kings, but I an I.

JUBIE: Is the only one, I an I, him claim. No other one that the King of Kings claim on the earth away from I an I. All the place where him trod I never hear. . . .

DADA: So I want to know if the King of Kings' dignity does not really have any power. And me hear little Manley say him go to England and him have Jamaican up there and him gwine repatriate them out of England and also America, towards the skill they have, for Jamaica is short of skill. Eh? And I don't hear no dispute from those governments saying that right here-so, and is three hundred thousand in England, you know. Where them gwine put them?

FATS: Better them send them go a yard [Ethiopia] you know; for if them come out ya it might be worse.

JUBIE: So is folly him talking about repatriating man here. Him don't even count the ones in Canada nor in Germany. For years this government has been exporting the people who has been the source of life and creativity.

The pronouncement by then Prime Minister Manley that Jamaicans abroad were welcome to return and help develop Jamaica with the skills they had acquired was interpreted by the Dreadlocks as a kind of Repatriation. They linked the matter to the unemployment situation in the country to show the apparent contradiction they saw underlying it. Nevertheless, they did not launch off on the favorite question of their own Repatriation to "yard" or Ethiopia. A possible reason was the desire of Bongo Floyd and Jubie to make more capital out of what was then the burning issue at that time, namely, the constitution supposedly left by Selassie.

They explored one aspect of this issue, the status of the state of Jamaica in the eyes of Selassie, a point on which they shared difference with Dada.

FLOYD: Bongo Dada, this ambassador which I overheard the I praising, there is no Jamaican flag hoist up anywhere in Ethiopia, whether at the office or nowhere. Why? Because for any ambassador to receive into a country, it must be that country recognize you status of Government. And Jamaica is not recognized; no existing nation where Jamaica is concerned. It is a fraud.

JUBIE: And to prove it, I an I know that the Jamaican Government has been pressuring the Ethiopian Government say—they don't tell I an I this, but I an I know—the Ethiopian Government let them know that the King has already Ilected [selected] ambassador here, who deal with the welfare of the people. So what they did expect now is that a ambassador would be sent from Ethiopia that look like them in them own Babylon ways, well trimmed and shaved, so they could invite him into certain things and overrule I an I rights. I an I know that lately Breda Foreman who was up there as ambassador have to return here, and where is the new ambassador that has been appointed to Ethiopia?

CHORUS: None!

FLOYD: All government rest upon His Majesty's shoulder.

JUBIE: And on I an I the King's son.

FLOYD: Jamaica is nothing recognized. Even our culture is not foundationable; it have to adapt; something imported through America, Italy, Rome and German, and French, all different pirate. And the people who inherit it likewise achieve nothing from it. It's black masses, and we have a black culture, not a white culture.

SHAKA: Charge the whole of them with the infringement of I an I rights!

VOICE: A house-to-house arrest, Ia!

FLOYD: For where I an I is concerned right now, the Coptic Church and the theocratic Government of His Majesty, unless I an I don't get to give the people them righteousness, then the whole place can go up in a human volcano, burst, and . . .

VOICE: Any Imes [time], any Imes!

FLOYD: I an I naa beg that, I an I *I*mands [demand] it!

JUBIE: Yet them say Job was the most patient man. I an I fulfill every prophecy where I an I have more patience than Job. I an I extend tolerance and let the people know that I an I King and Jah, Haile Selassie I, Jah Rastafari, say that I an I don't deal with violence. But is only if a man bring force to I an I and him refuse to learn any other way, even as it was in Ethiopia with Mussolini—it was the first time that 17,000 white men ever kill one place in Africa . . .

FLOYD: So even now if this colonial government down here does not submit his little dirty, nasty principle to I an I, the Coptic Church and Nyabinghi Order of Jah Rastafari Holiness, and let I an I freely give unto the people what belong to the people, so shall he get too!

VOICE: Calamity!

FLOYD: So, as a researcher, which personally we are not against your personal researching . . .

FATS: I love him as a brother, man!

FLOYD: . . . these sounds are to protect you also as a black man. Getting these sounds will enable you to know what to do towards your personal step, for you can only speak for yourself.

VOICE: Save yourself first, before you could save others!

On that pleasant note the ritualized aggression of the Dreadlocks came to an end. One by one they left the porch, either to look for supper or to smoke and reason informally in smaller groups of twos and threes, in which setting it was once again possible to converse with them without being subject to verbal abuse or aggression.

Discussion

We may therefore ask what was it all about. We, but especially myself, were put in the role of representative of the establishment, which either does not regard the Rastafari as serious and deserving of much consideration or—and this was the dominant mood—takes it seriously enough to devise schemes to keep it from realizing its expressed goals of liberating all Israel from the clutches of the white man. The reasoning has two levels of meaning, one situated at the level of form, the other at the level of content.

The Form

On the level of form, what took place was a ritual drama (Turner 1968) in which the main element was centered not around action, as in religious and secular rites, but around *words*. This may at first seem strange, but it becomes intelligible when examined against the background of the folk culture of the peasantry, among whom is a deeply rooted predilection for the spoken word. I have already referred to the ethnographical observations of Martha Beckwith in the 1920s. This aspect of traditional culture, however, goes much further back.

The historian and poet Edward K. Brathwaite identifies this tradition as being based on the Bantu concept of the *nommo* (Brathwaite 1971, 237–39), which, according to Jahn, is "the life force, which produces all life, which influences 'things' in the shape of the *word*" (Jahn 1961, 124). It is by naming that a child becomes a human being. Naming, says Jahn, is a creative act. "What we cannot conceive of is unreal; it does not exist. But every human thought, once expressed, becomes reality" (133). It is the *nommo* principle, says Brathwaite, that was at work in the plea of a slave mother that "Monk" Lewis change the name of her child in the hope of preventing it from dying, leading Lewis to draw the inference that the "name contains in it some secret power" (Brathwaite 1971, 237), and in the "mysterious power of sound" to which, as missionaries noted, the former slaves were susceptible.

Whether the nommo is an operative principle in folklife, it is a fact that there are aspects of the folk culture that admit such an interpretation. One's name is so personal and private that it is an offense against etiquette to shout out in public the name even of good friends. Instead one attracts their attention by clapping of the hands, or by the familiar hiss "Ssst!" The name may also be used to harm. Since duppies can "capture" the voice, people do not answer to their names at night, not even when they think they have recognized the voice of the caller, until after the third call.

As to the power of sound, analysis of the tonal messages of Revival and Pentecostal preachers among the lower class would reveal that as much store is put on their tonal variations and stylized pronunciations as on the content itself. In a later essay, Brathwaite examines this tradition in the emerging "nation language" (that is, Jamaican) poetry. Says he:

The poetry, the culture itself, exists not in a dictionary but in the tradition of the spoken word. It is based as much on sound as it is on song. That is to say, the noise that it makes is part of the meaning, and if you ignore the noise (or what you would think of as noise, shall I say), then you lose part of the meaning. When it is written, you lose the sound or the noise, and therefore you lose part of the meaning. (1986, 271).

To this characteristic of nation language poetry he adds a second meaning achieved in the context of a responding audience. To be fully intelligible, he argues, the "sound poetry" of the late Michael Smith and others who now use Jamaican must be heard, in the same way that the music of the contemporary song has to be heard.

They use the same "riddims", the same voice spreads, syllable clusters, blue notes, ostinato, syncopation and pauses, along with, in Smith's case, a quite remarkable voice and breath control, accompanied by a decorative S90 *noise* (the S90 is an admired Japanese motorbike) which after a time becomes part of the sound structure and therefore meaning of the poem. (Brathwaite 1986, 272)

According to Brathwaite, the orality of the contemporary culture is to be understood not so much as the prevailing effect of illiteracy but as the result of a deeply embedded philosophical concept, rooted in African culture, which gives language the ability to acquire deeper levels of meaning than the literal, to create and to destroy.

This "ritual of words" among the Rastafari, like "the dozens" among American blacks, represents an arena of verbal competition between the Dreadlocks. Although there were some fifty onlookers, only six principals emerged: Naia, Jubie, Dada, Shaka, Floyd, and Fats. These vied as to who could use words better, more effectively. For example, after Dada scored a big point with his "threat" of assassination, Floyd, who up to then had not spoken, tried to create a similar effect, using the word "temptation," before going on to correct a point Dada had made. Because the reasoning is competitive, every now and then a free-for-all takes place, out of which emerges one speaker. The length of time he occupies the floor depends on (1) his ability to sustain a point of argument, and (2) his ability to entertain, to elicit the other responses of the other Dreadlocks.

In a sense, therefore, the persons involved in the ritual, including myself, were actors, dramatis personae. The role each played was not that of his own personality, not the personality of Naia, Shaka, or Dada but of *Rastafari*. The two outsiders represented not themselves but *Babylon*. Throughout the entire two or three hours, no matter who the speakers were, all eyes were riveted on one of us, and wherever the pronoun "you" or its Jamaican form "unu" appeared, it meant us, the outsiders, the aliens, even in a sentence such as this: "Him write that him witness Jehovah, but him no tell the people that is the King of Kings and Lord of Lords who *you* beat I Rasta for," where I was addressed even though it was not meant personally. When the same speaker said, "All the come you come a wi yard is only one thing you can ask we for, 'Where is the ganja?'" he addressed me but meant the police. At this level of meaning the contumely heaped upon our heads was heaped upon Babylon. Clem, not understanding this, tried to step outside his ritual role and merited the ridicule of the Dreadlocks.

The language used in the ritual was, where possible, highly stylized and formal. To get the floor, one said "I pray thee." Here is a list of some of the formal phrases.

NAIA: We are a people of the royal family of creation.

JUBIE: Where[as] I an I . . . , so now . . .

SHAKA: Those are colonial celebration. They shall be leaving a hissing, without an inhabitant, a everlasting darkness, where the dust of this earth shall become brimstone. It will be a everlasting lake of furnace!

TIGO: That is the most seenry!

That is a state-ical procedure!

FATS: I an I have been still martyred.

DADA: Where would you have to spend your long eternal?

VOICE: Save yourself first, before you could save others.

To the Rastafari what took place was "only sounds." They have a slogan that says, "WORD, SOUND and POWER," a trinity. To them the word is both sound and power. It is sound not only because its effect is aural but also because it is capable of quality, capable of being "sweet," of thrilling the hearer. It is power because it can inspire responses such as fear or anger or submission. The articulateness, tonal variation, pitch, and formalisms are the Rastafari version of the sweetness of the sermons in lower-class churches, and to describe this level of expression they use the word "to chant." The persuasiveness of the words themselves reveal their power, as when Clem sprang to his feet in anger. The word is wind, but it has the power to pierce one's heart and make one respond, or, as in the case of Geoffrey in the preceding chapter, to engulf the shop of a slanderer in flames.

The Content

The ritual had a second level of meaning that may be found in its content, an examination of which will reveal that it consisted of a delineation of the ritual distance between the sacred and the profane. As Emile Durkheim (1965, 53) noted, these two categories are "so profoundly differentiated or so radically opposed to one another," as no other in all of human thought. This opposition became all the more necessary to maintain because as the session progressed, especially after the admission that they were dealing only with "sounds," the attitude toward us began to change from that of placing us on trial to that of treating us as potential converts. The phrase "careless Ethiopian" was used quite frequently to refer to us. All black men are considered Ethiopians, for that is the nationality of Selassie I, but some are wayward in that they do not recognize their true identity and instead call themselves Jamaicans. Shaka compared the careless Ethiopian (that is myself) to a prisoner in a sinking ship of colonialism. Both master and slave were about to go under, but there was time yet for the slave to save himself. "Where", asked Dada, "would you spend your long eternal?" No other place for the black man, answered Jubie, but Ethiopia. No, intoned Fats, for the joy of the whole earth is—and the chorus of all voices responded—*Mount Zion*! "Mount Zion," of course, means Ethiopia, the seat of God.

I strongly suspect that many of those young men and women from middle-class backgrounds become Rastafari through processes like this one: first, a kind of shock treatment, perhaps to leave a feeling of guilt, but definitely to mark a separating distance between the oppressed and the oppressor and the sacred and profane; and second, an appeal to step across the threshold and join the oppressed.

Proselytizing was not the only function, however. The oral aggression was a means of reinforcing the posture for which the Dreadlocks have been so well known. That Fats thought it necessary to reassure me that they were not going to assassinate me is an indication that the hostility was real. Afterward, a Dreadlocks woman, in the presence of her husband and another elder, commented that as grueling as the session had been it was nothing compared to the treatment they received as women. In making this comment she implied that we together with the women shared the same role in relation to the Dreadlocks. This could only mean that we both symbolized profanity. Aggression sharpened the line of separation between the sacred and the profane.

At the same time there was an apparent paradox, in that the aggression was only symbolic, not real. This came out when, responding to Clem's outburst, the Dreadlocks said they were dealing only with "sounds." As long as their aggression remained on the level of "sounds" no harm would be initiated against the person. In fact, they would not need to take such measures, for Selassie by his divine power could see to that.

Thus while the aggression was real in that the Dreadlocks in effect declared an incompatibility and a mutual hostility between Jah's children on the one hand, and oppressive Babylon on the other, there also was an admission that nothing could be done about it except by the action of God. In other words, they stopped short of political action to redress a situation of oppression.

This conclusion may also be derived from an examination of the main articles of faith that emerged in the course of the reasoning. Generally speaking, there were two groups; one might be said to constitute a *political opposition* to the government, and the other mainly centers on the concept of a *remnant*.

In the first group belong the following:

1. The emperor, Haile Selassie, left a constitution for his people with the Jamaican Parliament. This constitution clearly supersedes the Jamaican Constitution. It also follows from this that the duly constituted authority over Jamaica is the Emperor Selassie.
2. The education system is colonial.
3. Jamaican culture is a black culture, not a mixed or creole one.
4. The free smoking of ganja is a religious right.

Implicit in each of these four articles of belief is a criticism of the government or state, which, theoretically at least, could be addressed in the course of political action. Indeed, the Manley government had in one way or another acknowledged the criticism. The Constitutional Reform Program and hearings of the Parliamentary Committee on the Decriminalization of Ganja both underway in 1977 provided the Rastafari with a chance for real input. When Prime Minister Manley, addressing a gathering of youths in October 1976, cited Columbus's "discovery" of Jamaica as an example of history seen through the eyes of the European colonizers, not of the Arawak whom the navigator found already living here, nor of the African whom the colonizers later enslaved, he was indirectly paying tribute to the Rastafari. And in a similar way the criticism of Jamaican culture could be met by greater acknowledgment of the role of Africa in its development, as is widely done. The general point is that these four themes could, in theory, constitute a program for political action. Not so, however, with the second group of articles:

5. The slaves who came to Jamaica are the Remnants of an entire people.

6. The Remnant = Israel = Ethiopians = Royal Family. Those people who today refer to themselves as "Israelis" are impostors.

7. The Remnant is exiled in Babylon, or Jamaica.

8. The Remnant will be saved by Repatriation.

9. The Repatriation will take place in seven miles of ships in the context of a general upheaval of nature and natural forces.

10. The activities of natural forces are instruments of Selassie's divine action.

The main point to observe about this second group of beliefs is that the goal as conceived cannot be attained by any but divine action. These two groups were to become the focus of a split in the house.

9. Repatriation and Divination

Leadership of the Nyabinghi House resides in the elders. They derive their position not by appointment or election, but by virtue of the initiative they show. For example, out of fifty or more Dreads present at the ritualized aggression described in the last chapter, only about one-half dozen individuals dominated the three-hour reasoning. They happened to be the most knowledgeable or the most forceful participants, whether this knowledge or forcefulness derived from venerable age and experience in the movement, as was true of Naia, or from native intelligence, as was true of Jubie. An elder must also participate in the life of the house by attending the monthly duty called to discuss internal affairs and to plan events such as the celebrations. In mid-February 1974 I found my way to one of these private meetings at the invitation of the man designated as the Most Senior Elder, Bongo Paul, a first among equals. In taking it upon himself to invite me, Bongo Paul, strictly speaking, had violated the principle of collective decision making, but the decision, which was taken in Bongo Jose's yard, had the support of several other important members of the house, who passed through from time to time. Paul also lived in the same yard.

The headquarters of the house where all meetings took place were situated at Bongo Floyd's home three kilometers away. My presence at the meeting, naturally, came as a surprise for some of

the brethren who knew nothing about my invitation, and so Bongo
Paul rose and addressed the house on the matter, reassuring them
that I had promised to remain only as an observer. Ras Tigo, one
of the most respected of the elders, supported Paul thus:

Seeing that he was called here by an Elder, and already forewarned of the
sight of I an I that he can be seated only as an observer and don't disturb,
I an I don't have anything talking that no one can't hear outside. For if it
wasn't Bongo Paul, an upful elder of the Church, he wouldn't be here. So
he come here through I an I, seeing I an I accept him here.

His reason was twofold: the meeting was not so secret that
anyone who wanted to could not listen (the porch from which the
meeting was directed lay within three meters from the neighbor's
fence, and, moreover, Bongo Floyd had tenants in the yard who
were non-Rastafari), but more important, it was Bongo Paul who
had extended the invitation, and Tigo made sure to emphasize that
Paul was in good standing, "an upful member of the church." His
argument carried the weight of reason, although, as Paul himself
admitted, the decision to invite an outsider to this particular duty
had best been made by the house itself. There were a number of
Dreads, however, who persisted in challenging my presence, the
main antagonists being Bongo Floyd and Bongo Jubie, who succeeded in diverting the meeting from the stated agenda that included the plans for the Upper Clarendon exercise.

The house finally decided to allow me to stay, but it was not
until more than a year later that I was to learn the true meaning of
what was going on. I had been, for the duration of that particular
debate, at the center of a conflict that later split the house. The
split came about in the following manner.

Judgment Come

Several weeks before the 1974 celebration of the Anniversary of
His Majesty's Visit, the treasury of the house was stolen. The house
had a box of thirteen cubic inches (representing the Father and his
twelve children, the tribes of Israel), with two partitions, one for
coins, the other for notes. The lid had a lock. Keeper of the box was
Ras Tigo, whose home was on Newcombe Drive less than two
hundred meters from the headquarters of the house in Bongo

Floyd's yard on Morning Avenue. On the corner of that avenue and Newcombe Drive stood a Chinese shop. The elders in their wisdom decreed that the key should be separated from the box, and so they appointed Ras Jose to be the Keeper of the key. The box made its appearance at duties, the first Saturday of every month, when before the eyes of the elders all monies were pushed in through the apertures. The box was seldom opened. It was kept in case of contingencies such as assisting an elder who ran afoul of the law.

At the time in question, Ras Tigo, a mason by trade, was in the country finishing off a job that kept him there for three weeks. He was not present when the money was stolen, but the house charged him nonetheless because he was the one responsible for its safe-keeping. Living in Ras Tigo's yard were his wife with her small children and Tommy, the son of a very old Dread living in the country.

One Tuesday night as he stood by the gate looking out, Tommy was accosted and searched by a joint military and police patrol, one of many which could be found patrolling ghetto communities in a drive against violent crimes. They entered and searched the house too, inside and out, looking for firearms. Satisfied, they departed. Just then another patrol emerged from a rum bar and, concluding that their colleagues were not thorough enough, carried out a second search of Tigo's house. They found the box above a clothes press, and pried open the lock with one of the bayonets. Since Tommy had told them it contained the treasury of the house, one of the policemen warned him to keep his eyes steadfast on what they were doing to avoid any accusation that in carrying out their search they had stolen valuables. Satisfied again, they departed.

Acting responsibly, Ras Tigo's wife told Tommy that the open box was no longer safe in their home. It had to be taken to head-quarters. Tommy agreed and asked her to accompany him. Leaving the children alone, she was going the short distance with him when they saw Bongo Floyd riding up with his bicycle. They waited by the Chinese shop and had hardly begun explaining when the shopkeeper, seeing Floyd and Tommy, called Floyd to "tell him something." Floyd left them waiting. He spent a while there, and Sister Tigo, anxious about her children and considering her presence no longer necessary, decided to return home. What did the shopkeeper want? According to Floyd's testimony at the trial, he had lodged a complaint against Tommy: The Sunday before he was inside taking stock when Tommy and another youth pulled his shutters, entered, and asked to be sold some cigarettes. When he refused, Tommy replied angrily that he was going to want sale but unable to get it, and the two youths left. The shopkeeper asked Floyd to warn Tommy not to do it again, because he could easily have gotten Tommy arrested.

After leaving the shop, Floyd did not finish dealing with Tommy but told him to do whatever he wanted with the box and rode on up the avenue to his home, with Tommy following a distance behind. On reaching the yard, he is alleged to have said to his wife: "A judgment coming. Go deal with it for me." She met Tommy in the yard and began to abuse him at the top of her voice, saying she did not want the box in her yard. Tommy placed the box on the porch and left hastily.

Shortly after this scene, the Congos arrived to spend the night at Bongo Floyd's: Ras Congo, Maa Congo, and Iaata, their daughter, were on one of their frequent trips to Kingston to dispose of their craft work. Seeing the box, Ras Congo shouted to Bongo Floyd, who at the time was in the kitchen preparing supper, "It come home!" to which came the reply, "A so me see!" No other words were exchanged pertaining to the box, which remained on the porch until midnight when Floyd took it up and placed it in the living room, where the Congos were sleeping. In the morning, Maa testified, she saw it, took it up, and felt its weight. "It heavy!" she exclaimed, and put it back. Iaata testified that she did not touch it, but in tidying swept around it. Later in the day the Congos left. Wednesday night Floyd rode down to Bongo Paul's yard and there delivered the news: the money had been stolen, all gone except twelve dollars in notes and coins. The following Saturday night was to have been a monthly duty at which the upcoming Anniversary celebrations were to have been discussed. It was decided to deal with this matter then, but after a preliminary discussion the elders decided to wait until after the celebrations rather than divide the house and create bitter feelings at that time.

The trial was set for the last Sunday in April. Charged were Floyd, for obvious reasons; Sister Floyd, because she was a member of the household in which the crime took place; Sister Floyd's son, for the same reason as his mother; Tommy, because he had been left alone with the box after Sister Tigo's departure and for as long as it had taken to walk the eighty meters from the corner shop to the headquarters; Sister Tigo, because she and Tommy had possession of the box; the three Congos, because they slept in the room with the box; and Ras Tigo, because the box was his responsibility to guard—nine suspects in all. The trial was held neither at headquarters nor at Bongo Paul's yard, but on neutral territory. The selected "Ghana," Bongo Norman's yard in a community several kilometers away. Starting at about 8 P.M. the trial was well attended, for Dreads far and wide regarded it as quite serious. Into the night they charged and countercharged, argued and debated. Why did Floyd attend first to the shopkeeper before attending to his brother? Didn't the irregular sight of the box mean something was wrong? Why did Ras Congo, a senior elder at that, do nothing? There was no end to the suspicions. Floyd even suggested that Ras Tigo could have broken open the box before leaving for the country, with the intention of putting back the money. Bongo Paul testified, however, that Ras Tigo had borrowed four dollars from him for the trip and Tigo himself brought supporting evidence that he had borrowed money also from a woman in Duhaney Park for the same reason. At 3 A.M. Ras Tigo was the only one cleared, and there was still no progress in establishing guilt.

Then Bongo Paul made a motion: each of the remaining eight persons was to select a passage from Scripture, have it read, and let the house judge innocence or guilt by interpretation of the reading. It was a last resort. All eight were called up and required to stand in a line. Following are the texts that each one chose (Sister Tigo's could not be recalled):

Floyd	Psalm 94
Tommy	Psalm 28
Maa Congo	Psalm 91
Iaata Congo	Psalm 7
Floyd's son	Psalm 9
Sister Floyd	Psalm 27
Sister Tigo	
Ras Congo	Jude 1

Ras Congo chose not to announce his text but to "cut the book," that is, to open it randomly and accept as oracle the passage revealed. As presiding elder, Bongo Paul strove to make it clear that it was not the recovery of the money that was the main goal at that point, but establishment of the truth. It was important that if "Idrin" were living by certain principles, those principles be protected and vindicated.

It is necessary for us to know the text of Psalm 94 in order to understand the power play between Bongo Floyd and Bongo Paul. Tommy's father was appointed reader.

1. O Lord God, to whom vengeance belongeth; O God, to whom vengeance belongeth, show thyself.

2. Lift up thyself, thou judge of the earth; render a reward to the proud.

3. Lord, how long shall the wicked, how long shall the wicked triumph?

4. How long shall they utter and speak hard things? and all the workers of iniquity boast themselves?

5. They break in pieces, thy people, O Lord, and afflict thine heritage.

At verse 5 Bongo Floyd stopped the reader. Addressing the house, he said that he had a vision to declare. In his vision he found himself among a vast multitude of people traveling on a long journey. Looking around, he recognized no one except Bongo Jose and his wife Sister Maria. The rest were strangers. On and on they traveled until they came upon a green pasture, grass underfoot like a carpet. In the middle of the field, however, was a pit, but no sign of the earth that had been excavated. The pit was further concealed by the overgrown grass around the edge. As they neared it Jose fell in. The rest of the multitude waited for him to emerge, but he did not. Unable to wait any longer, Floyd cut a long stick, lowered it into the pit, and began to stir. The stench released by the stirring was so foul that the multitude ran.

Bongo Paul stopped him. Paul preempted the interpretation of the vision. "The pit, Bongo Floyd, is for no one else but you, the multitude carried you to show you the pit, so that if you don't amend your ways you will surely go down. Bongo Jose's fall into the pit is only symbolic to show that any man who falls in has no hope of returning." Floyd was dumbstruck. He uttered not a word; neither did the rest of the house. Perhaps only a few people, if any at all, really understood what Bongo Paul had done; they would have understood only if they really had known by heart what the rest of the psalm was all about. There was absolutely no doubt that Floyd knew—he had selected it. The reading continued:

6. They slay the widow and the stranger, and murder the father-less.

7. Yet they say, the Lord shall not see, neither shall the God of Jacob regard it.

8. Understand, ye brutish among the people; and fools, when will ye be wise?

9. He that planted the ear, shall he not hear? He that formed the eye, shall he not see?

10. He that chastiseth the heathen, shall not he correct? He that teacheth man knowledge, shall he not know?

11. The Lord knoweth the thoughts of man, that they are vanity.

12. Blessed is the man whom thou chastiseth, O Lord, and teach-est him out of thy law;

13. That thou mayest give him rest from the days adversity, until the pit be digged for the wicked.

At verse 13 the house let out a roar. Floyd's fate was sealed. He had been outwitted and outmaneuvered. Verse 13 made it clear that Bongo Paul himself had also known what the chapter was about, and that was why he preempted an interpretation. At the end of the reading the house found Bongo Floyd guilty.

Tommy was also found guilty. His text was a very bad choice: verse 10,

My heart panteth, my strength faileth me; as for the light of mine eyes, it is also gone from me,

indicated that there was a contradiction, according to Paul. "Tommy is a young man, then how could his heart be weak and his strength failing, were he not guilty?" verse 11;

My lovers and my friends stand aloof from my sore; and my kinsmen stand afar off,

Paul interpreted as reflecting the separation of the house from Tommy. And verses 21 and 22,

> Forsake me not, O Lord; O my God, be not far from me. Make haste to help me, O Lord my salvation,

applied appropriately, "through him worried." What is interesting in Tommy's case, and in all the others as well, was that there were verses favorable to the defendant that were ignored. For example, verse 12 reads:

> They also that seek after my life lay snares for me; and they that seek my hurt speak mischievous things and imagine deceits all the day long.

When I pointed this out Bongo Paul said nothing. He merely grunted until a verse was read that in his eyes established guilt. In short, Tommy was guilty because he could not prove he was innocent. Crucial had been his walk from the corner shop up to the headquarters, alone and in the dark. According to Paul, he could have taken, and probably did take, some though not all of the money. Moreover, unemployed at the time, he would have been in need of money. Thus, it was not the sacred Scriptures that condemned him as much as the area of doubt that he could not clear up. As long as there were reasoning and counterreasoning by all and sundry, his fate could not have been sealed. That was where the Bible came in as the infallible word of Jah, acknowledged by elders and accused alike for its power to sift the truth. But the interpretation given to the texts were by no means arbitrary. Those found guilty were in fact the only ones who could have taken the money from the box. That did not mean they actually had stolen; however, the Bible brought to an end the whole night of discussion, sealing it once and for all.

Although acquitted, Ras Congo was censored for not acting responsibly as a senior elder with more active years in the movement than Bongo Floyd. Sister Floyd was found guilty, by association or collaboration with her husband. Actually, whereas Tommy's verse was a bad choice for him, hers was not unfavorable, and verse 12 mentioned that "false witnesses have risen up against me." Nevertheless, the house found it necessary to condemn her. Sister

Floyd was a tall woman, who moved with fine grace, much taller than many of the Dreads and elders. When the reader came to verse 6;

> And now shall mine head be lifted up above mine enemies round about me; therefore will I offer in his tabernacle sacrifices of joy,

she was said to have looked at the elders, sweeping them with her glance. It was clear, said Bongo Paul, why she had selected that psalm: she was contemptuous of all the elders. On account of her haughtiness the elders refused to attend the next monthly meeting at the headquarters.

The trial did not bring about a sharp split immediately. A full year passed before the fissure widened into a deep rift between a very small but militant faction led by Bongo Floyd and Bongo Jubie on one side, and the rest of the house on the other.

Left, by the Bus

Among all Rastas there are four main events in the liturgical calendar:

Ethiopian Christmas	January 7
King's Anniversary Visit	April 18
King's Birthday	July 23
King's Coronation	November 7

In 1968, following the second anniversary of the King's visit, the house had decided to rotate each celebration from parish to parish. The main motive was to reduce the risk of police harassment, which was at its peak around that time, but the move had the additional advantage of exposing Rastafari to the people in rural communities. By custom the site of the next celebration was chosen before the current celebration ended. At the Upper Clarendon celebration in 1974, and before the trial, it was decided to celebrate the King's birthday at Portland Cottage, a small community near the Monymusk sugar estate in Lower Clarendon. Normally, the buses and trucks would have departed from headquarters, but in light of the dim view the elders had of the Floyds, they agreed to depart from Ras Tigo's gate only a short distance away. On reaching Bongo Floyd's gate, however, they sent to notify him of the departure, but he and Bongo Jubie, who now lived with him, sent word that they would arrive on their own. There were others, too, who for various reasons did not travel with the bus. So as the participants arrived one by one the following day, Bongo Paul went up to them and said: "Those that come with the bus and those that left, even if they did not intend to miss it, are the Right Wing and the Left Wing of Jah Rastafari Church." Jubie said nothing. This use of the "Right" and the "Left" was a characteristic play on words. Right meant those "in the right"; Left meant those who placed themselves in the wrong by being "left by the bus." Bongo Paul was pressing home his advantage, in an attempt to isolate the main contenders for hegemony over the house.

Again at the Christmas celebration at Bull Head Mountain, also in Clarendon, Jubie and Floyd did not arrive until the second day, once more refusing to travel with the main convoy. Main activities for that evening were a film show and the regular nyabinghi during which there was to be a "baby delegation," a ceremony in which boys three months old and girls four months old are presented and blessed. As I explained previously, these events generally attract onlookers. Just as Bongo Paul entered to start the binghi with the greeting, "Perfect Love!" Bongo Floyd rushed to the front and raising his arms said, "Brethren, remember, regardless of what happen, 11 Morning Avenue is still our headquarters!" The gesture had the opposite effect of that intended. Members of the house roared sounds of disapproval at this tactless exposure to the public of a private and internal matter. On the following day Bongo Paul began sending out feelers for the site of the next celebration, the Anniversary Visit, and found one in Sunning Hill, St. Thomas. At the end of the last day's service he made the announcement to the house. As soon as everyone broke up, Bongo Floyd and Bongo Jubie came to Paul and said, "We heard you announce Sunning Hill for the next Duty. We had in mind Payne Avenue." Paul replied, "The word of Jah has gone out already. *You* can call back the House and make the announcement to them!" Jubie declared that Sunning Hill was the wrong place. Paul replied that the house was large enough for two celebrations to be kept, but as for himself he was bound for eastern St. Thomas. And so in 1975 there took place two Anniversary celebrations, one in Sunning Hill, the other at the Haile Selassie Secondary School on Payne Avenue.

The Payne Avenue Anniversary

The First Document

In the weeks leading up to the Anniversary the Left faction circulated two documents under their new name of the Judah-Coptic Church. The first was a large poster entitled "THE ACCEPTABLE YEAR JAH RASTAFARI" and advertising a thirteen-day celebration to be held at the Haile Selassie Secondary School to mark the Anniversary of the King's visit. The language was millenarian. It referred in places to "the acceptable year of Jah Rastafari Isaiah 61:2, sela seventy five," the year when "every eye must behold the Lion!" and when Selassie would pay his "divine visitation to I an I Rastafari, his brethren," the year of "deliverance, redemption, repatriation and reunification of the ancient Black Church, prophesied by I an I elder brethren, the prophet Marcus Garvey."

The Second Document

The second document was longer and more complex. It listed five charges against the government of Prime Minister Manley. To put these charges in context, I will provide some background information. Michael Manley, who led the PNP to victory in 1972, had aroused decisive support of Rastafari youths by playing upon his visit to Africa, and in particular, to Emperor Haile Selassie in 1970. During the campaign he brandished his gift from the emperor, a "rod of correction" that was popularly believed to be a symbol of the mandate from Jah. Soon afterward, however, Jamaica underwent its first major postwar economic crisis. A very steep and sudden rise in the price of oil drove up the price of goods and services and triggered a downturn in production, leading to a recession. The government responded on two fronts. On the economic front a number of measures were introduced, including a unilateral levy against the bauxite mining companies and a speeding up of land reform in connection with which Manley visited the Dreads. On the political front democratic socialism was reintroduced into the ruling party. These measures were unable to prevent the steady decline in the material condition of the poor throughout all of 1974 and into 1975. The general situation confirmed the feeling among the Rastafari that Rastafari had been used by "party politricks."

The first charge "accused Prime Minister Manley, his party and Government of SACRILEGE." Here, after three years of his rule, they attacked his uses of the visit to Ethiopia and the rod, calling them "electioneering gimmickry" and "infamous fraud." They included in this charge violations of the constitutional rights to wear their dreadlocks and to practice their religious use "of a natural herb." The second charge accused the prime minister and all previous administrations

of knowingly and unlawfully collaborating in an immoral conspiracy to defraud the descendants of the slaves from the full rights and benefits of the Abolition Act of 1838; to deny the spirit and intent of Emancipation; and to seek through fraudulent and deceptious [*sic*] devices to illegally extend inhuman and degrading forms of servitude over the masses.

The main device alleged in this charge was the persecution of the Rastafari, the religion of the descendants of the slave, with the result that the masses had an "unfair and unjust handicap." Third, the document accused the Governments and administrations of genocide (presumably through birth control measures). Fourth, it charged Manley and his government of "an international conspiracy with multi-national news agencies and services to misrepresent events occurring in Ethiopia . . . spreading false reports, disseminating unjustified rumors; and distorting news dispatches in an attempt to cause harm, rebellion, bloodshed and confusion among Ethiopians at home and abroad." These devices were also used "to slander, propagandize and to libel" Selassie. Finally, the three administrations were accused of (since Independence in 1962) "extending the rule of the descendants of the slave masters through an allegedly independent constitution, which in reality and truth, is an order in Council of the British Parliament of the United Kingdom of Great Britain" and of breaching several articles of the United Nations Universal Declaration of Human Rights.

The document then went on to attack the two-party system:

Thirty-six years of two-party democratic partianship have left the masses of the people in a more degenerate, demoralized and mal-nutritioned condition than existed in 1938 when the solution of repatriation was persecuted into rejection in favor of capitalist experimentation.

Since adult suffrage has been forced upon the masses of illiterate and uneducated descendants of the emancipated slaves, successive governments have promoted insidious and discriminatory campaigns to ridicule, mock and discourage the reality of repatriation.

The style was quite bold and libelous, and the document scored a number of important points. The "gift" of the constitution from Britain, it argued, stood as a reminder that links with the former colonizers and slave masters had not been thoroughly severed by Independence, for the constitution retained Queen Elizabeth as also queen of Jamaica. And although not many Jamaicans had been bothered by this circumstance, it was a distasteful reminder to the Rastafari who had a strong sense of historical injustice. It is in this light that we must view the Rastafari's belief that Haile Selassie left them a constitution in 1966.

The "Left" denounced the two-party system for bringing demoralization and poverty, claiming that repatriation had been rejected in favor of capitalism by forcing adult suffrage on the masses, who, through lack of education, did not truly understand the "capitalist experimentation" they were getting into. If the people had understood the evils of capitalism when they voted in their first elections under adult suffrage in 1944, they would have opted for repatriation.

At the Payne Avenue Celebration

Declaration by the Left that the emperor would pay a "churchical" visit to Jamaica in 1975 became that faction's focus of the Anniversary celebration. Expectation of a visit explains the Left's attempt to site the duty at Haile Selassie Secondary School on Payne Avenue instead of Sunning Hill: the school had a symbolic link with the emperor who had turned over the first soil when the school was about to be built. According to a letter appearing in the *Daily News* from someone signing his or her name as "Teacher," the Rastafari had "captured" the Haile Selassie Secondary School and had disrupted classes. Indeed they had, for the school board had turned down the group's request to site the celebrations there. The police however, for some reason, failed to dislodge them from the school yard.

The imagined visit of Selassie was not the creation of Jubie's and Floyd's faction alone. The rumor had been circulating for some time throughout the movement. But what seemed to have stirred the Left into action was the Commonwealth Heads of Government Conference scheduled to take place in Kingston between late April and early May 1975. They probably anticipated that Selassie would be present. Indeed, Prince Emmanuel of the Bobo had himself asked me if Haile Selassie would be there. Why the emperor should be present was not clear, because Ethiopia was not a member of the Commonwealth.

At any rate, the Left declared repatriation to be the main item on the agenda of the conference and made it the main theme of the Payne Avenue celebration as well. But whether the Commonwealth conference dealt with and resolved the repatriation issue, repatriation must take place, for, according to the prophecy, if repatriation failed, Manley's head would roll and the brethren would sail home in a sea of blood. And this fate held true not only for Manley's head but also for the heads of "all careless Ethiopians," people like myself, "for cares not what the I think, the I is a Ethiopian." Once repatriation was accomplished, a theocratic government would be established. If therefore the repatriation issue were resolved at the conference, all would be well and good; if it failed, there would be bloodshed. Prophecies of Marcus Garvey proved that this was the year for such events to occur. Garvey had prophesied that "when you see a third party rise up in Jamaica it is the Brethren's time." That third party was the United Party, which broke off from the Opposition Jamaica Labour Party after the defeat in the 1972 elections. And again Garvey prophesied "when you see no more jangkro in Victoria Park, is time for the same brethren on the Dungle who you call 'jangkro' gwine rule." Manley had until September to effect the repatriation.

But the Brethren on the Left were not content to let prophecy have its course. They wanted to be accorded the status of delegates at the Commonwealth conference, and this desire explains the cordial manner of their reasoning with me, even though the "careless Ethiopian" argument was present. On Monday night preceding the opening, there was to take place at the large assembly hall of the University of the West Indies a solidarity rally in honor of the African Freedom Fighters, at which it was expected Zimbabwe delegates to the conferences would speak. Bongo Floyd and Bongo Jubie reasoned that because the rally was taking place in the assembly hall of the university, it must have the sponsorship of the university itself. They planned to attend in the hope of getting the university to push through a resolution declaring that they had the right to sit as delegates at the Commonwealth Heads of Government Conference. And being from the university I was to use my good offices to bring this about. The university, they argued, was the seat of learning without whose research and recommendations the government could not act, therefore it was of higher status than government. As a parting gesture I was given passages to read from two of the most millenarian of all books in the Bible, Daniel 2:22–24 and Revelation 13:17 and 19, because, they explained, the prophecies referred to therein are the ones now being fulfilled. The first passage contained Daniel's interpretation of the dream of the king of Babylon, Nebuchadnezzar, which ended with the promise of a kingdom to be established by God which "shall stand forever." The second passage covered the dream of the fall of Rome, symbolized as Babylon, and the investiture of Christ as King of Kings and Lord of Lords.

The Rally

The rally at the university was attended by a wide cross section of people. The Judah-Coptics came, as was their intention, but so did other Rastafari groups. Mortimo Planno, famous for having been on the 1961 Mission to Africa and for restoring control over the wildly enthusiastic crowd of Rastafari that prevented the emperor from disembarking at the airport in his 1966 visit, led a small group with several placards, one of which read:

The Rasta Movement Association was also there, and one of its leaders, Ras Historian, later helped chair the meeting. But the leading forces, which occupied the attention of everyone, were the Judah-Coptics and the Bobo led by Prince Emmanuel. Between them both, chaos reigned. On one side of the great echoing hall fifty Bobo—every single man, woman, and child among them dressed in white turbans and robes—were dancing to the rhythm of their own drumming and chanting and were waving sixteen flags and banners. It was an impressive sight. But not far away were grouped the Judah-Coptics, slightly fewer in number, chanting songs, reciting psalms, and trying to out-drum the Bobo. And in a far corner a group of ten Rastas were engaged in hanging the effigies of Vorster and other South African racists. To top it all, the Zimbabwe delegates were not going to arrive on that night at all, and therefore fresh arrangments had to be made to meet the needs of the rally. A Zimbabwe lecturer at the university was given the arduous task of filling in for his countrymen, and from the start it was clear that no matter the outcome, the rally was going to be dominated by Rastafari rivalry.

With a great deal of difficulty the drumming ceased, and the meeting began under the chairmanship of the Youth Forces for National Liberation, a Maoist revolutionary group. The Zimbabwe lecturer failed to satisfy the heightened anticipation of the audience. And the Judah-Coptics, in no mood to overlook his shortcomings, rebuffed his concluding suggestion that what Jamaicans could do for the Zimbabwe national liberation struggle was to support it with clothing and money, with a chorus of "Lightening! Fire! Blood!"

The next speaker called was Prince Edward Emmanuel of the Bobo. From the moment they had been asked to stop the drumming and dancing in order to get on with the meeting, the Bobo had sat down quietly, except for Prince who took up position at their head where he remained standing throughout. Now, called by the chairman, neither he nor any of his followers gave the slightest indication that they had heard. They stared steadfastly ahead, ignoring the invitation, giving the impression that they wanted to distance themselves from the boisterous Judah-Coptics. Amid shouts of "Come on, Eddie!" from the Judah-Coptics it was apparent that Prince would have been heckled. The antagonism came from Prince's claim to membership of the Godhead, which was why, Rastafari say, he was the only Rastafari at the official reception in 1966 to shake the emperor's hand with his glove on.

The chairman of the rally gave up, and possibly in the hope that a Rastafari chairman might be able to exercise control, handed over the podium to Ras Historian, who then called on Bongo Jubie. Jubie spoke for one and one-half hours, by which time most of the audience had left. He had even failed to raise the question of his own resolution. Some of the other Rastafari groups were quite furious and voiced contempt for Judah-Coptics' behavior. The meeting broke up with the end of Bongo Jubie's speech.

An Assessment

To return to the conflict over the box, it does seem an anomaly that all the affairs of the house except for the treasury were centralized at the Morning Avenue headquarters. In most organizations the treasurer receives, keeps, and disburses money. He or she *handles* the funds, for which reason treasurers are generally chosen for their probity and integrity. The house never appointed a treasurer as such, because the adopted procedures made the actual handling of money unnecessary and impossible. From that point of view, the box could have been entrusted to any reliable elder and could very well have remained at the headquarters, making it unnecessary to carry it to and fro once every month. Only one thing therefore could have accounted for this unusual arrangement, and that was mistrust. The leadership of the house for whatever reason apparently did not trust Bongo Floyd, either personally or possibly because of other circumstances such as the visitors it disproved of who frequented the headquarters. The principals in the drama understood this, hence the remark by Ras Congo: "It come home!"

Viewed in an episodic way, the debate over my presence at the private meeting of the house and the incident with the box amount to nothing more than tales of personality conflicts. But when treated as a sort of "extended case study" (Van Velsen 1967) different meanings begin to appear, and the drama over the theft of the resources of the House turns out to be a disguise for differences over more fundamental issues of orthodoxy. The struggle for leadership of the house was in reality a struggle for the *direction* of the house.

Repatriation

One of the most passionately sung hymns at Rastafari celebrations is the following:

Babylon is a wicked one [3 times]
O, Jah Rastafari O—Selah

Our forefathers were taken away [3 times]
O, Jah Rastafari O—Selah

Open up da gate mek I repatriate [3 times]
O, Jah Rastafari O—Selah

In this song is captured the essence of Rastafari belief that black people are in reality the captive children of Israel in Babylon and that, in repeat fulfillment of history, they will one day be set free. Repatriation is that freedom. That is why Dada, as he held forth before a group of one-half dozen younger Dreads attending the Black Rock celebration in St. Thomas in 1988, condemned those who talked of wanting to free up ganja, because "is not ganja not free, is man no free!" Freedom, however, will be coming soon, for every 2,000 years mark the end of an old and the beginning of a new dispensation. The coming dispensation will not find "I and I" here. There will be, he declared, ten miles of ships to take us home.

Dada went on to lecture the young Dreads that not all black men will be saved. He posed a riddle to them: holding up his knee-length locks he said, "You cannot be saved without this, but this won't save you!" When a baldhead who had joined the group asked him to explain, Dada said: "Don't when dem cut off hair dem used to put i' a' tree root and all [even] under dem?" There was an accompanying gesture to his crutches. "Yes," replied the baldhead, "an' it still goin' on, still goin' on!" "Well, alright!" said Dada.

Dada's meaning was that wearing dreadlocks symbolizes a break with the old and mistaken tradition and in this sense is a necessary prerequisite for salvation. But though necessary it is not of itself sufficient, because not everyone who wears dreadlocks is upright in the faith. Salvation through repatriation is therefore an act to be accomplished only by Jah, who alone knows the upright from the impostor.

Continuing his lecture he explained that it is the "conscious" black man, the Ethiopian, who will be saved by repatriation, whereas the brown man will remain here, for Jamaica is his home. Then he asked, "Who do you think represents the brown man, the American Indian?" Finding everyone wanting, he answered his own question, "Fidel Castro! Is the same spirit! The Spirit of life cannot die! Wha' me say? The spirit of *life!*"

These views were expressed by Dada but could have been the words of any of the other ancients present at Black Rock. They uphold the belief in the physical return to Ethiopia of the conscious, not the careless, Ethiopian and in the relinquishing of the New World by the white man, the European, to its true owner, the Native American represented here by Fidel Castro. Knowing that Fidel in not physically descended from Native Americans, Dada explains that the spirit of the Native American has passed to him.

The conviction that repatriation is to take place soon was also expressed by Bongo Stephen, who, in responding to my comment that the thatched roof of the imposing tabernacle at Black Rock would need replacement in ten or fifteen years, said that might not be necessary because "we all good fi gone before the new dispensation!"

Bongo Floyd and Bongo Jubie, on the other hand, while sharing the conviction that a new dispensation was approaching, believed in the direct intervention by man. Initially, their focus was on the alleged constitution left by the emperor in 1966, which would extend His Majesty's jurisdiction to Jamaica and give them the freedom to go home. From the word ritual of the previous chapter it is apparent that this view was shared by other Dreadlocks, but the effort to force the constitution out of the government through the millenarian threats and the Commonwealth Heads of Government Conference in 1975 distinguished Floyd and Jubie's faction from the rest.

The key to Bongo Floyd's conception was his position that for repatriation to come about, the Rastafari needed what he called "a central office of administration." This is what the church he built at his home on Morning Avenue was all about. But he sought sanction for his point of view in instructions he alleged to have received from the emperor to build the church for his second coming, to call it the "Royal Judah Coptic Church," and to have it registered so that the visit could be felt "churchically." These instructions were given during the state visit (and first coming) of His Imperial Majesty in 1966.

Registration of the Judah-Coptics remained Floyd's most tirelessly pursued goal, until January 1988 when the Joint Private Bills Committee of Parliament finally turned down his application for incorporation on the grounds that incorporation would tacitly sanction the use of ganja. The nonrecognition was felt keenly, he said, because it prevented him from acquiring the status of a clergyman and gaining legitimacy for a more extensive herbal practice. Thwarted thus, he called a press conference in March 1988 and publicly launched his African Comprehensive Party.

This step served to distance the Judah-Coptics from the house even further. Aware that his actions were seen by the house as trying to introduce politics into the Rastafari movement, Floyd publicly criticized "the attitude of some of the brethren . . . for the passive stand taken on issues involving 'indigenous cultures' of Rastafarians over the years." What did he mean?

According to Bongo Floyd, only the conscious Ethiopian will experience repatriation. But, he asked, what about the rest of the people? Although they might be careless Ethiopians, they were still Ethiopians. Hence it was the responsibility of the conscious to ensure that they left behind a country and a system that was just. He saw himself as continuing the struggles undertaken by such heroes as Garvey, Paul Bogle, and Nanny to bring about a just society right here in Jamaica. The other brethren spoke of love, but "if these men don't love what they see they cannot proves to me that they will love what they doesn't see."

Floyd's and the Coptics' position thus differed from that of the house in that he identified more than they did with other blacks, at least on the ideological level, and it was this that induced him to say that he dealt with redemption, not just repatriation. By redemption he meant negotiating with the "slave seller" and the "slave buyer" to accept responsibility for the compensation of the descendants of the slaves, as well as for the resettlement of those who, like himself, would be repatriated. In this view, repatriation would be a political act like that whereby the Jews having learned, he said, from their centuries of mistakenly passive expectation, finally forced the establishment of the state of Israel.

For his part, Bongo Jubie shared the view that "I an' I" had a responsibility to establish what he called "majority rule" here in Jamaica, but he gave a more theologically sophisticated argument for his position: Basically, black people may be divided into two categories, "those taken and those sent." Those taken were those captured and sold into slavery. But Jah, in his love for his children, chose some whom he sent among them to enlighten them and to be their guide in captivity, until the time for their redemption. The two groups were recognized by their knowledge or lack thereof. Those *sent* were the keepers of knowledge, "I an' I" Rastafari, who knew and are continuing to pass on to those who were *taken* the truth about Jah.

This argument bears some parallel to traditional Christian teaching about Jesus Christ's being sent by the Father. And in truth, Jubie saw Rastafari man as agent of Jah, as divine.

Some say that majority rule here is not possible, but not I. I say it can, but with *I*vine help, because we are on the threshold of a new dispensation. This *I*vine help is through human agency, for humanity is the seed of *I*vinity. I an' I are being refined as an *I*vine instrument. That's why I an' I have been adjusting mentally within a *I*vine perspective.

To Jubie, therefore, there is no contradiction between adherence to the traditional doctrine of repatriation as a divine act and working as men to bring it about. His activities described above were consistent with this conclusion. After those events, he went on in the early 1980s to become very active on the radio call-in programs, taking up public issues. Then in 1985, while still in collaboration with Bongo Floyd, he drafted a fifty-page political manifesto entitled:

The Ethiopian-African Theocracy Union Policy: EATUP
True Genuine Authentic Fundamental Indigenous
Original Comprehensive Alternative Policy: FIOCAP

The first characteristic of EATUP-FIOCAP was the claim to have inherited from the "national Patriot-Martyrs" the

divine national responsibility delegated by the circumstance of the purpose and choice of JAH Almighty to navigate a course of national reunification, reconciliation and internal revival in the land of our birth, without prejudice, conflict or opposition to the hope, sacrifice and the land, in which our illuminated forefathers were created.

In other words, without sacrificing repatriation, they believed the church had been given the mission to bring about reunification and reconciliation here in Jamaica, in the tradition of Sharpe, Bogle, Garvey, and other patriots.

Second, EATUP-FIOCAP set out the details of a "theocracy structure of governmental organization," the main features of which were the decentralization of administration at the level of constituencies, of which there were to be five per parish, making seventy in all; a National Ombudsman; Parliamentary Opposition; a Parliamentary Regional Executive Constituency Cabinet; and a National Legislature composed of an elected and a nominated House.

Third, the manifesto set out in detail the policies to be implemented by the eighteen ministries. The policies in essence mirrored the practices and teachings of the Rastafari. For example, the Health Ministry would liberalize ganja use and codify all herbs; Foreign Affairs would pass a "Repatriation of (Descendants of) Slaves Act," seek compensation for 420 years of slavery, and join the Organization of African Unity (OAU). Education would, under a national charter, "revive the divine glory and the golden era of ancient Ethiopian-African civilization." And Security and Justice would file a writ "seeking injunction against the crown & or government of those nations who initiated & or benefitted from the slave trade and the institution of racial commercial slavery."

Although they have gone their separate ways since the manifesto was drafted in 1985, Bongo Jubie was still defending it in November 1988 when I interviewed him, while Bongo Floyd used it as his campaign platform in the 1989 general elections. For Jubie it is a model to be implemented from even now, and that was why he declared himself the provisional head of Jah Rastafari Theocracy Government and said he was gearing himself up to contest the elections in the seat of the incumbent prime minister, Edward Seaga.

While members of the house criticized Floyd and Jubie for introducing politics into the Rastafari movement, Floyd and Jubie were equally critical of house members. Floyd charged them with inconsistency in approving of Garvey, even though Garvey was a political figure. He voiced his disapproval of their conduct at celebrations, saying that when they assembled to praise God "they do not fast; they eat, drink, nyam [eat]—a hundred pots all over the place. When there is a solemn duty, there shouldn't be any activity of this kind. If you hungry, nyam at home!"

Jubie expressed his criticism thus: for a divine culture to grow, separation is necessary, but the question is In what areas? The senior elders in the house are for total separation. But that is not possible, as they are now learning; for some of them, having just returned from a delegation abroad, must now know that they could not have gone had they insisted on their "African" rather than on their Jamaican nationality or had they not carried Jamaican passports. The folly of their insistence on rigid separation was exposed by the fact that most of their children, he said, were combsomes.

Death

On yet one other point of doctrinal significance, there is a difference between the Right and the Left trends. The traditional teaching on death remains very much present in the house. Since the end of my fieldwork in 1975, Bongo Paul, Bongo Anton, Brother Saasi, Badaman, Sister Maria, and many others whom I had known are dead, owing to disobedience, said Wato, up to 1992 the most senior elder or patriarch.

Bongo Stephen elaborates. There are two kinds of brethren: one holds that man is here but for a time; the other that man is put here to live forever. "I am of the second type," he says. Death, he explains, occurs because of some flaw, some imperfection, were it not for whose existence, those people who have passed away would be still alive. Such imperfection is not only moral but physical, depending on the type of food one feeds one's structure. Man's disobedience to Jah is what leads to death.

Stephen reminded me of the incident in which I had taken Brother Saasi to one of the university doctors in 1975 with a letter of introduction. The doctor sent him for a blood test, but when Saasi saw the equipment he panicked and ran. Stephen, who considered Saasi's behavior ingratitude to someone who had tried to help, refused to allow him back into his house. Rather than submit to the blood test, Saasi sought refuge with another *I*dren, who, on getting the full story from Stephen, also refused him shelter. Saasi eventually betook himself to the country and died there. According to Stephen, disobedience killed him.

Stephen had other examples: the Dread, who, objecting to Stephen's bringing a white man among the brethren in May 1988, took up a rock to strike Stephen in the head; and Tommy, who beat up Ras Tigo and left with Tigo's wife. Both were struck dead by the power of Jah. They were disobedient to the ways of Jah Rastafari.

The mere fact that Stephen admits that there are two kinds of Rastafari is indication enough of an unorthodox trend in the movement. Bongo Floyd reflects this unorthodoxy. "When you die it is Christ that take the life. You die in Christ. When they say you live, is because of your works. Is your good works that make you live forever. To die mean that you are dead and forgotten; and you leave no example for others to follow." Interestingly, Floyd used the name "Christ," rather than Jah or even Jesos. "To die mean that you are dead and forgotten" is a position not far removed from that which understands the meaning of the ancestors.

10. Rastafari and the Wider World

On a trip to Washington, D.C., a delegation of Nyabinghi Elders, including two women, is interviewed by Alona Wartofsky, a female journalist, for a feature story in the *Washington (D.C.) City Paper* (Sept. 15–21, 1989). Near the end of her story she writes: "For me, the aspect of Rastafarian lifestyle hardest to understand is the status of women, who are known as daughters or sistren. Although women perform with men, during our interview-cum-reasoning the two women sit quietly." Why? she asks. One of the men sums up the situation thus: "a woman is the minister of home affairs and health, the husband the minister of foreign affairs and defense." Then they invite Wartofsky to ask the sisters anything. With some prompting Sister Pam outlines the role of Rasta women. "The daughter must obey the king-man and the daughter must wear what the king-man says . . . no makeup. The daughter's head must cover and the daughter have a time to stay far from the king-man when we have a monthly period . . . and must not cook for the king-man." The elders are amused at Wartofsky's dismay. They ask whether she walks around Washington during her period. "Seven pairs of eyes bore into me as I decide against reasoning on the utility of tampons." Had Wartofsky known how unprecedented it was for a woman to take up her place alongside males as an official representative of the Nyabinghi House of Jah Rastafari, she might have expressed wonder at the change rather than shock at the patriarchy. Since the main research for this study was carried out in the 1970s, some further remarkable developments have been taking place among the Rastafari. Wartofsky's story captures two of them: the changing role of the woman in and the internationalization of the Rastafari movement.

The Changing Role of Woman

Up to the mid-1970s the ritually enforced subordination of the Rastafari woman to her Rastafari "king man" precluded any role outside of the domestic sphere. She took no part in public reasoning, seldom made the trip to a celebration, could never acquire the status of elder of the house, covered her locks from public scrutiny, observed menstrual taboos, and so forth. Now all this has been changing.

The one hundredth Anniversary of the birth of Jamaica's national hero Marcus Garvey on August 17, 1987 was recognized officially by the Jamaican government. The Ethiopian International Unification Committee led by Ras Michael Lorne, a Dreadlocks Rastafari lawyer, in association with the Nyabinghi House of Rastafari, held a rally in the Half-Way-Tree Park in Kingston, at which prominent elders such as Wato were active participants. The nonsectarian nature of the rally was underscored by the success in getting a Bobo who happened by to say a few words. There were no fewer than twenty speakers, including representatives from abroad.

During the speeches, a female journalist protested to Lorne that no Rastawoman had spoken or was scheduled to speak. He promised to correct this "oversight," and within twenty minutes Maa Ashanti was called upon and delivered a well-received speech from the platform. Such a manifestation was unheard of in the 1970s.

At Rastafari celebrations today, female Rastafari are noticeably present, and in large numbers. Most are young and of child-bearing age, and their main role is looking after the children. In the evenings they participate in the chanting and dancing, but maintain a symbolic distance by dancing behind rather than side by side with the males. The genesis of this gender-related development is from two directions: (a) externally derived influences and

(b) internally propelled struggle and accommodation. These two directions are treated differently only for the sake of convenience. In actual fact it is impossible to separate them completely.

External influences

Issue 94, September 1985, of *Rasta Voice,* a magazine published by Ras Historian, carried the following message by "Daughter Loi."

African women are in double jeopardy
My black brothers, your black sisters are not your enemy. Your black sisters are not a threat to your masculinity.
In this system she is in double jeopardy.
Just as the white man system provide for the use, abuse and refuse of the black race, so too is the system of the black man on black woman. At this point-in-time black sisters are forced to recognise their role in the black brethren scheme of things to be one of inferiority. She now see herself at the mercy of black men who, unfortunately have inherited much of the white man attitudes. Worst of which is now manifested in the use, abuse and refuse of black sisters. For black sisters who recognise themselves to be assets to our liberation struggle, the role of inferiority is unacceptable.
In the quest for the liberation and oneness of our people, the black man must discontinue the practice of subordination of black sisters, and come to grip with the facts; we are just as needed as the brothers in the struggle for liberation and continuous prosperity of the black race.

The Rastafari woman is becoming increasingly conscious of and opposed to her inferior status within the movement. Daughter Loi uses the Marxist paradigm of the double oppression of women to score the point that black (including Rastafari) women are op-pressed first as blacks and secondly as women. She challenges the meaningfulness of black liberation if at the same time black broth-ers oppress their black sisters. Her call is for equality.

The year 1985 marked the end of the United Nations Decade of Women, ten eventful years that brought about dramatic and quali-tatively new changes in the consciousness, organization, and politi-cal role of Jamaican women. International Women's Day came to be celebrated as an annual national event recognized by govern-ment and by all political parties and interest groups. Many organi-zations of women sprang up or were strengthened over the decade, and today the most important of these have joined together across political and ideological boundaries to form the Association of

Women's Organizations of Jamaica. Their effectiveness may be recognized by their success in winning legal sanction for maternity leave with pay in 1980; and again in 1985 when they forced the government to replace the male minister in charge of Women's Affairs as head of an official delegation of women to the End of Decade Conference in Nairobi. In both struggles Party women took public positions opposed to governments formed by their parties. These developments could not but exert a powerful influence on men and women throughout the society, sharpening the awareness of many, changing the outlook of some, and making possible significant changes in Rastafari practice if not ideology.

One of the women's organizations formed by working-class women in the 1970s and specializing in drama-in-education is Sistren Theatre Collective. Commissioned by Sistren, Imani Tafari Ama, a Dreadlocks Rastafari, conducted some original research on gender relations among the Rastafari. Her subjects comprised eighty Dreadlocks, evenly distributed between genders and spanning the major groupings, including the Nyabinghi House, the Twelve Tribes of Israel, and the Bobo. The research elicited separate views from males and females on four topics: domestic roles, sexuality, self-image, and ideology.

In the sphere of domestic roles, taking care of children turns out to be the greatest and most consistent feature of a Rastawoman's life, despite the expectation that the Rastaman will shoulder half the burden. In addition, many women are breadwinners. Most vexing is the tendency of their men to be involved with other, non-Rastafari women. For their part, the men say they fall short of the ideal notion of fatherhood, mainly because "secret polygamy" prevents them from spending adequate time with their children.

The Sistren research laid bare the underlying tensions in Rastafari sexuality over the recreational and procreational aspects of sexual intercourse. Some insist on a contraceptive method or device (rhythm or condom), others suffer having children, while still others become celibate rather than risk a pregnancy. Particularly controversial is the issue of polygamy. Those Rasta sisters who agree with the practice do so conditionally—it must not be at their own expense, emotionally or financially, and they must have a say in the selection of the second wife. Others were unconditionally opposed to the practice. On the issue of menstruation, the views were fairly uniform and depicted it not a period of uncleanness, but as a time when a woman is "under the influence and control of extensive powers" that are potentially dangerous to all males above seven years old and transmissible into food through her vibrations. Hence she should not cook. For their part the males were all in favor of polygamy but felt it should not be indulged purely on the basis of self-gratification; they felt that a sound economic base was an important precondition.

Turning to their own self-image, the women expressed resentment at the Rasta male opposition to their self-expression, the use of the title "Daughter," and the insistence on covering their locks. On this last concern, however, the female elders sharply disagreed: uncovering is "taking the seriousness out of one of the highest principles cherished by Rastafari." The male positions on these issues were surprisingly open, if somewhat contradictory. They were against any limits being placed on the Rastawoman's involvement in public life, but at the same time defined her role as essentially domestic.

On the fourth issue, ideology, whereas the males were most firm in defense of the authority of the Bible, the females unhesitatingly blamed the negative biblical sources for the imposition of an inferior status on them. This system of authority, they said, required sorting out.

The fact that the research was undertaken is itself significant. It belies the numerical growth of women in the movement since the 1970s. Particularly remarkable is the similarity between the Rastafari and the non-Rastafari populations on a number of counts: multiple partnerships by males; socialization of children by females; domestic work by women (except abstention from cooking by Rastafari women during their menstrual flow); recognition of the recreational aspect of sex; use of contraceptives. This last practice is the most remarkable of all, because of the well-known Dreadlocks opposition to birth control, which they used to call a "plan to kill off black people."

The research also brought out regional differences among the Rastafari, which future studies of the movement need to be sensitive to. The deep rural sisters are alleged to harbor stronger feelings of their own inferiority than are their urbanized sisters; they view the male as almost if not equal to Jah. The Montego Bay brethren and sistren seemed on the whole more liberal than their Kingston colleagues, possibly because they are further removed from the seat of orthodoxy. On the other hand, they seemed less tolerant of white consorts, Rasta and non-Rasta, no doubt because of the Rent-a-Dread phenomenon in tourism zones like Montego Bay.

The Internal Process

In an early reflection on the status of the Rasta-woman Sister Ilaloo (*Yards Roots*, Apr./May 1981, 5–7) offers what she believes to be the reason for the internally motivated changes in the movement. Traditionally, she explains, there was no such person as a Rastawoman, but a Rastaman woman, a girl taken from outside the movement and fashioned into the Rastaman's ways (Carole Yawney [1983] calls this process "Growing a Daughter"). But since the 1970s, women have been coming into the movement "independently of any man" and this has posed problems for the Rastaman.

If the Rastaman has problems in terms of changing power relationships, the Rastawoman also faces problems in terms of authorization of the new discourse. On what source or sources must she base her ideas of rejection of old traditions and calls for the formulation of new practices and modes of relationship? What should be her responsibility as Rastafari and as woman, and which must come first? Standing at the doorway between Babylon and Zion, which way should she set her face? Is she who has been quarantined now in danger of infecting Rastafari by her rejection of ritual contamination? Debate around these issues has begun, according to Yawney (1987), at the national level in Jamaica and among the Rastafari diaspora. Renee Romano and Elliott Leib's video *Rastafari: Conversations Concerning Women*, which allows Rastawomen to express their views, shows "that they are quite dissimilar in their attitudes toward and reactions to male-defined cultural norms, (e.g., restrictions surrounding menstruation, male dominated speaking roles/abilities, the spiritual subordination of women)" (Homiak 1986, 13). The sistren report found the same divergence of views.

I am not certain if Ilaloo represents a trend, but in her view the authority of the Bible has to be superseded. She grounds her position on the *over*standing that because His Majesty is the returned messiah the prophecies have been fulfilled "and now we are dealing with a whole other dispensation and we are building the laws which applies [*sic*]" (*Yard Roots*, Apr./May 1981, 5). On the face of it this position is quite radical, but building new laws may be nothing more than sanctioning Rastafari accommodation to the more radical ideas and practices of society. If that is so, what then becomes of the Rastafari as separate and chosen?

The polar opposite position would be that of Sister P. and Sister Bernie who "support the [Rastafari] practice of polygamy on cultural grounds" (Yawney 1987, 195), and that of the two elder sisters on the Washington delegation.

Maureen Rowe (1980) occupies the middle ground in the debate. Basically accepting the fact that the Rastafari is a patriarchal movement, she presents the positive side of the Rastaman's gender relationship: the Rastaman's respect for the Rastawoman, symbolized in the honorific titles he has for her. This position is not new, but it accentuates the positive that is generally overlooked. More than any other, this position approximates the attitude toward woman in Jamaican peasant culture, an attitude whose ambivalence is in practice as real as it is ideological. It is, within the current Rastafari context the most compelling position, for it allows the acceptance without polarization of significant if only symbolic change such as that noted by Sister Eleanor Wint (*Sistren Newsletter* 11 (2), 1989, 9): "The uncovered locks is another change, although always properly fixed up, wrapped up on itself or without a cloth so its [*sic*] not sticking out like a mad-women [*sic*]. One time we could never put our foot out the gate without our head being completely covered." Female public display of dreadlocks is now socially acceptable, provided, as Sister Eleanor Wint implies, it recognizes the shifting boundaries between being in society, "properly fixed up," and being out, the display of the derelict and insane.

According to Wato, "once upon a time the daata-dem used to be fearful, but now they are coming forward." By this he clearly implied that no longer are women reproved by males and that Dreads are more tolerant. Their increased presence, he said, was a sign of the growth of the house and a manifestation of Jah Rastafari. Bongo Stephen went even further and conceded to the woman greater skill than the man in organizing such things as fund-raising and certain aspects of the recent delegation abroad.

There was no better symbol of the growing demand among Rastafari women for equality and of the growing accommodation among Rastafari brethren to female equality than the entry of a young Dreadlocks woman with a rod, the symbol of male authority, into the Black Rock tabernacle where the nyabinghi marking His Majesty's Birthday was being held in July of 1988. She took up a position behind the males and there danced with the rod held firmly in her hand. No man objected; no man seemed to care.

Internationalization of Rastafari

Ken Bilby (1983) correctly attributes the overseas stage in the recent development of the Rastafari movement to two factors: migration of Jamaicans and the "international trade in vinyl." Whereas migration has resulted in centers of Rastafari presence in Canada and Britain, the general influence of reggae is responsible for the spread of Rasta to the African continent, Europe, Japan, Australia, New Zealand, and other parts of the world. These two factors have merged in some countries.

Most First World scholars who have written on the Rastafari have based their studies on research conducted in Jamaica. With the exception of scholars who have conducted research in Britain, few have examined the movement elsewhere in the industrialized world.[1] One reason for this lag I believe is that in the past Rastafari abroad were Jamaican migrants or children of Caribbean migrants. Only recently has Rastafari begun to take root among nationals. What follows focuses on Rastafari's development in the United States.

The Role of Migration

In chapter 1, reference was made to the migration of Jamaicans to parts of Central America, Cuba, and the United States up to

1. Pieter Buiks's study (1981) is available only in Dutch. Stephenson's study (1987), mentioned later, is the only study I know of in the United States that is based on Rastas in that country. Currently, Randal Hepner is studying the movement in Brooklyn, New York (personal communication), while Neil Savishinsky has recently completed his fieldwork studying Rastafari in Africa (personal communication), both for doctoral dissertations.

the Second World War. Afterward, external migration was first directed to Britain. Between 1953 and 1962 when that country changed its immigration laws, approximately 175,000 Jamaicans from town and country boarded the banana boats destined for London, Liverpool, and other British ports. It was the children of these immigrants and of other migrants from other Caribbean islands whose crisis of identity found resolution in Rastafari.

Canada became the next destination, starting in the mid-1960s. Jamaicans settled mainly in Toronto and Montreal. However, since the 1970s the United States has been absorbing the overwhelming majority of the 20,000 Jamaicans migrating annually. These figures refer only to those who migrate legally, and do not reflect the underground movement of illegal immigrants, who acquire bogus visas or who defect as migrant farmworkers and visitors, even after the 1988 amnesty granted by the United States. The main host cities are those on the eastern seaboard (from Boston to Miami), Houston, and the cities of California. There the pride that Rastafari enjoyed in Jamaica for their proverbial nonviolence, integrity, and honesty was overshadowed by the media perception of them as being associated with crime. This was most unfortunate and with competent research into the movement could have been avoided, for in Jamaica of the 1970s no such confusion arose, because there it was recognized that the youths, including criminals, had taken over the symbols of Rastafari but not the religion.

From the mid-1960s through to the 1970s in Jamaica, Rastafari captured the minds of the urban youth (Chevannes 1981). All the main Rasta symbols—colors, language, food ways, and, for those independent of parents, hair—became sources of identity for the youth. To reach these youths, one had to enter Rastafari discourse, which Michael Manley did through the symbol of the rod, and he won a handsome victory mainly because of the youth vote (Stone 1974).[2]

Had Jamaican politics remained at the level of symbolism, not much harm would have been done. However, starting in the 1960s,

2. Edward Seaga, a leader in the ruling, center-right Jamaica Labour Party who understood well the importance of symbols, paraded his "rod," denouncing the other as stolen. Adam Kuper (1976) was quite right in noting the seriousness behind this seemingly amusing battle over symbols. See also Olive Senior (1972).

the political system in Kingston's inner-city areas became paramilitarized, as gangs of youths were recruited and armed with guns to capture or to defend political strongholds or both. By the mid-1970s, political violence had escalated to a level unprecedented in the history of the country. In 1980 alone, after a general election was called, more than nine hundred people, most of them youths, were killed, the victims of "partisan politricks".[3] During this period many of these youths began to take up residence in the United States, some to escape reprisals, others to arrange for the smuggling of arms back to Jamaica. In the aftermath of the "war" they were joined by many of the vanquished youths who fled the mopping-up operations carried out by the Jamaican security forces. The victors too were not long in following, as the economic recession in Jamaica emptied the pork barrel and pushed many of them into the international cocaine trade. Thus, by the early 1980s, the United States had become a mecca of boundless opportunity for some of Jamaica's most wanted outlaws. They took with them not only the fearlessness of seasoned gunmen and a high level of organization but also the main trappings of Rasta symbols that were all part of the youth culture up to the beginning of the 1980s—the dreadlocks, Rasta colors, I-talk, and the hatred of Babylon. What they could not take, because they did not have them, were Rastafari religious values. These outlaws were as far from the Rastafari most Jamaicans know and respect as the parasitic group of hustlers described in chapter 7 were from the other Dreadlocks who had likewise journeyed to Westmoreland to chant praises to Jah at their binghi.

Up to this time, the only thing most Americans knew of the Rastafari, if anything at all, was related to reggae king Bob Marley and other exponents of this new music. In 1979, however, members of the Coptic Church based in Miami (not to be confused with the Judah-Coptics) received national publicity following a court action that sought to declare them a public nuisance. CBS screened a documentary on the group in its program *60 Minutes*, hosted by

3. From the popular poem of the late Michael Smith, "Mi seh mi kyaan believe it." Mikey became the tragic victim of the same "partisan politics" he denounced, when he was identified by political thugs and stoned to death near the constituency headquarters of one of the parties in Stony Hill.

Dan Rather, in which the Coptics defended their use of ganja as a sacrament. The Coptics were not well known in Jamaica until the late 1970s. Indeed, during my fieldwork in 1974, I found a small secretive group of them on Drummond Street in Kingston. The offshoot of a small sect founded in the Papine-August Town area of Kingston by a man known as Brother Lover, they held Marcus Garvey, rather than Haile Selassie, to be the true Rastafari and as a consequence were hostile to the Dreadlocks, whom they would ridicule as "rope head." They themselves did not wear dreadlocks, and they further emphasized their sectarian stance by the spelling of God as "Goud" and Love as "Louv." Suspicious of strangers, they used to take turns disappearing into "the woods" of St. Ann to plant the herbs for export. When therefore the church went fully public a few years later, it was as the owner of vast tracts of land in the parish of St. Thomas, several large trailer trucks, and a supermarket outlet in Kingston that provided cheaper prices on vegetables, fruits, and household articles. They were widely believed at the time to have been a conduit for the illegal importation of guns, though this was never established.

It was as drug addicts, unfortunately, that the Rastafari were first introduced to the American law enforcement establishment and through it to the print and electronic media. When CBS screened a second documentary in December 1980, Dan Rather raised two concerns with Professor Rex Nettleford, one that Rastafari were part of the "Cuban-Soviet axis," and the other that the movement "represents a large criminal element." Nettleford's emphatic denial obviously had little effect. Thus by the time Jamaican posses, cited by some as the most vicious organizations ever seen in the American criminal world, began to control the drug trade in the northeastern United States, Rastafari was already confirmed in the minds of many as a new and dangerous sect. This was most unfortunate because the essential attributes of Rastafari as a spiritual and cultural movement found themselves struggling like wheat among tares.

Added to this criminal image was the "strange" appearance of the dreadlocks. Americans, who had for centuries been used to Africans cropping their hair short and who had just got over the threat of cultural independence represented in the "Afro" and "bush" hairstyles, were now confronted with yet another hair statement by blacks: a symbolically aggressive profusion of kinks. Dreadlocks were not only strange (even to African-Americans); they were intimidating as well.

These were the reasons why Edward Lawson was "detained and questioned by police 15 times during a two-year period while walking or hitchhiking in predominantly white areas of San Diego" (*Washington [D.C.] Post*, July 6, 1983, 1). These were also the reasons why Jack Anderson's first column on the Rastafari was not about Rastafari culture or beliefs but about the fear of "Rastafarian Violence." Anderson basically relayed to his readership sections of a secret report, circulated by the New York City Police Department among its officers, that spoke of menacing, "criminal elements of the Rastafarian religious sect," trained by Cuba in guerilla warfare and Marxism and having links to then former Prime Minister Michael Manley (*Washington [D.C.] Post*, June 29, 1983, 11).

The "secret report" itself was a professional product based on research conducted in both New York and Jamaica. Its author understood very clearly the religious character of the Rastafari, their raison d'être, and certain important aspects of Rastafari beliefs, and cautioned against viewing all Rastas as criminals. Nevertheless, in addition to its many inaccuracies, such as the finding that "an important and extremely complex set of ideas cluster around reincarnation"[4] —reincarnation is not as central a concept as the report alleges—the report had a major flaw: it confused Rastafari beliefs with what were in fact aspects of the street culture of the ghetto youth. In effect the report isolated Rastafari as the ideological underpinning of criminality among the Jamaican immigrants, altogether missing the distinction between ideas originating in Rastafari and ideas originating in the youth subculture. And this flaw unfortunately was the main source of the distorted communication transmitted to the American public about Rastafari—needlessly, because in Jamaica no such distortion exists, despite the longstanding animosity between Rastafari and the police (or "Babylon").

4. *Caribbean Review* 14 (1), Winter 1985, 12. The journal's editors in publishing the report mentioned that background material had been written from as early as 1977, a date that coincides with the beginning of the influx of Jamaican gunmen.

No doubt this report of the New York Police was shared with police departments in other cities, for it included "information that criminal Rastafarians have plans to assassinate law enforcement officials in this country." Two years earlier in October 1981 a New York City police officer had been shot five times by a Jamaican "suspected of having drug dealings with the Rastafarians" (*New York Times,* Oct. 12, 1981, B3). Now, it was alleged, police officials were to be targeted. The Houston police department in fact was circulating a memorandum in November 1982 advising its officers to be on the lookout for Rastafarians, who it said were known in New York to be organized criminals.

As it was, police in other cities had already formed their own false impression of Rastafari. In Washington the murder of a young Jamaican informer working with the Immigration and Naturalization Services (INS) was attributed to "members of a West Indian religious cult" (*Washington Post,* Jan. 27, 1980, 1), on whom he had passed information. The story alleged that the boy's neighbors and friends were living in fear "that the Rastafarians will return." This misperception linking Rastafari to crime was later to embarrass the Washington Police when its Operation Caribbean Cruise netted only twenty-eight arrests on drug charges, firearm violations, and fugitive charges (*Washington Post,* July 3, 1986, D3). Black policemen had been kept out of the planning.

In Philadelphia, the *Philadelphia Inquirer* of September 27, 1981, carried on its front page the story of a Rastaman "shot fatally in the head, apparently by wolves in sheepskin" in the Main Line area of the city. Experts, the article said, painted a scenario that began with "isolated crimes among the Rastafarians themselves—shoot-outs, robberies, assaults" that before long take on organized proportions, with more killings, even of innocent bystanders. The experts pointed to the situation in Brooklyn, where in 1980 alone "there were more than 25 homicides involving the Rastafarian community in Flatbush."

And in Boston in September 1981 a "self-styled 'general' in a Jamaican cult" was arrested for shooting an employee of the *Boston Globe* fifteen months before (*Boston Herald American,* Sept. 9, 1981, 1). The employee was permanently paralyzed below the waist. Searching for possible motives, one report alleged that he was simply trying out the gun he had just bought. From the pictures of his arrest, the suspect did not appear to be wearing dreadlocks, but, according to the *Herald* he was "allegedly a member of a violent sect of cultists who loosely associate themselves with Rastafarians" (*Boston Herald American,* A7).

As the years wore on, however, verbal association of Rastafari with criminality declined in frequency, though the pictoral association remained. *U.S. News and World Report* (Jan. 18, 1988, 29ff.), for example, carried a feature story on the developing interethnic and transnational cooperation and ties among criminal gangs. In discussing the Jamaican posses, though no mention was made of Rastafari, three of the four gang members whose pictures were reproduced were young Dreadlocks. The same trend was apparent in *Newsweek.* The issue of March 28, 1988, reported that posse gunmen preferred shooting their victims in public, particularly at reggae clubs, but made no mention of Rastafari. And in the issue of October 24, the same year, in reporting the arrest of over two hundred members of the Shower posse during Operation Rum Punch II, carried out in twenty states by the U.S. Bureau of Alcohol, Tobacco and Firearms, the word *Rastafari* did not appear even once, but in the photograph one of the suspects held wore below shoulder-length dreadlocks.

I believe that one reason for this shift in the way Rastafari was being portrayed in the American media was the slow but increasing recognition the movement had begun to gain as a spiritual force in the United States itself. For example, Hazel Myers, in response to Jack Anderson's statement that their dreadlocks were the identifiable mark of the criminal Rastas, wrote that "I and several of my associates wear our hair in the dreadlock hairstyle . . . as a symbol of pride in our heritage" (*Washington Post,* July 3, 1983). Articles were already appearing, if not sympathetic to the Rastafarian outlook, then certainly of more objective quality. One article in the *Atlanta Journal and Constitution* (Mar. 18, 1984) examined how Rastafarians, "most of them Jamaicans but also including a few Americans," were coping under the Marxist regime of Mengistu Haile Miriam. In 1986 the celebrated Peruvian writer Mario Vargas Llosa in the widely read *New York Times Magazine* (February 16) told the story of his son's conversion to Rastafari while studying in England and of his own shock and amazement at the discovery while attending the Berlin Film Festival as a member of the panel of judges in 1984. And in 1987, Nikke Finke, staff writer of the *Los Angeles Times,* wrote two sympathetic articles, one introducing readers to the origins, beliefs, and practices of the Rastafari, the other explaining why white middle-class adolescents in the eastern United States as well as in southern California were taking to it. Because of its similarities to the hippie movement of the 1960s, Finke argued, most adults were not much concerned about police-based newspaper reports linking Rastas to violent and drug-related crimes and were instead seeing its adoption as a phase.

Further proof of the shift in law enforcement attitudes were certain court rulings that had the effect of recognizing Rastafari as a bona fide religion. In 1990 the U.S. Supreme Court upheld a 1986 ruling by the New York State Appeal Court "that New York State prison officials could not constitutionally require inmates who adhere to the Rastafarian religion to cut their hair" (*New York Times National,* Oct. 10, 1990, A19). In this manner Alfredo Lewis, who had not cut his now four-foot-long dreadlocks for twenty years, won historic recognition in a legal battle lasting several years and exhausting the legal system of the United States. Imprisoned Rastafari were not so fortunate over the kind of foods they ate; a U.S. district judge dismissed a motion filed by two Rastafari prisoners in Virginia that their rights of freedom of religion were infringed "when they were given food with preservatives, salt, artificial flavoring and additives" (*Jet,* Aug. 3, 1987, 12). I do not know whether this decision was being appealed. The ban on the use of marijuana, of course, has not been tested.

Articles and court actions such as those just cited were helpful in producing the shift in attitude. However, the main kudos must go to the powerful influence of reggae.

Reggae

Peter Lee began a warm memorial tribute to Bob Marley by citing the love for Marley's music as the common bond linking a blues guitarist in Mississippi, a black South African soldier serving in Namibia, a young accordion player in a South African township, and a group of Australians, New Zealanders, and Scotsmen in London (*Guitar Player,* May 1991, 82).

Robert Nesta Marley, O.M.,[5] did more than any other person or group to introduce Rastafari, reggae, and Jamaica to the rest of the world. Even in death his influence is still being felt. Long before Bob had become an international star with his *Catch a Fire* and *Natty Dread* albums, he was easily the most popular reggae composer and singer in Jamaica, whose songs were memorized and sung as people jammed to them, for they echoed the way Jamaicans felt then about themselves and their society. As Alice Walker perceptively wrote, he not only "loved Jamaica and loved Jamaicans and loved *being* a Jamaican, . . . but . . . knew it was not meant to limit itself . . . to an island of any sort" (*Mother Jones,* Dec. 1986, 43–44). After being shot in 1976 Bob left Jamaica. For the next four years he virtually toured the world, taking his music and message to its four corners: Europe, the Americas, Asia, and, of course, Africa. Those final years of Robert Nesta Marley may yet prove to be the most decisive turning point in the history of Rastafari movement, and in future decades could well be regarded as the Rasta version of Paul's decision to preach to gentiles.

Because the United States is the single largest market in the world of popular music, successfully penetrating the U.S. market is the goal of every artist aspiring to international recognition. Bob Marley was no exception. When news of his cancer broke out, he had only just begun his second tour of the United States with a tour de force performance before a capacity crowd at the Madison Square Gardens in New York City, rated by his biographer Timothy White as the event "that could prove to be a turning point for commercial recognition of reggae in this country" (*Rolling Stone,* June 25, 1981, 25). That was his legacy.

His death in 1981 was carried by all the major newspapers and magazines in the United States, where he was the subject of many tributes. By 1983, he was being immortalized alongside other black heroes in "This Week in Black History" (*Jet,* May 16 1983). But

5. Order of Merit, the third highest national honor, behind National Hero (awarded to seven Jamaicans, four from the eighteenth and nineteenth centuries and three from the twentieth, including Marcus Garvey) and Order of the Nation (reserved for Governors General).

Marley was just as compelling in death as in life. In the December 1986 article cited earlier, Alice Walker describes how she first really discovered and became transfixed by his music, while writing the screenplay for her novel *The Color Purple*. "It was as if there had been a great and gorgeous light on all over the world, and some-how I'd missed it" (44). Then followed her transformation—"I felt my own dreadlocks begin to grow"—climaxed by a pilgrimage with her family, "as neophyte Rastas," to the mausoleum shrine of this great prophet, there to experience her own redemption. Bob Marley having blazed the trail, other stars followed, burning the message of Rastafari through the power of reggae music—Peter Tosh, Third World, Black Uhuru, Sly and Robbie, Pablo Moses. Non-Jamaican reggae groups like Steel Pulse and UB40 became living testimony to the association between being exponents of reggae and adopting the dreadlocks.

Through the music itself many came in touch with what Isaac Fergusson (*Essence*, Nov. 1982, 18) called "a political and spiritual force in today's music." One such person was Gary Himelfarb, a Jew, who fell in love with reggae as early as 1972 and spent the next few years building up an enormous collection of several thousand albums. Himelfarb, with full grown beard and shoulder-length dreadlocks, made his pilgrimage to Jamaica in 1977 and there spent three months walking the island and absorbing its culture. Returning home to Washington, D.C., and adopting the radio persona name "Dr. Dread," he started a Sunday night reggae show on WHFS-FM called "The Night of the Living Dread" that became a major success. In 1981 he gave up the show to launch his own RAS label, by 1987 a million-dollar business that handled Jamaican reggae artists. "'A lot of the beliefs and principles of the Rastafari are the same as my beliefs,' he says. Is Himelfarb, then, a Rasta? 'Yeah, to a degree'" (*City Paper*, June 12, 1987).

Dr. Dread's was not the only reggae radio show, of course. Doug Wendt, in an article entitled "Reggae in Crisis" (*Reggae and African Beat* 6 (4), 1987, 9-11, 47), bemoaned the fact that certain negative developmens in the music had forced the resignation of Roger Steffens from his "Reggae Beat" show on KCRW and the cancel-lation of Roger and Hank Holmes's "Reggae Beat International" heard on over 130 radio stations. The developments referred to were the use of reggae as a front for laundering drug money, the instant-star complex of some reggae artists, and the get-rich-quick attitude on the part of others. Following Wendt's argument, one would have to conclude that reggae artists were their own enemies. Another writer argued that the prejudice of American radio, particularly African-American radio, imposed the barriers (*Variety*, July 1988, 58). At any rate, whether the Jamaican reggae artist or American radio, or both were to be blamed, reggae continued to attract an audience in America.

An important symbol and expression of the triumph of reggae was, and still is, the annual event since 1978 known as Reggae Sunsplash. Until 1993 when its venue was changed to Kingston, Sunsplash was held in Montego Bay for a week during the month of August at what has since 1981 become the Bob Marley Centre for the Performing Arts. It has been attracting large followings of reggae aficionados and visitors from all over the world, among them "Japanese kids with corn rows and WASPafarians from the United States" (*Washington Post*, Aug. 25, 191, G8). Sunsplash is followed closely by most reggae and music magazines in the music capitals of the world, and it too has evolved with an international character, attracting artists from Europe and Africa. Versions of Reggae Sunsplash have been exported to California and Japan. Zambian Rastafarians and reggae artists and fans have been staging their own Sunsplash outside Lusaka every September since 1990. In this respect, mention should be made of the important role that Caribbean festivals hosted by Caribbean immigrants in some of the major cities on the east coast have played in promoting reggae music and Rastafari lifestyle: the Cambridge River Festival in Boston, the African Street Festival in Brooklyn, New York, and the Annual Reggae Festival in Washington, D.C., to name a few.

A sign of the native growth of Rastafari in the United States has been the rise of local American reggae bands and reggae artists. Healin' of the Nations and Jah Ma Roots, both based in Boston, See-I and Babylon Warriors, based in Washington, D.C., and Riddim Section, Roots Reggae, now based in southern California, not only have adopted names drawn from Rastafari, but most members are Rastafari. Founded by the Steele brothers, Jah Rootz and Zbo, See-I creates music that challenges people "to take a righteous stand until they see the good and perfect coming of JAH RASTAFARI" (undated brochure). All the members of the American punk group, Bad Brains, are "devout Rastafarians" (*Guitar Player,* July 1990, 60). Dr. Know, the leader of the band, describes their music as "'Jah rock'—it's rock and roll, and Jah is the influence" (60).

Bad Brains' music is one example of crossover reggae, which some reggae specialists argue was necessary for reggae to make it in the United States, and they point to Peter Tosh's fusion with rock as an example. In this way white groups like Blondie and the Police have staked their claim as reggae bands. But attempts have also been made to fuse reggae with jazz, some of them successful, some not, according to Norman Weinstein (*Down Beat,* Mar. 1987, 83). What makes trumpeter Leo Smith the most successful, argues Weinstein, is that Smith is "an active believer in the faith of Rastafarianism, [and he] brings this spiritual perspective directly into the heart of his recent compositions." Smith is "dreader than dread," saxaphonist Oliver Lake "less than dread," and others like guitarist Kuzumi Watanabe and trumpeter Lester Bowie "dreadful" variations between. The point I wish to make is not who is better than whom, but that all are experimenting with the vitality of reggae and spiritual force of Rastafari.

To summarize, reggae music has been a powerful medium of communicating the message and spirit of Rastafari in North America, succeeding in neutralizing the negative impact of the movement's misperceived association with crime and violence. The consequences are many. First, not since Marcus Garvey have African-Americans and their African-Jamaican siblings found such common ground. Dera Tomkins does not disguise the fact that she is an American, but as a Rastafarian she "frequently speaks out for [Washington] D.C.'s Caribbean community" (*City Paper,* June 12, 1987). In Rastafari she has found "a true black identity" (*Washington Post,* Feb. 23, 1986, A18). In California, where Edward Stephenson conducted doctoral work in which he interviewed sixty Rastafarians from Santa Cruz, Oakland, and Los Angeles, the theme of identity was voiced by many of the African-American members: "I got involved in Rasta when I realized the amount of years that I did not have this certain sense of identity"

(Stephenson 1987, 71); or "Here in America . . . we don't identify with our roots" (87).

But more than Garvey, Rastafari in the United States has found common ground also with white Americans. Deborah Davis (*Everybody's Magazine,* Aug. 1983) tells the story of five whites, including herself, who became Rastafari. They were all born into families that instilled in them tolerance, compassion, and a sense of justice, so that they grew up exposed to other races and ethnic groups. Having become Rasta, through the combined influences of Bob Marley, reggae, and friends, they now feel a sense of being touched and chosen by Jah, and have found an "alternative way of living." Unhappily for many parents of the "Blond Rastas" from California to Connecticut, Rastafari does not appear to be a passing phase for their children. Many who have been touched by Rastafari, even though they later shed their locks, are said to retain the inner sense of harmony and oneness with God and nature the teaching propounds. Sensing this, American Rastas have quietly enforced their own understanding of the movement's guiding philosophy. For example, Healin' of the Nations reggae band used to call itself "Healin' of the Nation." The pluralizing of the word *nation* reveals an understanding that passes beyond a narrow interpretation of the doctrine of black supremacy. Similarly, See-I speaks of their music heralding the day "for all of Jah Children—red, yellow, black, white, and brown—to realize Jah made us all and we ALL are members of HIS UNIVERSAL FAMILY."

The proud wearing of dreadlocks by many African-Americans, not necessarily accompanied by other teachings of Rastafari, is yet another manifestation of the rootedness of the movement. To be sure, there is the faddish aspect to wearing the locks—"Fashion Dread," to borrow Gregory Stephens phrase (*Whole Earth Review,* Summer 1988, 60)—but wearing them also embodies spiritual recognition. I have already made reference to the letter of *Washington Post* reader Hazel Myers. Ken Jones (*Essence,* Oct. 1985, 8), a journalist, spent two years grappling with the "spiritual, political and pragmatic realities" of growing dreadlocks, before deciding to grow them himself. He was first drawn by Rastafari musicians and artists, whose "Pan-African messages and flying locks radiated an energy unlike any I'd ever witnessed. . . . Theirs was the walk of Black spirits reaching back to Africa." Undaunted by the negative reaction of his peers and his mother's disdain, "[o]nce I started to dread I knew there was no turning back." His dreadlocks are not "some whimsical eccentricity . . . here today and gone tomorrow." They are, he says, "the manifestation of the spirit of a Triumphant God within me." Only the most cynical would dismiss testimonies like this. Kelly Dalton, an elementary school student wrote to the *Philadelphia Inquirer* and inquired, "when did people first start putting their hair in dreadlocks?" The reply of the "Q and A" columnist was itself instructive. Noting that dreadlocks became common after Selassie was crowned emperor in 1930—an error I hope this book has corrected—the columnist said, "The dreadlocks are a symbol of humans in their natural state." With this for an answer Kelly Dalton is unlikely to become a fashion Dread.

So far I have been discussing the impact of migration and reggae music on the development of Rastafari in the United States. These two factors remain, as Bilby (1983) observed, the principal causes for it. However, I wish to cite one other factor that may be considered as an adjunct to both, but which is best discussed by itself. I refer to the role Rastafari elders in Jamaica have been playing in the recent years by trodding into the very heart of Babylon.

It was only a matter of time before the house dealt with the spread of the movement to the rest of the anglophone Caribbean, to the United Kingdom, and to North America. This was first dealt with by a series of three International Conferences: Toronto, in 1981, Kingston in 1985, and London in 1986. Besides, elders were hosted by brethren in St. Lucia, Barbados, and several of the smaller islands in 1982 and again in 1986. These conferences and "trods" brought together the leaders and main ideologues of the Nyabinghi, on the one hand, and Rastafari dispersed in the diaspora, on the other, to bear witness to the power of Jah and growing influence of the movement. The conferences served to broaden the concept of the House of Nyabinghi from being narrowly Jamaican to being international, with branches in the United States, Canada, the United Kingdom, and so on.

But in the late 1980s, a series of visits to the United States ushered in a new stage.[6] Partly in response to the adverse publicity suffered by the false association of the movement with criminals, members of the Rastafari community in Washington, D.C., with the assistance of the Smithsonian Institution, sponsored an official delegation of the house in 1988. The delegation visited and performed to audiences of primarily students at Howard, Johns Hopkins, Southeastern, and Morgan State universities and at the Smithsonian itself.

The second delegation took place a year later in connection with the Festival of American Folklife sponsored by the Smithsonian Institution. Again, the Washington community, including African-American Rastas, provided the delegation with airfares, accommodation, and transportation. On this occasion, audiences were less university-based, since the two-week festival attracted more of the general public. During the festival the delegation took time off to view the Odundu festival in Philadelphia and to participate in the street festival in Brooklyn. Staying on afterward they journeyed to Chicago where they appeared on radio before returning to participate in the Washington Reggaefest Festival in early August and appear on radio in Baltimore.

The third visit was sponsored by the American Natural History Museum in New York City and lasted for only two days. However, the elders again spent time circulating in the Rastafari community in Brooklyn, Baltimore, Richmond, Virginia, and Washington, D.C. Yet again African-American Rastafari and, significantly, Ethiopian Rastafari all pitched in to assist.

The final visit was in 1991 at the invitation of the Anacostia Museum and involved a one-night performance of nyabinghi chanting and display of ital food, in a program entitled "Celebration of the Lion and the Lamb."

The third and fourth visits were not official delegations from the house, but they have to be taken into account in assessing the impact of elders moving in and out of Rastafari communities in

6. I am grateful for a personal communication from Dr. John Homiak (August 14, 1992), acting director of the Human Film Archives within the Department of Anthropology at the Smithsonian Institution. Dr. Homiak was personally involved in the arrangements of the visits.

the United States. In the first place, the visits have served to put the stamp of legitimacy on the fledgling movement in that country and to counter the negative images of the movement's being a drug-infested cult. Performances included lectures and question and answer sessions. This is not to say that the problems with the law enforcement agencies are over, but rather to suggest that the visits have gone a long way in repairing the damage done by the drug posses in the 1980s. These visits also provided most of the African-American Rastafari (and many migrants from the Caribbean, including Jamaica) with their first insight into who and what an elder was and with their first taste of a real nyabinggi. Indeed, these visits most likely succeeded in confirming the faith for most African-American Rastafari, for outside of formal presentations there were extensive reasonings with the elders in the homes where they stayed. Some perhaps learned by participation the sacramental value of a reasoning. As Ras Peddie, a member of the delegation to the Folklife Festival, said, it was a way of ministering to "those who have not had the opportunity to discourse and reason for a number of years with the Elders (*Washington [D.C.] City Paper,* September 15–21, 1989). The visitors, in turn, (and by proxy the house in Jamaica), would have received greater confirmation of their status as elders in the movement. In addition, the visits served to bring each of the various Rastafari communities closer. Rastafari individualism is well known and in some ways provides the movement with its dynamism. But that brethren were able to come together to raise funds in support of the visits meant they were also delineating paths to greater cooperation and unity.

So vitalizing were the visits, particularly the first one, that several Rastafarians, including brethren of Caribbean origins, subsequently undertook pilgrimages to Jamaica.[7] For, without participating, how might anyone describe a binghi in Jamaica, surrounded by hundreds of Dreadlocks, young and old, roaring "JAH! RASTAFARI!" every time firewood from the sacred bonfire cracks, splintering its cinders; who settle down either into the common sleeping area or find their own corner, or who sit around reasoning in the charac-

7. John Homiak, personal communication (August 14, 1992).

teristically informal and yet still so formal manner? How might the feeling be described when the drummers "tuok" the bass, suffusing the gathering with that divine spirit that enables brethren to prance in the air and to sing for hours without ceasing? As Carole Yawney (1988) argues, the binghi in Jamaica is a state of devotional discourse, in which there is no audience, no performer, but all are participants. One can find no substitute but to "trod" for oneself to the land where Rastafari—in the language of Rastafari—is made manifest, where Bob Marley rests, Jamaica. But as they keep coming so will the elders keep going, especially those who have little difficulty obtaining visas. Internationalization has brought Rastafari to a new stage.

The house has already recognized and sanctioned this development, but is in somewhat of a dilemma as to how it should be handled. One example of what I mean will suffice. The first delegation was in actual fact quite successful, but it was not without some internal squabbling reminiscent of the controversy over the box that split the house in 1974. One of the elders on the delegation, having retrieved a film on the movement that the house claimed was being used to enrich the Americans who made it rather than the Rastafari, took the decision to leave it in the care of the Washington community for fund-raising purposes, he said, instead of bringing it back with him. A second elder, presented with a video production of the visits and performances of the delegation, took the decision to sign a contract on behalf of the house, he said, to acquire 50 percent of the distribution rights. The house heard their report and expressed its displeasure. Some members voiced their suspicion that the two senior elders had sought to aggrandize themselves at the expense of the house, while others charged them for acting ultra vires. Debate around the issue dominated the last days of the binghi in honor of His Majesty's Birthday in July 1988, and in the end both elders were debarred from future international delegations. One thing is clear from the episode: few elders will want to take initiatives of this sort, while even fewer will want to allow it. But at the same time, given the strong sense of individualism among the Rastafari, who can blame the house for its suspicion? No doubt, guidelines could be developed to prevent recurrence of situations like that, but they cannot cover all eventualities. Since the rise of the Dreadlocks, democratic principles have guided the conduct of the house. The real issue is whether these principles can continue unmodified if the house is to meet the new challenges.

Bibliography
Index

Bibliography

Abrahams, Rober. 1983. *The Men-of-Words in the West Indies: Performance and the Emergence of Creole Culture.* Baltimore: Johns Hopkins Univ. Press.

Agorsah, E. Kofi. 1992. "Archeological Perspectives on Maroon Heritage in Jamaica." Paper presented at "Born out of Resistance," the International Interdisciplinary Congress on Caribbean Cultural Creativity as a Response to European Expansion, Utrecht and Soesterberg, The Netherlands, March 25–28.

Barrett, Leonard. 1968. *The Rastafari: A Study in Messianic Cultism.* Río Piedras, Puerto Rico: Univ. of Puerto Rico Press.

———. 1977. *The Rastafarians: The Dreadlocks of Jamaica.* London: Sangster's and Heinemann Educational Books, Ltd.

Beckwith, Martha. 1929. *Black Roadways: A Study of Jamaica Folk Life.* Chapel Hill: Univ. of North Carolina.

Besson, Jean. 1987. "A Paradox in Caribbean Attitudes to Land." In *Land and Development in the Caribbean,* edited by Jean Besson and Janet Momsen. London: Macmillan Caribbean.

———. Forthcoming. "Religion as Resistance in Jamaican Peasant Life: The Baptist Church, Revival cult and Rastafari movement." In *Rastafari and other African-Caribbean World views,* edited by Barry Chevannes. London: Macmillan.

Bilby, Kenneth M. 1983. "Black Thoughts from the Caribbean." *New West Indian Guide* 57, no. 3/4: 201–13.

Braithwaite, L. E. S. 1953. "Social Stratification in Trinidad." *Social and Economic Studies* 2, nos. 2–3.

———. 1960. "Social Stratification and Cultural Pluralism." In *Social and Cultural Pluralism in the Caribbean,* edited by Vera Rubin. Annals of the New York Academy of Sciences, no. 83, New York.

Brathwaite, Edward Kamau. 1971. *The Development of Creole Society in Jamaica, 1770–1820*. Oxford: Clarendon Press.

———. 1986. *Roots*. Havana: Casa de Las Americas.

Breiner, Laurence A. 1985–86. "The English Bible in Jamaican Rastafarianism." *Journal of Religious Thought* 42, no. 2: 30–43.

Brodber, Erna. 1986. "Afro-Jamaican Women at the Turn of the Century." *Social and Economic Studies* 35, no. 3.

Broom, L. 1953. "Urban Research in the British Caribbean: A Prospectus." *Social and Economic Studies* 2, no. 1.

Buiks, P. 1981. *Surinamse Jongere op de Krauskade*. Van Loghun Slaterus.

Campbell, Horace. 1980. "Rastafari and the Culture of Resistance." *Race and Class* 22, no. 1:2–22.

———. 1985. *Rastafari and Resistance: From Marcus Garvey to Walter Rodney*. London: Hansib Publishing, Ltd.

Cassidy, Frederick. 1961. *Jamaica Talk: Three Hundred Years of the English Language in Jamaica*. London: MacMillan.

Chevannes, Barry. 1971. "Religion and Black Struggle." *Savacou* 3.

———. 1976. "Repairer of the Breach: Reverand Claudius Henry and Jamaican Society." *Ethnicity in the Americas*, edited by Frances Henry. The Hague: Mouton.

———. 1981. "The Rastafari and the Urban Youth." In *Perspectives on Jamaica in the Seventies*, edited by Carl Stone and Aggrey Brown. Kingston: Jamaica Publishing House.

———, ed. Forthcoming. *Rastafari and Other African-Caribbean World Views*. London: Macmillan.

Chirenje, J. Mutero. 1987. *Ethiopianism and Afro-Americans in Southern Africa, 1883–1916*. Baton Rouge and London: Louisiana State Univ. Press.

Clarence-Smith, W. G. 1986. "Runaway Slaves and Social Bandits in Southern Angola, 1875–1913." In *Out of Bondage: Runaways, Resistance and Marronage in African and the New World*, edited by Gad Heuman. London: Frank Cass.

Clarke, Colin. 1973. "The Slums of Kingston." In *Work and Family Life: West Indian Perspectives*, edited by Comitas and David Lowenthal. New York: Anchor Books.

———. 1975. *Kingston, Jamaica: Urban Development and Social Change, 1692–1962*. Berkeley: Univ. of California Press.

Clarke, Edith. 1957. *My Mother Who Fathered Me: A Study of the Family in Three Selected Communities in Jamaica*. London: G. Allen and Unwin.

Comaroff, Jean. 1985. *Body of Power, Spirit of Resistance: The Culture and History of a South African People*. Chicago and London: Univ. of Chicago Press.

Comitas, Lambros. 1973. Occupational Multiplicity in Rural Jamaica. In *Work and Family Life: West Indian Perspectives*, edited by Lambros Comitas and David Lowenthal. New York: Anchor Books.

Cundall, Frank, and Izett Anderson. 1927. *Jamaican Negro Proverbs and Sayings*. London: West India Committee.

Curtin, Phillip. 1955. *Two Jamaicas: The Role of Ideas in a Tropical Colony, 1830–1865*. Westport, Conn.: Greenwood Press.

De Montagnac, Noel. 1899. *Negro Nobodies: Being a series of Sketches of Peasant Life in Jamaica*. London: Fisher and Unwin.

Dominguez, Bernardo García. 1988. "Garvey and Cuba." In *Garvey: His work and Impact*, edited by Rupert Lewis and Patrick Bryan. Mona, Jamaica: Institute of Social and Economic Research and Department of Extra-Mural Studies, Univ. of the West Indies.

Durkheim, Emile. 1965. *The Elementary Forms of the Religious Life: A Study in Religious Sociology*. Glencoe, Ill.: The Free Press.

Eigen, Keith vom. 1987. "A Comparison of Physicians and Folk Healers in Jamaica." Proposal for Anthropological Research. Department of Anthropology, Teachers College, Columbia Univ.

Eisner, Gisela. 1961. *Jamaica, 1830–1930: A Study in Economic Growth*. Westport, Conn.: Greenwood Press.

Elkins, W. F. 1977. *Street Preachers, Faith Healers and Herb Doctors in Jamaica, 1890–1925*. New York: Revisionist Press.

Engels, Frederick. 1967. *The Peasant War in Germany*. Chicago: Univ. of Chicago Press.

Evans, Arthur S., and David Lee. 1990. *Pearl City, Florida: A Black Community Remembers*. Boca Raton: Florida Atlantic Univ. Press.

Evans, William McKee. 1980. "From the Land of Canaan to the Land of Guinea: The Strange Odyssey of the Sons of Ham." *American Historical Review* 85: 15–43.

Furnivall, J. S. 1948. *Colonial Policy and Practice*. London: Cambridge Univ. Press.

Garvey, Amy Jacques, comp. 1986. *The Philosophy and Opinions of Marcus Garvey, Or Africa for the Africans*. Dover, Mass.: The Majority Press.

Geertz, Clifford. 1960. *The Religion of Java*. New York: The Free Press.

Gordon, Derek. 1988. "Race, Class and Social Mobility in Jamaica." In *Garvey: His Work and Impact*, edited by Rupert Lewis and Patrick Bryan. Mona, Jamaica: Institute of Social Economic Research and Department of Extra-Mural Sudies, Univ. of the West Indies.

Hall, Douglas. 1978. *Free Jamaica, 1838–1865: An Economic History*. London: Caribbean Univ. Press.

Hamilton, Beverly. 1988. "Marcus Garvey and Cultural Development in Jamaica: A Preliminary Survey." In *Marcus Garvey: His Work and Impact*, edited by Rupert Lewis and Patrick Bryan. Mona, Jamaica: Institute of Social and Economic Research and Department of Extra-Mural Studies, Univ. of the West Indies.

Hart, Richard. 1985. *Slaves Who Abolished Slavery: Blacks in Rebellion*. Vol. 2. Mona, Jamaica: Institute of Social and Economic Research, Univ. of the West Indies.

Henige, David. 1982. *Oral Historiography*. London and New York: Longman.

Henriques, Fernando. 1953. *Family and Color in Jamaica*. London: Eyre and Spottiswoode.

Herskovits, Melville. 1958. *The Myth of the Negro Past.* Boston: Beacon.

Heuman, Gad. 1981. *Between Black and White: Race, Politics, and the Free Coloreds in Jamaica, 1792–1865.* Westport, Conn.: Greenwood Press.

Hill, Robert. 1981. "Dread History: Leonard P. Howell and Millenarian Visions in Early Rastafari Religions in Jamaica." *EPOCHÉ* 9: 31–70.

———, ed. 1983–85. *The Marcus Garvey and Universal Negro Improvcement Association Papers.* 7 Vols. Berkeley: Univ. of California Press.

Homiak, John. 1986. "Daughters of Zion by the Rivers of Babylon." Review of *Rastafari: Conversations Concerning Women,* by Renee Romano and Elliott Lieb. *Reggae Times* 1, no. 6.

———. 1987. "The mystic revelation of Rasta Far-Eye: Visionary Communication in a Prophetic Movement." In *Dreaming: Anthropological and Psychological Interpretations,* edited by Barbara Tedlock. London: Cambridge Univ. Press.

———. Forthcoming. "Dub History: Soundings on Rastafari Livity and Language." In *Rastafari and Other African-Caribbean World Views,* edited by Barry Chevannes. London: Macmillan.

Hurston, Zora. 1939. *Voodoo Gods: An Inquiry into Native Myths and Magic in Jamaica and Haiti.* London: J. M. Dent and Sons.

Jahn, Janheinz. 1961. *Muntu: An Outline of Neo-African Culture.* London: Faber.

Kuper, Adam. 1976. *Changing Jamaica.* London: Routledge and Kegan Paul.

Langer, Susan. 1951. *Philosophy in a New Key: A Study in the Symbolism of Reason, Rite and Art,* 2d ed. New York and Toronto: Mentor Books.

Lewis, Rupert. 1987. *Marcus Garvey: Anticolonial Champion.* London: Karia Press.

Lewis, Rupert, and Patrick Bryan, ed. *Marcus Garvey: His Work and Impact.* Mona, Jamaica: Institute of Social and Economic Research and Department of Extra-Mural Studies, Univ. of the West Indies.

Lewis, W. A. 1936. "Evolution of the Peasantry in the British West Indies." Mimeo.

Littlewood, Roland. 1993. *Pathology and Identity: The Work of Mother Earth in Trinidad.* Cambridge: Cambridge Univ. Press.

MacCormack, C. P., and Alizon Draper. 1987. "Social and Cognitive aspects of Female Sexuality in Jamaica." In *The Cultural Construction of Sexuality,* edited by Pat Caplan. London and New York: Tavistock.

Mansingh, Ajai, and Laxmi Mansingh. 1985. *Hindu Influences on Rastafarianism.* Caribbean Quarterly Monograph. Mona: Univ. of the West Indies.

Martin, Tony. 1976. *Race First: The Ideological and Organizational Struggles of Marcus Garvey and the Universal Negro Improvement Association.* Westport, Conn. and London: Greenwood Press.

———. 1983. *The Pan African Connection.* Cambridge, Mass.: Schenkman Publishing Company.

Mills, Charles W. 1987. "Race and Class: Conflicting Paradigms?" *Social and Economic Studies* 36, no. 2.

Mintz, Sidney. 1974. *Caribbean Transformations*. Chicago: Aldine Publishing Co.

———. 1990. "Labor Needs and Ethnic Ripening in the Caribbean Region." *Anales del Caribe* 10.

Munroe, Trevor. 1977. "The Marxist Left in Jamaica, 1940–50." Working Paper, no. 15. Institute of Social and Economic Research, Univ. of the West Indies, Mona.

Nadel, S. F. 1954. *Nupe Religion*. London: Routledge and Kegan Paul.

Olivier, Lord Sydney. 1936. *Jamaica, The Blessed Isle*. London: Faber and Faber.

Ong, Walter. 1982. *Orality and Literacy: The Technologizing of the Word*. London and New York: Methuen.

Owens, Joseph. 1976. *Dread: The Rastafarians of Jamaica*. Kingston: Sangster.

Paget, Hugh. 1945. "The Free Village System in Jamaica." *Jamaica Historical Review* 1, no. 1.

Parry, J. H., and P. M. Sherlock. 1957. *A Short History of the West Indies*. London: Macmillan.

Patterson, H. Orlando. 1964. *Children of Sisyphus*. London: New Authors.

———. 1967. *The Sociology of Slavery: an Analysis of the Origins, Development and Structure of Negro Slave Society in Jamaica*. London: McGibbon and Kee.

———. 1970. "Slavery and Slave Revolts: a socio-historical analysis of the First Maroon War, Jamaica, 166–1740." *Social and Economic Studies*, Volume 20, Number 3.

Post, K. W. J. 1970. "The Bible as Ideology: Ethiopianism in Jamaica, 1930–38." In *African Perspectives*, edited by C. H. Allen and R. N. Johnson. Cambridge: Cambridge Univ. Press.

Potter, Philip. 1988. "The Religious Thought of Marcus Garvey." In *Garvey: His Work and Impact*, edited by Rupert Lewis and Patrick Bryan. Mona, Jamaica: Institute of Social and Economic Research and Department of Extra-Mural Studies, Univ. of the West Indies.

Rathbone, Richard. 1986. *Out of the House of Bondage: Runaways, Resistance and Marronage in Africa and the New World*. London: Frank Cass.

Roberts, George. 1957. *The Population of Jamaica*. London: Cambridge Univ. Press.

Robotham, Don. 1981. "'The Notorious Riot:' The Socio-Economic and Political Bases of Paul Bogle's Revolt." Working paper, no. 28. Institute of Social and Economic Research, Univ. of the West Indies, Mona.

———. 1985. The Cry of the Cuckatoo. *Social and Economic Studies* 34, no. 2.

Rodney, Walter. 1982. *How Europe Underdeveloped Africa*. Washington, D.C.: Howard Univ. Press.

Rowe, Maureen. 1980. "The Women in Rastafari." *Caribbean Quarterly* 26, no. 4.

Rubin, Vera, and Lambros Comitas. 1975. *Ganja in Jamaica.* The Hague: Mouton.

Schuler, Monica. 1979. "Myalism and the African Religious Tradition in Jamaica." In *Africa and the Caribbean: the Legacies of a Link,* edited by Margaret Crahan and Franklin W. Knight. Baltimore: Johns Hopkins Univ. Press.

———. 1980. *"Alas, Alas, Kongo": A Social History of Indentured African Immigration in Jamaica, 1840–1865.* Baltimore and London: Johns Hopkins Univ. Press.

Senior, Olive. 1972. *The Message is Change: A Perspective on the 1972 General Elections.* Kingston: Kingston Publishers Limited.

Shepperson, George. 1953. "Ethiopianism and African Nationalism." *Phylon* 14: 9–18.

———. 1968. "Ethiopianism: Past and Present." In *Christianity in Tropical Africa,* edited by C. G. Baeta. London: Oxford Univ. Press.

Simpson, George Eaton. 1955. "Political Cultism in West Kingston, Jamaica." *Social and Economic Studies* 4, no 2.

———. 1956. "Jamaican Revivalist Cults." *Social and Economic Studies* 5, no. 4.

Smith, M. G. 1965. *The Plural Society in the British West Indies.* Berkeley: Univ. of California Press.

Smith, M. G., Roy Augier, and Rex Nettleford. 1960. *Report on the Rastafari Movement in Kingston, Jamaica.* Kingston: Institute of Social and Economic Research, Univ. of the West Indies, Mona.

Smith, R. T. 1967. "Social Stratification, Cultural Pluralism and Integration in West Indian Societies." In *Caribbean Integration: Papers on Social, Political and Economic Integration,* edited by Sybil Lewis and Thomas G. Matthews. Río Piedras: Institute of Caribbean Studies, Univ. of Puerto Rico.

Stein, Judith. 1986. *The World of Marcus Garvey: Race and Class in Modern Society.* Baton Rouge, La.: Louisiana State Univ. Press.

Stephenson, Edward G. 1987. "Rastafari." Ph.D Diss., Univ. of California, Santa Cruz.

Stewart, Robert. 1983. *Religion and Society in Jamaica, 1831–1880: Conflict Compromise and the Christian Churches in a Post-Slave Colony.* Ph.D. Diss. Univ. of the West Indies, Mona.

Stone, Carl. 1974. *Electoral Behavior and Public Opinion in Jamaica.* Mona, Jamaica: Institute of Social and Economic Research, Univ. of the West Indies.

Sundkler, Bengt. 1961. *Bantu Prophets in South Africa.* 2d ed. London, New York, and Toronto: Oxford Univ. Press.

Troeltsch, Ernst. 1950. *The Social Teachings of the Christian Church.* Vol. 1. London: George Allen and Unwin.

Turner, Victor W. 1968. *The Drums of Affliction: A Study of Religious Processes among the Ndembu of Zambia.* Oxford and The International African Institute: Clarendon Press.

Vansina, Jan. 1973. *Oral Tradition: A Study in Historical Methodology.* Harmondsworth, Middlesex: Penguin.

Van Velsen, J. 1967. "The Extended-Case Method and Situational Analysis." In *The Craft of Social Anthropology,* edited by A. L. Epstein. Social Science Paperbacks. London: Tavistock.

Warner-Lewis, Maureen. 1990. "African Continuities in the Rastafari Belief System." Mona, Jamaica: Department of English, Univ. of the West Indies.

Wedenoja, William. 1989. "Mothering and the Practice of 'Balm' in Jamaica." In *Women as Healers: Cross-Cultural Perspectives,* edited by Carol Shepherd McClain. New Brunswick and London: Rutgers Univ. Press.

Weisbord, Robert G. 1970. "British West Indian Reaction to the Italian-Ethiopian War: An Episode in Pan-Africanism." *Caribbean Studies* 10, no. 1: 31–41.

White, Timothy. 1983. *Catch a Fire: The Life of Bob Marley.* London: Elm Tree Books.

Williams, J. J. 1979. *Psychic Phenomena of Jamaica.* Westport, Conn.: Greenwood Press.

Willoughby, Neville. 1977. Neville Willoughby Interviews Kapo. *Jamaica Intercom* 2, no. 1.

Wilson, Peter. 1973. *Crab Antics: the Social Anthropology of English-speaking Negro societies in the English-speaking Caribbean.* New Haven: Yale Univ. Press.

Witter, Michael, and Claremont Kirton. 1990. "The Informal Economy in Jamaica: Some Empirical Exercises." Working paper, no. 36. Institute of Social and Economic Research, Univ. of the West Indies, Mona.

Yawney, Carole. 1976. "Rastafarian Attitudes to Race and Nationality." In *Ethnicity in the Americas,* edited by Frances Henry. The Hague: Mouton.

———. 1983. "To Grow a Daughter: Cultural Liberation and the Dynamics of Oppression in Jamaica." In *Feminism in Canada,* edited by A. Miller and G. Finn. Montreal: Black Rose Books.

———. 1987. "Moving with the Dawtas of Rastafari: From Myth to Reality." In *The Caribbean and Latin America: Papers Presented at the Third Interdisciplinary Colloquium about the Caribbean,* edited by Ulrich Fleischmann and Ineke Phaf. Berlin: Verlag Klaus Dieter Vervuert.

Index